THE APOSTLE

THE APOSTLES' CREED

THE APOSTLES' CREED AND ITS EARLY CHRISTIAN CONTEXT

PIOTR ASHWIN-SIEJKOWSKI

t&t clark

Published by T&T Clark International
A Continuum Imprint
The Tower Building   80 Maiden Lane
11 York Road   Suite 704
London SE1 7NX   New York NY 10038

www.continuumbooks.com

British Library Cataloguing-in-Publication Data
A catalogue record for this book is available from the British Library.

Typeset by RefineCatch Limited, Bungay, Suffolk
Printed and bound in Great Britain by CPI Antony Rowe, Chippenham, Wiltshire

ISBN-10: HB: 0–567–00175–X
        PB: 0–567–32821–X
ISBN-13: HB: 978–0–567–00175–7
        PB: 978–0–567–32821–2

Contents

Acknowledgements

I would like to express my special gratitude to a group of friends whose generous assistance enabled me to write this book. They are: Alyson Barr, Fr Philip Bevan, Howard Cattermole, Rev Dr Allan Jenkins, Penny Francis, Kevin Norris, Rev Neil Summers, Martin Warner and Shirley Wallis. They all kindly gave their time in order to help me edit my manuscript, and they also provided invaluable comments on the first draft of my book. I am also most grateful to the very supportive staff from the library of the University of Chichester, who provided me with all necessary literature during my work on this project. I also wish to express my gratitude to Thomas Kraft, my editor, for his interest in this project. My special gratitude belongs to my wife Sarah, who, as always, was enormously patient and supportive, although the revision of this manuscript has happily coincided with the first months in the life of our daughter, Anna Elizabeth.

I dedicate this book to the memory of my dear friend, Rev Peter Gooderick (1926–2007), who was an excellent Anglican parish priest and a great companion with whom I had endless theological debates. I miss him and those conversations very much.

Introduction

This book is an outcome of two kinds of inspiration. First, my academic interest in the history of early Christian doctrine, my real joy in teaching 'Patristic Theology' at the University of Chichester and addressing the students' questions, prompted me to prepare a basic 'guide-book' through the complex labyrinth of early Christian thought. Secondly, my parish ministry in Richmond Team Ministry (Richmond/Surrey) inspired me to offer an introduction that would explain the crucial message of the Apostles' Creed and its early Christian context. The Apostles' Creed, so popular in the Anglican liturgy, provides a perfect gate to open the amazing, rich and colourful 'garden' of early Church theology. One of its commentators calls it 'the creed of creeds'[1] in the Western Church, and it was admired for its simplicity and brevity by Luther and Calvin, and also by both Roman Catholics and Anglicans.[2]

I have also been thinking of a way to introduce the Creed and its difficult jargon to a much wider group of readers even than my students and parishioners. However, I am aware that there will be a number of Christians for whom this Creed is incomprehensible, even irrelevant. For them the Apostles' Creed could be put on a shelf of the British Library to gather dust, and not many people would notice its disappearance from the liturgy. Against this way of thinking, I would like to argue that the theological content of this specific Christian confession may still inspire our faith, and at the very least challenge our intellect. It may stir up a new desire to know more about the history of Christianity. The early Christian theologians are not mummified, static saints or villains from Madame Tussaud's Museum of Wax Figures. Some of them were later labelled 'heretics', but I treat them with respect. All of them,

1

the 'good' and the 'bad', are still very much alive and the Apostles'
Creed echoes their important theological quarrels. Those ancient
Christians were passionate about God and their relationship with
the divine. This book will explain more about their disputes.
However, I don't approach the early Christian theologians on my
knees, and neither do I encourage my readers to do so. I cannot
hide the fact that I admire some of them, while others I would not
invite to dinner, but the voices of the latter are still recorded in the
following chapters.

1

The reader is invited to reflect on the Apostles' Creed, which is
based on an Old Roman Creed thought to date from the third
century,[3] and has many connections with the Western part of early
Christendom.[4] My examination of the confession is limited to only
the first three centuries of our Common Era, and excludes, for
instance, Origen. His enormous theological legacy had more
impact on the Creed of Nicaea (325 CE). Still, I hope that the
variety of literary evidence provided by this study will reveal the
richness of early Christian theology. Using the Apostles' Creed as if
it were a time-machine, we will make a journey back to the period
of the formation of the New Testament. The Bible is treated as
the necessary introduction to this particular article of faith. The
Apostles' Creed will take us back to the ancient world, which for
some readers may conjure up the images of Spielberg's *Jurassic
Park* full of 'pre-historic', rather unpleasant monsters, demons
and weird ideas. I believe that this world is still very much alive
and not only the subject of nightmares. On the contrary, it is a
fascinating, colourful, fresh world when Christians, like young
children, looked around with new eyes, trying to touch, name
and express their feelings to the surroundings in which they
found themselves. They tried to communicate their joy of being
born to the world of a new faith to those around them, including
their natural family and relatives: the Jews and the Greek philosophers. Some of those Christians were born more into one
ethos, but they certainly inherited characteristics of both parents.
This is the reason why we cannot neglect the essential link
between early Christian thought and its historical milieu, particularly, the first two centuries.

The Apostles' Creed is a part of a larger experience which
includes endless efforts to express God's reality, and his divine
project of bringing salvation to humanity based on the limited
language of analogy. This language faces a permanent crisis as it

tries to reach the transcendent God and speak about Him or Her through a code of semiotics. How can any language, including music and arts, possibly articulate what is beyond words such as God's nature, incarnation and resurrection? How can the human mind even with its lofty abstract notions and sophisticated terms comprehend and explain God's mystery, particularly the unity of God and plurality of the divine persons? Should not silence or silent contemplation be the most appropriate 'theological narrative' of all? Even if we agree that silence is the most appropriate way to 'talk' or bear witness to God, still our paradox is not comprehensible. Further, those who seem to experience God's mystery, the so-called mystics, instead of remaining silent, write many vast volumes communicating with others about the experience of being 'caught up as far as the third heaven' (2 Cor. 12.2).

The faithful believers, every Sunday all over the world, recite one or another form of the Christian Creeds, but this routine does not often inspire them to reflect upon the context of their publicly proclaimed faith. Recognising these attitudes we must remember that Christianity is not an immobile, soundless 'gazing into the sky' (Acts 1.9–11). Christianity has not come into being in order for us to remain in silent awe of the transcendent Absolute. On the contrary, it is a religion of the Word (Gr. *Logos*), it bears witness to the dialogue between the Creator and the creatures, and thus it is called to communicate in an intelligible, coherent and stimulating way. The language in which it does so is by its very nature historical and is shaped by a multifaceted context. This includes social, historical, ideological and religious elements, not forgetting the whole issue of gender and psychology, and is the only available means to pronounce the human fascination with God. The role of language is central, and rightly so. But this is not a modern or postmodern discovery. The early Christian theologians were fully aware of the nature of the divine revelation. Communication of God's message to the human community, which always exists in a particular language and cultural framework, creates an important ambivalence. Each language facilitates the encounter of a specific generation with God, but as language is rooted in particular sets of symbols and idioms, it may alienate other generations from the core of Revelation.

2

The Christian faith, unlike contemporaneous beliefs such as Hellenistic Judaism, mystery cults, or the official state religion of the Roman Empire, generated a distinctive and unique collection of creeds. The history of religions shows that it is possible to distinguish, among various traditions, more or less specific intellectual doctrines of salvation, ethical codes, liturgical practices and elements of mystical experience. But only Christianity from its very beginning called its faithful followers of Christ to *confess* a particular *faith* which was much more than just an emotional adherence to Jesus. It supplied also an intellectual elaboration and pronouncement of this faith. The emergence of Christian theology begins with the Easter experience of the risen Lord. However, very soon Christianity encouraged people to receive baptism in the name of 'the Father, the Son and the Holy Spirit'. From early on this faith also expected the imminent return of the Saviour, and spoke of everlasting life in his kingdom. The Apostles' Creed, although its first appearance in its current form was in the eighth century,[5] and the final Latin formula dates from the sixteenth century,[6] reveals in its core the original, early Christian faith. But it also reveals the history of theology. This Creed at its heart presents a specific response of the so-called Great Church, towards three main challenges: the aftermath of the painful break with Judaism; the sharp criticism of gentile intellectuals and the alternative theories of God and salvation held by other Christians. The last point needs clarification. A naïve picture of early Christianity may suggest that our spiritual fathers and mothers lived a blessed life in 'peace and unity'. This is far from the case. Early Christian struggles about theological truth or 'correctness' engaged theologians and whole communities in fierce battles which were not only rhetorical but sometimes led to the martyrdom of representatives of both sides. We must remember that the Apostles' Creed voices the truth of the winning party, but this book pays some, although limited, attention to the lost cause of the defeated as well.

But it is not only polemic that prompted some Christians to establish a distinctive set of pronouncements which summarised their understanding of God and experience of faith. There was also another important factor. The first disciples of Christ were left with a commandment to *make disciples of all the nations and to baptise them* (Mt. 28.19; Mk 16.16; Lk. 24.47). That doctrine and its particular expressions in the creeds emerged as a form of catechesis practised by the early Church. There is a strong evidence of the practice of asking, usually three, questions during baptism, to which the neophyte responded three times saying, 'I believe'. That is also the reason why the baptismal confession took the form of a dialogue, of questions and answers which were later replaced by an official statement of faith. One among many examples of this baptismal practice is recorded by the *Apostolic Tradition.*[7] The neophyte was well prepared to respond to these questions not only with faith but also with the necessary degree of knowledge about the history of salvation. It would have been natural for the local churches or provinces to develop their own variations of the questions to the neophyte, as well as their own particular practices of preparing the candidates, and even variations in the rituals of the baptism.

Thus, what we see today as the Apostles' Creed is like a massive tree. But it started as a 'seed' that was grown in a particular soil and with specific climatic conditions. These elements will be examined through a commentary on each statement of belief.

3

I own to the reader of this book one important explanation related to the terminology. In order to identify theologians who later were labelled as the forerunners of 'orthodoxy' (Gr. *orthodox*, 'correct-thinking') I will use a term 'proto-orthodox'.[8] I am aware of its semantic awkwardness as well as the fact that for readers who are not acquainted with theological vocabulary, this term sounds rather disconcerting. Still, this term is helpful as it points to the important distinction between the authors of mainstream 'cath-olic' or 'orthodox' version of Christian belief and other early Christian theologians, labelled by their opponents as 'heretics'. By the term 'proto-orthodox', I denote the specific tradition within pre-Nicene Christianity, which later on was identified with the origin of the orthodox doctrine of the Apostolic and Catholic/Universal Church. As the notion of 'orthodoxy' is problematic in this early period, I use the term to refer to theologians and concepts later accepted as representatives of the doctrine of the Great Church. However, I am not saying that 'orthodoxy' or 'proto-orthodoxy' was the primordial, earlier established correct Christian doctrine which then was corrupted, intentionally or not, by erroneous 'options', or selective 'choice' (Gr. *hairesis*). In the second century, Irenaeus, the Bishop of Lyons, wrote his polemical work *Against Heresies* in which he argued that heretics diverged from orthodoxy that is from the tradition that he represented. In Irenaeus' view, heresy and heretics diverged from orthodoxy usu-ally either through intellectual arrogance or moral corruption, or a combination of both. Those erroneous teachers and doctrines then challenged the faith of the Church. Early Christian 'proto-orthodox' theologians commonly accepted Irenaeus' theory and were convinced that from the beginning the Great or 'Catholic' (here this adjective does not mean the Roman-Catholic) Church had held orthodox doctrines. These 'correct' doctrines were

clearly distinguishable, in the view of those apologists, from
erroneous beliefs, now called 'heresies'. This ancient or classical
model has been seriously questioned by modern scholarship as
thanks to the new discoveries, which include ancient documents,
we are able to see the definition of orthodoxy as a gradual process
which occurred through debate with alternative theologies ('heresies'). Therefore it is inaccurate to understand 'orthodoxy' as the
original, pure and innocent stage of Christian doctrine, and 'heresy' as its later corruption and degeneration. Thus, I present early
theological debates in this light of competitive struggle between
various Christian schools or traditions. One of them, soon dominant, I call 'proto-orthodox', that is, the 'archetype' of later Christian normative doctrine accepted and confirmed by the Councils
and Synods.

4

I hope these necessary preliminary remarks will make our encounter and intellectual dialogue with the Apostles' Creed easier.
Even so, the reader will encounter some difficult terms, and therefore I would advise beginners to consult the glossary at the end of
the book. More advanced readers may find the bibliography useful,
which lists a number of recent studies related to different statements of the Creed. My hope is that this very brief, introductory
encounter with early Christian theology will stimulate further study
of the theology and history of this period. Prof Avril Cameron
identified this fascinating time as one of the greatest importance in
shaping Christian identity:

> The second century, in particular, was a battleground for the
> struggle of Christians to control their own discourse and define
> their faith. Indeed, the continuance of that struggle, which has
> characterised Christianity throughout its history, is demonstra-
> tion enough of the crucial importance of text in historical
> growth and the acquisition of power.[9]

I Believe in God . . .

'Since you want the doors of understanding opened to you, it is
right that you should first of all confess that you believe'.
  Rufinus of Aquileia, *A Commentary on the Apostles' Creed*, 3[1]

There is no escape from the significance of the first word of the
Apostles' Creed. It calls for our special attention. The Creed begins
with a strong accent on the personal faith of a believer. The grammar
of the first sentence highlights the specific nature of the Apostle's
Creed. Unlike other creeds used by the Christians in late antiquity,[2]
the Apostles' Creed opens with *I* believe and not *we* believe. This
surprising formula, which emphasises a personal response of the
believer to God's revelation, echoes its original version, the so-
called 'Old Roman Creed' preserved in its Latin version from the
early fifth century.[3] Naturally then, introduction into the whole
complexity of the Apostles' Creed begins with this preliminary
reflection on personal faith, covering a whole range of meanings.
Faith once confessed needed further strengthening through theological teaching and daily *praxis*. These aspects of the faith of the
early Christians have not changed. However some similarities to
modern experience of faith do not overshadow the significant differences of their contexts. This context will be sketched only
briefly to emphasise the novelty of the Christian faith.

Origin

The Apostles' Creed, as any other Creed, preserves the origin of all
Christian affirmations of faith, which later took on a specific form
of 'confession of faith'. It reflects the early Christian baptismal
interrogatory custom, when a catechumen was directly asked three

main questions about his or her faith and responded to them as an individual with three straightforward answers. The Apostles' Creed reveals this form of the original practice, that is the preparation for baptism and a new life as the believer who identifies Jesus of Nazareth with the Messiah, 'God's anointed' (Gr. *Christos*). An ancient document called the *Apostolic Tradition* (3 CE) shows an example of this kind of liturgical interrogation and dialogue between the presbyter and the candidate:

> '– Do you believe in God the Father Almighty?
> And the candidate shall say: I believe. (. . .)
> – Do you believe in Christ Jesus, the Son of God, who was born of the Holy Spirit and the Virgin Mary, who was crucified in the days of Pontius Pilate and died and was buried, and rose the third day living from the dead and ascended into the heavens, and sat down at the right hand of the Father and will come to judge the living and the dead? (. . .)
> And the candidate shall respond: I believe.
> – Do you believe in the Holy Spirit in the Holy Church and the resurrection of the flesh?
> And the candidate should confirm: I believe'.[4]

The Creed retains the ancient tradition of a public, liturgical interview which emphasised the individual's choice to become a Christian and to follow a particular religious model of life as set by Jesus of Nazareth and his followers. With the development of more complex theology, this basic three-part form became the foundation of the compound architecture of all credal statements, which later accommodated further specifications of Christian understanding of God and salvation. Even so, the personal *faith in* remained the core of all confessions. This *faith* as an attitude and a style of life found its specific expression in the language of the first generations of Christians who were trying to articulate their unique relationship with God, now called 'Father' through Jesus of Nazareth, proclaimed as his 'Son'. Of course, the attitude of *faith* as an expression of personal trust and commitment was not a Christian invention. This aspect of *faith* was very well known to the Jewish people, who remained faithful to their Hebrew theology and their covenant with God through the Mosaic Law. But, in comparison with the Jewish ethos, Christian *faith* was totally Christ-centred. It is right to say that the essence of Christian faith affirmed the very exclusive notion of salvation uniquely through Jesus, as Christ, the sole Saviour of all humanity. This new aspect of *faith* originates in one of the first apologies of Christian faith by the Apostle Peter according to Luke (Acts 4.12):

> There is salvation in no one else, for there is no other name
> under heaven given among mortals by which we must be saved.

This short uncompromising statement expresses the core of the
first Christian dogmas and some of the theological axioms, which
was the basis of the further formation and use of all creeds. Here in
the Lukan elaboration, the Apostle Peter stresses the specific
understanding of God's relationship with humanity through the
crucial role of the only mediator authorised by God: Jesus Christ.
This theology is far from any concession to religious pluralism, as it
unquestionably affirms that all need to be saved by Jesus, and that
faith in Jesus leads to salvation. This rhetoric distinguishes a particular mode of the new covenant, now through Jesus, from the
previous ones, such as through Moses, and fearlessly declares its
true, ultimate and universal character. Soon, this line of persuasion
will be adopted by other early Christian documents where again
Christianity is asserted as the ultimate religion, that is the fully
true relationship with God, the Creator of the Universe. Early
Christians boldly stated publicly, on various occasions and against
different critics, the exclusiveness of Jesus Christ as God's chosen
representative. It did not matter whether those Christians were
questioned by Roman persecutors or Jewish critics: the same
religious determination to confess Jesus as God's unique mediator
set the crucial frame of Christian self-understanding. Obviously
this determination led those believers to an adamant attitude and
the rejection of all pagan[5] cults as idolatrous. In consequence, they
had to pay the highest prize for their commitment to the new
religion. In addition, their uncompromised attitude brought upon
them and their new *belief* a substantial amount of suspicion,
mistrust and even derision.[6]

Context

Christianity came into being as a departure from Jewish tradition
and ethos, and this process took place gradually during the first
and second century of the Common Era.[7] When the separation
began to appear Jews and Christians shared a monotheistic faith in
one God alongside other features such as the Hebrew Scriptures,
various elements of Jewish liturgy and a common esteem for the
patriarchs, prophets and martyrs who throughout the history of
Israel bore witness to Hebrew monotheism. This was a direct,
strong and natural source of the Christian self-understanding. As
far as we can say, neither Jesus of Nazareth, nor Paul or Peter,
intended to invent 'a new religion', but to a varying extent, they

understood 'the Way' (Acts 9.2, then in, e.g. the *Didache*, 1.1–6.2; *Epistle of Barnabas*, 19.1–2; 20.1–2) as based upon the core belief of the Hebrew covenant with God, now reinterpreted and proclaimed to a new or 'third race' of people.[8] It is right to say that at this early stage, the Christian confession *I believe in God* contained all the essential elements of Hebrew theology with the crucial imagery of God as the Holy and Living Creator and the Sustainer of the universe, the Father and the Protector of his people, a God of justice and mercy. But, unlike various forms of Judaism, different trends of Christianity recognised the crucial, irreplaceable role of Jesus as God's self-revelation and His communication with the whole of humanity. Therefore when their Jewish cousins summarised their faith in the famous words of *Shema Ysrael* (cf. Deut. 6.4–9), Christians having repeated the same confession immediately added *and in Jesus Christ* (cf. 1 Cor. 8.6) through whom they claimed to know the full truth about the nature of God. With this Christological amendment, the followers of the 'Way' still shared with their Jewish relatives the same feeling of religious awe, obedience and fear of their God. Reciting *Shema*, the early Christians, as far as we can say from the evidence of the Scriptures (e.g. 1 Pet. 4.16), saw themselves not as 'reformed Jews' but as the followers of Christ. Therefore their *belief in God* included a whole range of new aspects which were not accepted by those who remained faithful to the 'faith and practices of our forefathers'. Judaism never created any form of a creed, but it has no need of it, as the prayer of affirmation – *Shema* expressed the essence of faith and commitment to the God of Israel.

The Jewish roots aside, Christianity soon appeared among and interacted with the Gentile neighbours. It must be noted, although briefly, that *faith* played a rather limited role among the worshippers of many gods as well as those who believed in one. In the Gentile context *faith in gods*, or rather acceptance of their existence was a common, popular conviction based on the narrative of colourful traditional mythologies. But for those non-Christians, including a number of intellectuals, *faith* and *religion* were mainly a matter of a regular participation in a public cult, not a subject of dogma or even a claim of exclusive truth about the nature of gods.[9] As noted by one modern scholar, one of the leading characteristics of religion from Hellenistic-Roman times was its non-exclusiveness, as worship of a particular deity did not preclude belief in others.[10] Another contemporary scholar rightly points out that the term which describes the core of the religious mind-set of those non-Christians was *piety* (Gr. *eusebeia*, Lat. *pietas*).[11] The word originated in the context of family ethos and highlighted the importance of reverence to ancestors and godparents. Later, this term was used to signify loyalty and obedience to the traditions of Rome such as laws, but also reverence towards the noblest men of previous generations as well as to the founders of Roman culture. With the passing of time, the term found its place in religious language and mentality, as it denotes devotion to the gods and to the practices, public or private, which honoured the gods. I would like to suggest that if the Romans had had 'a creed' as a common symbol of self-identification, its first words would have been: 'I honour' or 'I promise to honour the gods of Rome'. This is one of the characteristic differences between early Christian self-understanding, and the self-assessment of their neighbours. Similarly, those pagans who were involved in esoteric cults of oriental deities did not attempt to formulate any credal, common and relevant elaboration of their belief, but rather sought personal contact with and experience of their gods. As it is possible to see from this sketch of the Jewish and Gentile elements, early Christianity offered a new insight into the meaning of *belief in*, which now needs to be explored.

Novelty

Early Christians approached their *faith* in an innovative way in comparison with the values which Jewish and Gentile attached to this term. Principally, *faith* was a gift of God (Acts 16.14) freely given to all humans, not just members of an ethnic group or bought for money (Acts 8.18–24). Anyone and everyone who looked on Jesus of Nazareth as God's Chosen Saviour of all people shared the faith with other members of the emerging Jesus' movement. Therefore all people were called to put their hope and trust of reconciliation with God in Christ. Secondly, *faith* was not just a one-off act, but rather a long process of transformation (Gr. *metanoia*) that led to baptism which made a neophyte a full member of the Church (e.g. Gal. 3.27). Thirdly, one's *faith* inspired the whole of one's existence and offered a new self-understanding and a new perception of the visible and invisible world, its rules, events and destiny (e.g. Col. 1.15–20; 1 Pet. 2.13–19; Rev. 17). Fourthly, *faith* established a specific fraternal relationship of love/charity between an individual and the Christian community (1 Jn 4.11). Last but not least, since the first generations of Christian believers found themselves misunderstood, castigated and persecuted, their *faith* called for an intelligible and convincing defence (1 Pet. 3.15). Together these factors formed the specific nature of Christian *faith*.

The novelty of the Christian understanding of *faith*, and the act of believing as well as the continuous process of *belief* hints at the holistic nature of that free involvement in God's self-disclosure in Jesus of Nazareth, which as a commitment encompasses all possible areas of human existence and experience. The Christian notion of *faith-belief* cannot be separated from its original Hebrew roots and theology. However, against this natural background this new *faith-belief* proclaims a distinctiveness of Christianity. For Christians Christ is not a new Moses, he is much more than Moses, and the nature of Jesus Christ, elaborated in the next statements of the Creed, separates him from all holy men and women from Israel's history. Secondly, the Christian notion of *faith-belief* remains focused on the paradox of God's self-limitation to a particular, local character and flavour. An eternal, transcendent and perfect God became visible, heard and understandable 'in' and 'through' Jesus of Nazareth. The universal and divine became a specific human and mortal. The latter claimed to represent, even to embody the former. Thirdly, the Apostles' Creed stands out as the very personal confession of faith capsulated in this first sentence. It emphasises the personal religious, intellectual and spiritual journey of faith of the believer. These three outcomes of the Apostles' Creed reaffirm its value as testimony to the Christian understanding of God.

Consequences

Soon the strong affirmation of *faith in God* in its crucial Christological context drew the attention of the Christians' closest relatives: the Jews. One of the aftermaths of the tragic war with Rome (66–73 CE) was the collapse of the centralised Jewish authority, already in crisis, represented by the priestly and theological groups around the Jerusalem Temple. The material destruction of Jerusalem created room for competition for spiritual authority over the nation. Two movements emerged as the most serious contenders to leadership: Jewish Christians and the rabbinic sages. Steady growth in power by the rabbis meant that the Jewish Christians, at least in Palestine, were marginalised. At the same time, the rabbinic representatives reorganised the core elements of Jewish identity, literature and ethics in a new, post-war context. It took place in the coastal small city of Jamnia (Yavneh), where the Jewish teachers, among many tasks, reaffirmed the canonicity of Hebrew Scriptures, rejecting any 'divine' inspiration of the Greek books (the Septuagint)[12] used now by Christians. They also responded to the Christian claim about Jesus of Nazareth as the promised Messiah, whom the Jews saw as a magician. Jesus' followers, who posed a significant danger to the integrity of the Jewish life and communities, were divided into two categories by the rabbis: those who were Jews by birth and those who were not Jews, therefore still pagans or people outside the valid Covenant.[13] Thus the main concern of the rabbis was focused on those Christians who were converts from Judaism, and now became heretics (Hebr. *minim*). Against those and other apostates and renegades a special prayer ('Eighteen Benedictions') was introduced imposing their excommunication. That liturgical form of the prayer affirmed that Jewish Christians ought to be excluded from the synagogues and ostracised in a social and possibly commercial context.[14] From the genuine and orthodox Jewish perspective, Jewish Christians at the very least misused the Holy Scriptures, then declared the divine authority of the so-called 'Gospels' thus introducing a serious confusion about the nature, role and identification of the Messiah. Christian pronouncement of the *belief in God* was castigated as an invalid alteration, as a sort of a sectarian breakout and even as an anti-Jewish sacrilege.

The second group of early Christian neighbours, the Gentiles, had a rather different approach and concern about this new Christian *belief*. At first, the early Christians appeared to be yet another 'oriental' sect who had much in common with the Jews, but unlike the Jews, were spreading their secretive message and organising rather esoteric meetings in private houses and even in other suspicious places such as cemeteries. While some Romans respected the old and venerable Jewish monotheism, and were familiar with the Jews as members of society with some privileges, the newness of the Christian cult raised only suspicion. In addition, Christian language was not very helpful. Christians shared 'a meal', where not everyone was invited, showing a lack of hospitality and the mystifying nature of their cult. This 'meal' was interpreted by them as the consumption of the 'flesh' and 'body' of their 'saviour'. Therefore an accusation of cannibalism was waiting to be deployed in a time of crisis of confidence. Then, Christians called each other 'brothers' and 'sisters', slaves were 'equal' to their masters, while women to men; they also exchanged 'the kiss of peace'. Practices and language provoked a further suspicion, this time of anti-social behaviour.

Finally, Christians stubbornly rejected any involvement in the Roman public religion, thus showing a lack of respect for the tradition of Roman values and Roman gods. This attitude, as a consequence of their *belief in God* produced a label of 'atheism' that was soon attached to Christians. From a Roman point of view, the detail of Christian *faith in God* did not matter at all, but a gesture of honour to the gods was all they required from those members of the new cult. This simple gesture would show that Christians also participated in the life of their community, that they equally revered and feared the power of the divine, that they expressed solidarity with non-Christian citizens of the local city and the whole state. But those 'atheists' were ready rather to face all the tragic consequences of their uncompromising *belief in God* than to compromise it. In the light of existing Roman documents, Christian faith appeared to be bizarre ('Jesus' resurrection'), extremely intolerant ('there is only one Saviour of humankind') and based on highly emotional attachment to their 'Christ' ('Jesus is the Lord. Amen'), who from the Roman point of view was a local Jewish criminal, executed in Palestine under the rule of Pontius Pilate. Therefore, Christian belief aroused suspicion, mistrust or even mockery. It is not surprising that the pagans saw the Christians as a minor, esoteric sect awaiting the imminent end of the visible world, including the end of the Roman Empire, and judgment over it. Christian belief in God, unlike the already established Jewish cult, centred on the monotheistic notion of the divine, was full of logical paradoxes, such as the coexistence of 'dead/alive' Jesus, then further incomprehensive jargon such as 'humiliation/ glorification', 'divine/human', 'weakness/strength', 'faith/knowledge'. In the relation to philosophy, Christianity promoted the attitude of *faith-belief*, and those Christians were very proud of their faith. That Roman intellectual world with its philosophical values, where Plato's legacy was still admired, saw faith as the lowest grade of cognition. 'Faith' characterised the lowest rank of society, the uneducated.[15] Therefore educated pagans saw themselves as representing 'reasoned conviction' while the Christians were, in their view, people of 'irrational faith'. Contemporary adversaries of Christianity such as Galen openly criticised Christians for their readiness to accept everything 'on faith'.[16] This pagan denigration soon brought accusations of 'superstition', 'ungodliness', 'magic' or even immorality. Christian faith was labelled a 'new and mischievous superstition' (Lat. *superstitio nova ac malefica*).[17]

If that was the common pagan view of the Christian faith, how then did the early Christians themselves understand their faith? Some answers we can find in collections of documents describing Christian martyrdom as 'hagiographies' (Gr. *hagios*, 'holy'),[18] composed in order to commemorate the martyrs and to promote the example of their extreme dedication. Although those documents present Christian saints in a highly pious, if not uncritical by our standards, way, still they give us insight into a sense of commitment to Christian faith. One of those accounts, the *Martyrdom of Bishop Carpus* provides an example of the early[19] self-awareness of

Christians. The confession of Carpus was brief but it had severe consequences as he gave witness to his principle by choosing suffering and death. Carpus' testimony, echoed in many further accounts of different martyrs who like him made their declaration, contains the essence of the new faith as an uncompromising and firm statement. *To believe* was *to confess* in public. This radicalism or even extremism was a quite common characteristic of many early Christians. In the light of that strong, unyielding faith human life also received a particular meaning as it was totally dedicated to Jesus Christ. God appears to be of supreme importance to all Christian martyrs, as he was for the Jewish martyrs (2 Macc. 7.1–42). Therefore any form of compromise with pagan polytheism, or even the cult of the Emperor, was out of the question. This radicalism outlined very well the character of Christian faith, as it from now on promoted the ideal of subordination of one's will to the will of God, which soon will be identified with the doctrine of the Great Church. Obedience to the Church will emerged as an extension of the original emphasis on the faithfulness to God and will provide 'catholic' Christians with another axiom of their self-understanding, as we shall see in Chapter 10.

*

In conclusion I would like to highlight that the original character of the opening statement of the Apostles' Creed called for a very personal and deliberate dedication to God. While Christian commitment, faith and trust had much in common with its natural Jewish ethos and Hebrew theology, nevertheless it differed, in that the crucial emphasis was put on Jesus of Nazareth: a new and ultimate mediator between the whole of humanity and God. Early Christians, like their contemporary neighbours, valued common rituals and the visible signs of belonging to a religious group, but unlike pagans, they prioritised a personal, often emotional attachment to Jesus as the only 'Lord', and therefore their inclusiveness had much stricter limits. At this early stage with only few 'dogmas' about the nature of God, salvation and the Church, the dominant element in Christian faith linked each and every believer with the Saviour, and through the Saviour with God and the rest of the fellow believers. *Faith in God* revealed by Jesus of Nazareth provided Christians with a fresh understanding of their fellowship, which soon expounded across ethnic boundaries, social classes and philosophical schools. New *faith* brought with it a new dynamism which gradually reshaped parts of Judaism and the boundaries of the Roman society within which this *faith* was proclaimed.

. . . the Father Almighty, Creator of Heaven and Earth

God's tripartite title ('Father–Almighty–Creator') is not a straightforward, predictable result of the fact that early theology was formulated exclusively by male intellectuals. This title should not lead to a simple conclusion that Christian doctrine came into being in a culture dominated by a patriarchal mentality, which projected its image and values on the Deity. Other religions of this period were male-centred too, but unlike Jews or Christians, they had female divinities. Equally, it would be an oversimplification to suggest that the imagery of late Hellenistic culture or some philosophical notions had no influence whatsoever on the Christian notion of God, as if theology could develop in cultural seclusion. These two views, like Scylla and Charybdis, must be carefully navigated. Although, there is substantial New Testament evidence of applying to God the title of 'Father' this practice was not an obvious indication that the Ultimate divine being was a male. Among the first generations of Christ's followers, there were also those, labelled by their 'catholic' opponents as 'Christian Gnostics'[1] who presented an alternative view of the Deity. In my view, the Gnostic theology played an important part in challenging proclamation of God's fatherhood that laid the foundation of the first sentence from the Apostles' Creed. Let's begin then with polyphony of voices on the fatherhood of God.

Fatherhood of God – Grammar and Theology

The passionate conflict between emerging proto-orthodox[2] view of God's fatherhood and other dissimilar notions is clearly noticeable during the first and second centuries. Although almost all of

16

polemical evidence comes from only the victorious party, it is possible to say that theology of the Gnostics was more open to accept
the female characteristics of the Absolute. This alternative view of
God, as an opposition to 'catholic' (Gr. *katholikos,* 'universal') doctrine, promoted the theological idea of masculine and feminine
elements as the Source of spiritual life and reality and some theologians of this orientation even understood the Deity as an androgyne.[3] This kind of exegesis seriously worried the proto-orthodox
polemists who saw those attempts as a dangerous modification of
the 'original' and 'genuine' Christian doctrine, at least represented by those authors. In this context I wish to introduce our first
important theologian: Irenaeus, the Bishop of Lyons.[4] Irenaeus'
theology responded to claims of his various Christian opponents
about the nature of God and salvation, therefore as an apologetic
reply was deeply connected with the Gnostic questions. The crucial
evidence of Irenaeus' 'correction' of heretical errors comes from
his main oeuvre, *Against Heresies* in which he presents an account of
the following Gnostic poetic theology.[5] Although God is ineffable,
this could be represented by metaphors which combine male and
female characteristics. The masculine and feminine elements in
the divine remain in balance and from them emanate further pairs
of masculine and feminine spiritual beings. This vision of God as a
pair of male and female eternal divinities finds its parallel in many
other documents.[6] One scholar notes[7] that the Coptic word for
'father' translating the original Greek term *pater* is also used to
designate the androgyne divinity. This philological observation
revises the use of male names for the principal Deity and introduces male–female terminology in many documents from the so-
called Nag Hammadi Library discovered in Upper Egypt in 1945.[8]
That note suggests that in some Gnostic theologies, the Highest
Deity accepted the idea of androgyny within the divine nature. The
theological model of God as male–female at the same time is well
documented in Gnostic writings.[9] The strong emphasis of the
proto-orthodox authors on the fatherhood of God must be seen as
a rejection of an option originating in the various Gnostic theological schools and communities. Among those Gnostic Christians
there was a room for an open appreciation and proclamation of
the female aspects of the 'Unknown God', which then had some
influence on role for women in local communities.[10] Other Gnostic
treatises suggest that Jesus' true Mother was the female Holy
Spirit[11] or that the Christian God is 'father and mother'.[12] God's
Spirit appears in Gnostic imagery to be, female. Similarly divine
spiritual beings such as Wisdom,[13] Silence,[14] Womb[15] or Thought[16]
receive female characteristics and become the maternal element in

God. Since Gnostic communities existed as a part of the Christian movement these few examples of their theology of God show a very pluralistic approach to the divine. There is a striking contrast between these Gnostic notions that underline the female ability of the divine to conceive, care for and nourish offspring, and the view of 'catholic' Christians who, in response emphasised God's fatherhood. The Gnostic Christians reflect on the story of the creation of the first human beings (Gen. 1.27) as 'icons' of God, as if their gender reflected God's masculine/feminine qualities.[17] At the same time the mainstream Christianity underlined the fatherhood of God as a guarantee of order, domination and organisation of the creation.

The works of the so-called 'Apologists'[18] of the second century[19] were engaged in the debate with pagans particularly on the language used to describe the nature of God. One of them, Justin Martyr provides us with a good example.[20] Both of his *Apologies* offer some examples of that hermeneutical approach. His theology of God and salvation showed an obvious connection between God's function as the Creator and 'the Monarch' (Gr. *monarchos*) over his creation.[21] Interestingly, Justin described God as the Creator using the Greek term *pater*, suggesting that fatherhood includes governing the world and taking care of it by his providence. Justin linked the title of 'Father' with the title of 'the king of heaven'.[22] More analytical insight into his terminology shows that the Platonic idiom 'Father of all'[23] inspired Justin's understanding of God's role. The analogical connection between the name of God as *Pater* and his functions as 'the ruler' or 'king' appeared frequently in Theophilus of Antioch.[24] Theophilus, the Bishop of Antioch in Syria expressed God's role in a very poetic way as 'the pilot steering the ship' that is the universe.[25] He perceived the whole of reality as 'God's monarchy'.[26] God, the Father, took care of the living and the dead and that care is his all-providing government.[27] Justin and Theophilus underlined that God's 'administration' embraces everything, including this material world. The fatherhood of God, a strong grasp over the changing and unstable reality of the world, seems better to express the human needs that were hidden behind addressing God as the male Governor.

It is interesting to note that fervent polemic against Gnostics and pagans motivated and consolidated the effort to promote by 'catholic' movement a specific image of God with male characteristics. The male God, a father-type figure arch-patriarch guaranteed, at least in the proto-orthodox persuasion, all necessary features of the divine ultimate authority, mainly his strength, stability and justice. These characteristics responded to a particular need of the religious people.

God Almighty – the Rhetoric of God's Might versus Fatalism and Astrology

The Greek title *pantokrator*, which emphasises God's absolute might, occurred in early theology firstly as the primary feature of Godhead.[28] In the light of the meaning of God's fatherhood this term strengthens the idea of God's unquestionable dominion over the world and all creatures. The scriptural narrative of God's sovereignty together with the philosophical climate of the late Graeco-Roman culture formed the axiom of God's transcendence, domination and independence from any other elements of reality. His powerful, unquestionable, autonomous governance and care includes historical events and the well-being of people. The three categories of God: oneness, fatherhood and omnipotence appear one after another and emphasise the true nature of God. The early theologians agreed that human beings cannot comprehend the essence of the Father, as he is incomprehensible. But because of his self-revelation through the nature of the created world and in Jesus of Nazareth, we are able to recognise and experience the divine Father's involvement in the present world. Faith in *Father Almighty* clearly underlined his omnipotence, omniscience and omnipresence. But it was neither academic speculation nor philosophical curiosity about God's nature that brought a philosophical category into the Creed. Experience of different sorts of evil in this world raised the fundamental question about God's response to it. The early Christians, like many other people at the time, needed faith in a God who could protect them from many forms of evil and they were genuinely searching for an answer to the question 'why are we persecuted?' Faith in *God the Father Almighty* responded to that very human feeling, fear of insecurity and vulnerability, leaving the believer with the conviction that individual life is precious in the eyes of God.

Christian affirmation of God's might, while it echoed classical Hebrew theology, addressed the pagan philosophical concept of determinism. This notion was related to astrology, as the stars were administrators of the universal, cosmological destiny. Astrology and belief in fate questioned the Christian concept of God's providence and his autonomy, in which everything that exists is dependent on God and remains under his rule.[29] Belief in fate and the power of stars found a well argued response among the Apologists. Athenagoras of Athens, for instance, having rationally demonstrated the existence of the One God convincingly argued that this divine Monarch exercises the power of governing his creation which cannot be shared with any other god.[30] God not only created the whole universe, but also sustains it and even nourishes it.[31] The same Father who is also the absolute Sovereign, the Source of all existing power and authority[32] oversees the matters of this world, which means sustaining its order.[33] Creating the world, he gave it his law[34] but angels and human beings since they were given reason, could make choices and experience freedom. That potential freedom if rightly used will be rewarded or, if misused, will find its just punishment.[35] Justin says that as justice is a characteristic of fatherhood, it is a very proper attribute for God.[36] This kind of persuasion constituted a strong argument against the assumed lack of freedom, predestination and the limitation of God's power, which undermined the Christian notion of God as the Father of all. According to early theologians human freedom and God's providence do not exclude each other, but they may co-exist in harmony. Therefore theologians such as Justin the Martyr,[37] Irenaeus of Lyons,[38] Tertullian,[39] Hippolytus of Rome,[40] to name just a few, defended the title of God as Father as related to God's providence, while upholding human freedom and personal responsibility. It is clear that they insisted unanimously, although with reference to different arguments, that God's plan of salvation echoes his nature as the caring Father. For better illustration, let us turn to some examples of that Christian rhetoric.

Justin elaborated a theology of God that helped him defend the Christian faith in almighty Creator of the universe.[41] Justin's treatise the *Dialogue with Trypho* while addressing a critic of a certain Trypho, a Jewish theologian, reveals that a good God[42] can do and does whatever he wills.[43] God created the world out of his goodness for man's sake[44] and he cares for the universe and particularly for individuals.[45] Justin's theology of God presented a synthesis of his philosophical Platonic convictions about the divine being, which is transcendent, immovable, ineffable, Cause and Ruler of the Universe,[46] and biblical descriptions, for instance, of a loving, caring Father. God is thus *pantokrator* and that title is the name that Christians rightly apply to God.

Irenaeus' understanding of God as *Almighty* contains some characteristics from his incessant polemic with his adversaries of dualistic tendencies. Irenaeus persistently emphasises that God the Father is omnipotent since visible, material reality is not an outcome of a cosmological catastrophe caused by an evil, uncontrolled Demiurge.[47] God is free from any external compulsion, he is absolutely autonomous and he can never be the slave of necessity.[48] All creation must submit to his will which has universal dominion.[49] All things are subjected to his will and, to highlight this, Irenaeus calls him 'God over all' and confirms that he is 'the cause of being to all things'.[50] Irenaeus' theology underlined the positive character of God: there is no other Source of being. God, the Father is one, creator, omnipotent and free. God is perfect in all things, he is the source of all good things; he lacks nothing because he is self-sufficient. But he gives other beings existence by creating them and this free act shows his governance over all reality.[51] And Irenaeus added that God's acts are marked by his power, wisdom and goodness.[52] God's will brings all things to existence and reflects his goodness and wisdom. Therefore, as the Creator, the Father acts in the following manner: bestowing harmony on all things and assigning them to their own place.[53]

Other theologians such as Tertullian[54] and Hippolytus of Rome both noted the title of omnipotent in their theological works.[55] But Tertullian understood the title as applicable to a God free from any limits, and that God is able to transcend the law of contradiction.[56] Interestingly, Tertullian also clearly stated that this title can be attributed to Jesus, as it refers to a characteristic of God's nature not just to the person of the Father.[57] A similar theological approach can be found in Hippolytus' *Against Noetus*, where the title *the Almighty* refers to Jesus Christ.[58] Only these references to various authors show that the effort to reaffirm faith in the Almighty God was important to Christians from different regions of the Roman Empire as they advocated against common theological, philosophical and psychological thread which diminished human freedom and divine protection, while overstated the might of invisible, hostile and dark powers.[59]

The Divine Creator of the Heaven and Earth

Faith in God, as the Creator of the visible and invisible realities was not taken for granted by early Christians as they encountered a number of other theological and philosophical theories within the Christian communities as well as outside them. In this short section I wish to sketch the most significant challenges to this credal belief.

First, within the inner-Christian circle, the Gnostic notion of 'emanation' of the whole spiritual reality from its divine Source presented the origin of the invisible world as a necessary, unstoppable and uncontrolled overflow. According to the 'catholic' critics, this kind of emanationism did not leave any room for a conscious, purposeful and free act of creation, but everything was determined by 'automatic' procedure which produced abundant spiritual beings ('Aeons'). The Gnostic poetic narratives, in its essential structure, presented the origin of the invisible realm as a gradual emanation of less and less perfect beings within the sphere of the divine, and that multiplication of levels, like a metaphysical pyramid with the divine, utterly incomprehensible Monad on the top, ultimately led to a catastrophe on its lowest level: creation of this evil world.[60] As we shall see, Irenaeus refuted this pessimistic scenario in his chief work.

In the same Christian context, yet another challenge appeared with the question of the co-existence of good and evil spiritual powers, raised in a radical way by Marcion.[61] This time it was not the gradual multiplication of the spiritual beings, but rather radical separation of two causes of the whole reality. It seemed that Marcion attacked the idea of one, good God-Creator and suggested the existence of two divine Rulers: one, the God of the Jews, the God of Justice and rather an autocratic, even cruel figure, and the second, an opposite – the Good Father, revealed by Jesus Christ, the source of Love, mercy and compassion. This antithesis emphasised the tension, at least among some Christians, between the faithfulness to the letter of the Law and the life of the spirit.

Tertullian's response underlined the unity and continuity in the history of salvation, as the God of the 'Old Testament' is also the Father of Jesus Christ. On another level, the Creator of the Universe is at the same time the author of its beauty and harmony. Imperfection noticeable in the visible world does not suggest imperfection in its Creator, but rather his will to call into being the whole range of creatures, including the insects. Often opposites found in nature expressed God's richness, originality and creativeness. God, according to Tertullian created all things: material and immaterial, animate and inanimate, vocal and silent, mobile and static, expressing in this way the symphony of all creation.[62] The evil spirit or Satan is not co-eternal with God the creator, but he has his own particular history. The evil spirit is a rebellious angel, originally as good as the rest of creation, who misused his freedom.[63] God postponed the annihilation of Satan and evil in order to give all humanity the opportunity to reject it and cooperate with him in re-establishing the original harmony and perfection.[64] Satan will be finally defeated by his former victim and the glory of God will be even more evident as he in his goodness offers human beings the chance to come back to their original place, which is paradise. Against Marcion, Tertullian highlighted the might of God by revealing to his readers a theological perspective in which the original tragedy of sin becomes transformed by God into the final glory. And that is possible only through God's governance and power.

Secondly, outside of the Christian milieu, there were at least two kinds of opinions regarding the Absolute's connection with the visible world, which provided a competitive model to the Christian 'catholic' concept of *the Creator of everything*. Although they represented an outcome of philosophical speculation, their popularity among intellectuals seemed to attract enough of common attention that they were scrutinised and considered untrue by the theologians representing the Great Church. First, the belief in *the divine Creator* refuted the philosophical (Platonic) concept of pre-existent matter, as the emerging doctrine of the creation of the universe 'out of nothing' highlighted God's absolute, unquestionable might. The proto-orthodox theologians responded with an original and controversial idea, which is usually referred to the Latin idiom: 'creation out of nothing' (Lat. *creatio ex nihilo*). This concept brings together all that has been said about God so far in the Creed: he is One; he is the *Father Almighty* and now: he is *the Creator of everything*. However it asks a lot of good will from those believers who were well educated in the classical Greek philosophy and knew the ancient axiom that 'out of nothing, nothing comes'. This time the proto-orthodox polemists aimed to reverse this paradigm and claimed that 'all come out of nothing', as a unique miracle of mighty God.

Another philosophical opinion, which was confronted by the belief in the *Creator of heaven and earth* proclaimed that although the reality was called into being, however, it is not a 'body' or an 'extension' of its divine Source. In this way another Greek theory, so called 'pantheism' (Gr. *pan* = 'everything' and *theos* = 'god'), was rejected. From a Christian proto-orthodox point of view, the universe and God are not 'mixed together'. The opinion that 'God is everything' and at the same time 'everything is God' in the way that the matter contained divinity while divinity was perceived by the material universe, was untrue. This Stoic concept was assessed by early theologians as a dangerous confusion of the Creator and the creation, which may lead to divinisation of the human and natural element, while deifying what was created. Rejection of these two concepts did not leave theologians in silence on the subject of God's relationship to the creation. On the contrary, they hoped to clarify the correct understanding of their belief in *the Creator of everything*.

The early, proto-orthodox thinkers approached these and other difficulties with a steadfast conviction that God is the sovereign, almighty Creator. For instance, Theophilus of Antioch interpreted

God as a Being is without beginning, immutable and immortal of ineffable essence. But the same God, unlike the Deity from Gnostic narratives, is the good Creator who is engaged in the existence of his creatures. The beauty of creation is a specific 'fingerprint' of its good Creator. He is not 'alien', certainly not 'evil' but on the contrary he is loving and caring, somebody who is 'inside' of the world as well as transcends it.[65] This interpretation of God appears to be of somebody who is present among his creatures, is concerned about them, supports and mercifully sustains them, but who is also totally other than this world. The biblical narrative, particularly the New Testament, and the philosophical, particularly Platonic, presuppositions about a Father and Creator of all things[66] came together in the proto-orthodox theology of this period. This one example shows how closely evaluation of the visible reality was connected with understanding of its invisible Author. This relationship is highlighted even more by Irenaeus of Lyons. Some of the dualistic Christian theologies presented the visible world as 'an abortive product', 'a shameful disease' and 'a place of darkness'. Irenaeus' response to this radical negative assessment of the material world introduces terminology echoed in the Creed:

> I should begin then, as it is important, with the first and the most important statement about God the Creator, who made the heaven and the earth, and all things which are within. His creation these people [i.e. Irenaeus' opponents] call blasphemously 'the fruit of a defect', and then I will demonstrate that there is nothing either above Him or after Him; nor that, He was influenced by any one, but of His own free will, He created all things, since He is the only God, the only Lord, the only Creator, the only Father, alone containing all things, who called all things into existence.[67]

This anti-dualistic statement openly defends the nature of visible and invisible reality as a positive, good and purposeful result of God's free act. Irenaeus' response to the pessimistic or even nihilistic evaluation of the universe is based on the nature of the Creator that is God's goodness.[68] Irenaeus emphasised that *the Creator* is directly responsible for the creation of the world. Good God is the intelligent architect of the beautiful universe and its creation reflects the personal characteristics of the divine Artist. To Irenaeus, God is a cosmic Mind who not only 'thinks' and 'creates' but also as an Artist, he uses his perception to create universe of harmony, beauty and light. Irenaeus' theology of God is fascinated with the motif of order and intentionality. Everything has its place, the whole history of salvation develops according to God's plan, and nothing is accidental. Therefore the whole reality is a symphony composed by the divine musician. He is a genius as he joined all created visible and invisible elements in concord of one choir. Of course there are some voices who do not sing the same melody as the rest of the creation, but still, in its final act everything will be brought to the original harmony and glory.

*

The first sentence of the Apostles' Creed summarise a fervent debate about the nature of God. All three selected God's epithets, recorded by the Apostles' Creed, aimed to explain the unique relationship between God and his creatures. These three titles emphasise God's autonomy, goodness as well as the positive value of the visible and invisible world. In a period of fear of the gods, the unpredictability of fortune, in the time of belief in the power of astrology and ubiquitous fate, this simple sentence encouraged the believers to put their trust in the name of their God. This belief offered neither immediate answers to daily dilemmas nor naïve consolation. But as a signpost it directed the minds of early Christians to their Creator, who was pictured by this pronouncement as the caring Monarch, the ultimate Governor of all reality but also as a very personal protector as a Father.

. . . and in Jesus Christ, His only Son our Lord

I am a Christian, and because of my faith and the name of my Lord Jesus Christ I cannot become one of you.

Martyrdom of Carpus[1]

This statement of the Apostles' Creed introduces a whole new section focused on *Jesus Christ*. It is about a Jewish man of Nazareth, who for his followers became the *Messiah/Christ*. The New Testament documents highlight different characteristics of Jesus as the *Christ*, unveiling specific theological interests which lay behind various theological accounts of Jesus' life and mission. From the common Christian perspective Jesus of Nazareth claimed his exceptional familiarity with God and had a special relationship with the divine Father as his 'Son'. This unique relationship produced the core of the Christian faith. But Jesus' death/resurrection and its Scriptural evidence developed more than just one line of interpretation of Jesus' life and his role as the 'Son of God'. The last Christological designate was not unique, as the New Testament contains forty two titles.[2] This natural pluralism of terminology, idioms and narratives provided the next generations of Patristic theologians with a great choice of material about Jesus of Nazareth. Later in history, under pressure of various doctrines, this material became theologically refined and summed up in the creeds. One of them, the Apostles' Creed, boldly states the distinctiveness of Jesus Christ as God's Son, while leaving out more complex theology on the nature of the Saviour.

From Jesus of Nazareth to Jesus the Christ –
Testimony of Early Theology

The earliest Christian literature openly proclaimed Jesus of Nazareth as the promised *Christ*. The Messianic idea gained its importance particularly in relation to the Jewish eschatological expectations and from there it was transferred to early Christianity.[3] It is therefore right to see the biblical prophecies as the direct source of the new Christology. The Christ-centrism of theology declared Jesus as the embodiment of the Hebrew concept of *the Messiah*, 'the Anointed one' and *Christ* of 'the last days'. The creed reflects the original association between those two inseparable elements: the Biblical prophesies about *the Christ* and the New Testament testimonies about their realisation in the life and works of *Jesus of Nazareth*. The gradual separation of early Christians from their Jewish background arose from the significance that the Christians attributed to the role of Jesus of Nazareth as *the Messiah/ Christ*. This case is well illustrated in Justin Martyr's debate with Trypho, the Jewish theologian.[4] This document, composed about 160 CE, demonstrates exceptionally well the Christian effort to identify *Jesus of Nazareth* as *Christ* to Justin's Jewish interlocutor. Through the mediation of the Scriptural evidence, Justin aims to present Christian self-understanding more clearly.[5] For Justin, Christianity is a natural, positive and final development of Judaism, with *Jesus* the central figure as he fulfilled the messianic promises of the Old Testament.[6] For Trypho, Christianity betrays the Tradition and the Laws, and by misusing the Holy Scriptures misleadingly asserts that Jesus is the Christ.[7] As expected, the whole debate between these two theologians and traditions focuses on the person and the mission of Jesus. Christians represented by Justin believed that they understood the mission of God's *Messiah* better than their Jewish opponents. Justin's debate gives evidence of that stance in which the concept of *Christ* become fully 'Christianised' and proclaimed to the Jews. The crucial part of that 'new interpretation' is the emphasis on the reality of incarnation, where divine Logos becomes human being – *Jesus of Nazareth*. Justin shows all the characteristics of this line of persuasion. At the same time to the Jewish audience, the Christian insistence upon the 'divinity' of the Messiah remains yet another proof of their erroneous exegesis, since it is hard to conclude the divine nature of the Messiah from the evidence of the Hebrew Scriptures. Nonetheless Justin is adamant about his belief that *Jesus Christ* was both divine and human. The crucified *Jesus of Nazareth* was the first-born of the unbegotten God. In Justin's theology the pre-incarnate divine

Logos which as a concept was known to the Jews, is identified with
Jesus, the Palestinian Jew. *Jesus Christ* is thus at the same time
divine and human, eternal and able to suffer and to die. He was
begotten by his divine Father and born of a human mother. This
paradox or Christian effort to join together what otherwise
does not have a common ground, is in the core of early Christian
apologetics, represented here by Justin Martyr.

The title *Jesus Christ* reflects the Scriptural bonding of Jewish and
Greek theological semantics. Yet, it is more than that. It also
indicates the moment of the theological departure of Christology
from its natural Jewish origin. It echoes, although indirectly, the
religious separation of Judaism and Christianity and the growth of
the Greek element over the Jewish-Christian one. The Hebrew epithet *the Messiah,* as the Greek *Christos* not only becomes more popular among Christians as a pragmatic, pedagogic amelioration, it
also magnifies the New Testament characteristic of *the Christ* who is
fully identified with *Jesus of Nazareth.* And that act of identification
of a historical character, a Jewish Rabbi of Nazareth, with the
Saviour of the World divine by origin is a matter of faith. But this
line of development of the belief in *Jesus Christ* soon came to the
next crucial questions: why had the divine being to be incarnated
in the first place? Why is there a need of mediation of salvation
'through' or 'in' human nature? There were a number of early
Christians, including the Christian Gnostics, who had their serious
doubts about the possibility of 'incarnation', or 'embodiment' of
the perfect divine element in deficient human flesh. Can fire be
mixed with water? Can unlimited spiritual reality become visible
and tangible as any other material thing? One of the best early
Christian answers to this question came from Irenaeus of Lyons.

Irenaeus' Christology put emphasis on the mission of *Jesus Christ*
to establish a new relationship between the creation and God the
Creator.[8] That new covenant is a real fact as the person who made it
possible is *Jesus Christ,* who in Irenaeus' view was fully divine and
human alike. Although being the eternal Word, this divine Logos
came down and appeared as a real human being, a historical man.[9]
The idea of the embodiment of a god in human flesh was quite
popular in various pagan mythologies, but the Christian belief in
incarnation had much more serious implications than just a conviction that the divine being can appear in human form. According
to the main line of Irenaeus' interpretation, *Jesus Christ,* a true
Man and true God, is the climax of God's revelation and
therefore through him people have access to new life,[10] new status
and new dignity. Christ is a spiritual and material 'bridge' who
brings together the two realms of divinity and humanity, God and

creation, as nobody before, because no human being was divine. As Christ is fully divine, only through *Jesus* we can learn about God himself. In Christ's visible humanity the divinity of the invisible God has been revealed to people.[11] It is uniquely through Christ that human beings can recognise their own identity, their purpose of life as renewing its likeness to God and the means to achieve it. Christ is then the central, historical point for humanity, and furthermore, *Jesus Christ* is the centre of the universe and of salvation. The Bishop of Lyons underlines this essential connection between the human and divine elements in *Jesus Christ.* In his view they are not a part of sophisticated speculation about the nature of the Saviour, rather they are the indispensable conditions of our salvation, which reached its fullness in Jesus. Irenaeus' famous statement asserts that: 'God become Man in order that man may become god'.[12] Only Christ can lift up the whole of humanity to its original place and status which was lost through the disobedience of Adam and Eve. There the original break took place, but in Christ, a 'new Adam', the final restoration takes place, and this motif is one of the crucial ideas of Irenaeus' theology. Therefore the doctrine of Christ is directly related to the doctrine of salvation, which in consequence means that an erroneous understanding of the first produces a false, invalid hope of eternal happiness with God in his dominion. Herein lays the reason why later debate on the two natures of Christ became a matter of life and death not only for theologians but also for many lay Christians. The descent or incarnation of the divine Logos, we may conclude from Irenaeus' visionary thought, is God's ultimate channel of communication with humanity. But also *Jesus of Nazareth* is the perfect apotheosis of humanity.

'Our God has begotten a Son' – Christian proclamation and context.

From the mythological, and especially the pagan perspective, the story about 'a god has begotten a son' was neither new nor even scandalous. It was a well-known literary fact of many ancient theogonies that gods like humans, procreated and had children.[13] In Hebrew theology the idea that the eschatological Messiah was called 'the son of God' had a long tradition[14] but it did not suggest literarily the divine origin of the Messiah. The Hebrew monotheism does not allow seeing any kind of 'division' within God and it put strong limits on the anthropomorphic image of YAHWE. Therefore all references to the idea of 'sonship', either particular individual or the whole nation, were read in the context of their symbolical and pedagogical function and their place within the rhetoric of Hebrew theology. Christian theologians, however, crossed over this boundary. The important transition from the title 'the son of God' to the new epithet 'God the Son' took place at the end of the first and during the early second century, and was later ultimately confirmed and proclaimed by the Creed of Nicaea (325 CE).

First, the Apologists made an effort to explain to Jewish and pagan critics the meaning of their belief in the exclusivity of the relationship between God the Father and his *Son*, Jesus Christ. The confession of the human nature of Christ was accompanied by an increasingly bold confession of his divinity.[15] At the end of the second century there was already a strong conviction about the divine element of Christ's nature, which balanced his humanity. One of the first and most elaborate attempts is found in Athenagoras' *Embassy for the Christians*, with a confirmation of faith in the *Son of God* as coeternal with his Father.[16] God the Father and his Son are 'one' in that they share the same divine nature, but according to Athenagoras, the Son of God is the Word of the Father. The Word coexists with his Father and remains equal to the One who has uttered him. But soon this still vague understanding of the relationship between the divine Father and his Son became challenged by a number of speculations and efforts to comprehend the mystery of the origin of Jesus Christ.

One such, radically separated the divine nature of God the Father from any other being, including Jesus of Nazareth and treated Christ as the 'adopted' rather than natural son of God. The divine Creator cannot have 'a son', but God elected a man, Jesus of Nazareth, to be his unique representative and messenger. This kind of Christological interpretation became known as 'adoptionism'. The adoptionist affinity in Christology states that Jesus, the son of Mary and Joseph, was a man endowed with divine powers by God, and thus Jesus was in a way elected as God's 'Son'. Originally adoptionism was confessed by the Jewish-Christians communities known as 'Ebionites' (Hebr. *ebyon* – 'the poor men'), who even had their Gospel, called 'the Gospel of Ebionites'.[17] This Christology accommodated the uncompromised monotheistic tendency, which in its view of God rejected any compromise with polytheism.

Another theory[18] was taught in the second century by Noetus of Smyrna and Praxeas.[19] Both theologians identified the Son with his Father saying in fact that the Father was born as the Saviour that is Jesus Christ, then suffered and was crucified.[20] Both put such a strong, if not extreme, accent on God's inner ontological unity as the one divine being, that any real distinction between the person of the Father and the Son becomes either an illusion of our human perception or a way 'mode' (Lat. *modi*) of God's self-disclosure for the sake of our limited comprehension. Noetus believed that the divinity of Christ was indisputable as the Son/Father was the true, eternal God, who was incarnated as the Saviour and went through passion and resurrection.

• In response to Noetus' interpretation Hippolytus of Rome composed a treatise *Against Noetus*, preserved only in fragments, and further, he ostracised Noetus in *Refutation of all heresies*.[21] This important example of theology in the Roman milieu re-examines the Scriptures and proves the real distinction between God the Father and his Son, reaffirming faith in *the Son of God* as a separate person but of the same, divine nature as his Father.[22] What emerges from Hippolytus' Christology, which is mainly his reinterpretation of John's Gospel, is not only the protection of the real difference between the persons within the Holy Trinity, but also his unwillingness to call the second person of the Trinity by the term 'Son' before his incarnation. In his view, prior to his historical manifestation *in flesh*, the second divine person was the Word of God.[23] The incarnation of the Word of God that is Jesus of Nazareth revealed the distinction within God that otherwise would never have been discovered by humans. God's unique revelation through his *Son* also brings us knowledge about the particular roles of the Father, the Son, and, as we shall see, the Holy Spirit in our salvation.

The greatest contribution to Christology at this stage of theology came from Tertullian. Again, his intellectual skills helped to clarify and communicate what previously was a matter of confusion. Addressing the controversy provoked by yet another form of belief that God the Father, identical with the Son, suffered on the cross,[24] Tertullian argues that the true faith of the Church, the faith originating in the John's Gospel, pronounces that:

> The one only God has a Son, his Word who has proceeded from himself, by whom all things were made and without whom nothing was made; that this Son was sent by the Father.[25]

Tertullian develops all the implications of that statement, which leads him to an affirmation of the unity within God, while he maintains the real difference between the Father and the Son as two persons. Tertullian believes that before the foundation of the universe God remained alone.[26] But this 'solitariness' must be understood not as loneliness. God never was 'lonely', even before the creation of the invisible world. God was always with his Reason (Lat. *ratio*), or 'Mind' which in Johannine tradition, was personified by the Logos and represented yet another synonym of God's

Son. It is possible to see that Tertullian is assimilating in the Christian context, the philosophical, Stoic, notion of the divine 'Mind', 'Word' or 'Ruler' of the universe. This eternal Mind, which governs the whole reality, is to Tertullian, a very helpful metaphor for the Son of God. As God's Mind has no beginning or no end, as it shares with God the same nature, it is co-eternal. But Tertullian knows from the Christian revelation, that this 'Mind', God's Reason is not an abstract rule, but the Mind of God is a person. He thinks, he has a will and has independent personality from the one of God the Father. Tertullian translates the philosophical specula- tion into a more accessible, visual example. In his famous example, the relationship between God, the Father and the Son is similar to the one of a tree and its root, a river and a fountain, the sun and its ray.[27] Therefore Son's existence is rather an extension of the divine nature, not a separation.[28] This essential difference between two persons does not in any way mean that for Tertullian Christian faith accepts the existence of two 'gods'. Both the Father and the Son, manifest *one, undivided substance* that is the *nature* of God.[29] They share the same nature, but they do so as two individual beings.

Jesus' Lordship

This third Christological title is the culmination of the previous debate about the nature and origin of Jesus Christ and the son of God. This time the Apostles' Creed highlights the Lordship of Jesus, which in the context of the early Christian theology, expresses the same faith, that Jesus is more than just a noble human messenger, he was and is *the Lord* (Gr. *Kyrios*) and the Saviour of humanity. It also points to the important shift in theological imagery from the original Jewish setting to a more Graeco-Roman terminology. Certainly this transition followed the sociological change within the Christian communities.[30]

In order to unveil the original meaning of the title, we have to look back to the Greek translation of the Hebrew Scriptures, known as the *Septuagint* (or the *LXX*) which played an immense role in the formation of the Christian theology[31] and Christology.[32] The Jewish authors of the *Septuagint* translated bravely the name of God *YHWH* into Greek as *Kyrios*.[33] This original act of interpret- ation of the Hebrew revelation into the Hellenistic mentality brought a whole range of new theological opportunities and prob- lems first for Jewish theologians,[34] and later for their Christian opponents. The Almighty becomes known as the *Lord*, or rather as the true Lord, as his might and authority have no equal in the universe. The Greek title applied to the Hebrew God brought also a number of new aspects, such as political references, but it soon becomes a synonym of the Eternal God of Israel. With the appearance of the first Christians, the title *Lord* is now commonly applicable to both: the earthly and the resurrected Jesus. As the *Kyrios*, Jesus assimilates not only a great many of the characteristics applied to God such as the 'ultimate Authority', or 'the Ruler' but also in the liturgical and ecclesiastical context, Jesus is worshipped as *the Lord* of Christians.[35] In fact, the title reaffirms the divinity of Jesus.[36] The secular, pagan or late Hellenistic semantic attached to this title, was welcomed by Christians as they saw Jesus as their Saviour (Gr. *Soter*), Deliverer, Benefactor and Protector of the world.[37]

In addition to this line of development, this title reflects another important change in early Christian theology: the shift of theological attention from the future second coming of *the Messiah/Christ* as testified by some New Testament documents, to his present role as *the Lord is here* in the later Patristic phase. After the very strong early eschatological emphasis in the New Testament, particularly in Paul's theology, and the focus on the imminent return of Christ and the end of time,[38] a different attitude emerges in second century documents. Theology looked more carefully at the historical existence, in the current world and time, and began to highlight a belief that *the Lord* is present in his Church. From the position of proclaiming the Saviour 'coming on a cloud' focused on the second coming of the Lord in the near future, there is a shift towards a confession of his existence within the visible Church here and now. This emphasis starts to bind the Christology and theology of the church in a new, significant way.

*

In summary, I wish to point out that the simple statement from the Apostles' Creed refers to a very complex theology of Jesus Christ. As we have seen, that theology was never static, but had developed on many levels. The first transition took place when Christians claimed that Jesus of Nazareth was actually more than a mere man, and that he was fully human and fully divine, as God's Son and the promised Messiah. In order to defend this view Christian theologians reinterpreted the Hebrew prophecies in a way which accommodated their own faith and the need of its proclamation. The second move took place in the social context when the majority of Christians were former pagans and therefore the earlier link with Hebrew, then Jewish-Christian Messianic imagery, weakened as new metaphors and idioms were assimilated for the sake of a more comprehensible communication to the new audience. The third move, less discussed in this chapter, appeared with the greater use of late Hellenistic philosophy and philosophical notions about God. Awareness of at least these three elements that underpin the current credal statement is absolutely crucial. But even with this knowledge we may in the pronouncement find an echo of a theological struggle, which may be summed up by the following questions: how to remain faithful to Christian monotheism, while accommodating God's revelation in his Son? How to comprehend the unity of God's nature, while reaffirming the real difference between the persons of the Father and the Son? These early Christian voices articulated only the beginning of the long and unfinished process of giving answers to these crucial questions.

CHAPTER 4

. . . Who was Conceived by the Holy Spirit, Born of the Virgin Mary

and He is acknowledged by the Holy Spirit to be the son of the most high God, who came down from heaven for the salvation of men. And being born of a pure virgin, unbegotten and immaculate He assumed flesh.

Aristides of Athens, *Apology*, 15[1]

We are about to explore one of the most controversial statements of the Creed, at least to a modern reader. Although the previous declarations contain a great number of miracles and assume a strong faith, this one seems to go even further. It appears to be openly 'untactful' and suggests that the early Christians were obsessed with the idea of 'purity', 'abstinence', 'life-long virginity' or 'sexual pollution'. Hopefully, the following examination will prove that the theology promoting this specific pronouncement had a different agenda than appears from a literal reading of the line above.

While paying attention to the grammar of the sentence, we may see that this article of faith underlines the direct connection between the divine 'by' (Lat. *de*) and human 'of' (Lat. *ex*) factors which facilitated the Saviour's incarnation. This syntax addressed some Christian views, which were happy to 'reduce' the nature of Jesus, to just one, either divine or human origin. Therefore the article is the sign of a theological battle which took place within the early Church. The present pronouncement refutes some of the alternative views already existing concerning the nature of Jesus Christ. As *the Holy Spirit* and *the Virgin Mary* are named by this declaration of faith, the two divine and human elements are established as essential to the proto-orthodox Christology. As to the

Holy Spirit, one important remark is needed. The second must refer to the virginity of Mary.

First, our reflection upon this statement must take into account that before the fourth century, the Holy Spirit was understood mainly as 'the creative power of the Most High' rather than a distinctive divine person of the Holy Trinity.[2] Although the specific nature of the Holy Spirit might have been less clear in the early period of Christianity (2–3 CE) the Apostles' Creed gives evidence to the intuition of early belief in the necessary involvement of both divine and human factors in Jesus' incarnation.

Secondly, Mary's virginity was perceived by early theologians as a way of protecting Christ against the corruption inherited from Adam and Eve. Mary was needed to be pure in order for her offspring to remain immune from the corruption shared by all human beings. The creative power of the Most High and the Virgin Mary appeared alongside each other in the most ancient of all Creeds, the archetype of all: 'The Old Roman Creed'. Mary is reaffirmed by this pronouncement as *the Virgin*, which is related to early Christian rhetoric competing with pagan, female deities. The importance of Mary's physical condition expressed the basic intention of those theologians to elevate the status of Mary above not only all other women, but also above all divinities known from mythologies and cults. Mary the Virgin triumphed over all other 'mothers of heroes' (paganism) and 'mothers of prophets' (Judaism).[3] Mariological piety introduced also an important female element into the mainstream Christian doctrine of a male-type God. However, Mary was never proclaimed to be divine but a creature closest to the divine. Mary was presented as 'pure virgin' totally consecrated to God, sanctified by the presence of the holy child in her womb. This expression and pedagogy responded to a specific theological and emotional need of early Christians, and flourished in and through the colourful, Mariological tradition.

Holy Spirit and the Virgin Mary – Their Roles in Incarnation

In one brief sentence of the Creed two aspects of the coming of Christ to this world are suggested. The first underlines his divine source and the second his human pedigree. Two lines of his descent into this world are interwoven: the one from Christ's divine Father, and the second from Jesus' mother. The guarantee of that connection is secured by the role of the Holy Spirit. This statement also attempts to respond to different Christological challenges during the first and second centuries such as Docetism[4] and the already mentioned adoptionism.[5] To resist those views, which represent either the reduction of Jesus to a divine being without flesh, or to a man, without any origin in the divine, the proto-orthodox theology had to bring together the Holy Spirit and Mary and affirm their role in the same sentence. The radical meaning of the declaration gives evidence to a serious crisis in the early Church as the connection between divine and human natures in Christ, was neither obvious nor even necessary. A careful, although limited, reconstruction of that historical background may help to assess the value of the link between the Holy Spirit and Mary, made in the credal declaration.

Our investigation begins with the leitmotif of early Patristic theology expressed by the following question: why was it so important for early Christian theologians to stress that Christ was divine and human at the same time? In order to provide a coherent, convincing answer, the early theologians presented a specific line of exegesis of a passage from 'the prophet Isaiah' (63.9)[6] in the Greek translation (the *LXX*) about God's own intervention which was central to early Christian Christology:

> It was no messenger or angel
> but his presence that saved them.
> in his love and his pity
> he redeemed them
> he lifted them up, carried them
> all the days of old.

For the proto-orthodox authors this prophecy was about the coming of the Christ/Messiah as messenger simultaneously human and divine. This passage directly inspired the Christology of Irenaeus[7] and Tertullian.[8] The appearance of the historical person of Jesus of Nazareth, who was recognised by his disciples as the Saviour, called for a theological formulation which would express the incomprehensible: the divine origin of a human being. Faith led to theological reflection, which later became doctrine written in the form of a Creed. If Jesus was 'the Son of God', and he was to his followers, he must have had only one Father, that was God himself, therefore his earthly, historical life must have been from this divine origin. This theological line of interpretation, which coherently traced Christ's divinity not from the point when, for instance, he was accepted as 'God's son' at his baptism, but to his divine nature, called for a special, miraculous intervention of God. This was formulated as conception *by* (Lat. *de*) *the Holy Spirit*.[9] But one danger must be avoided by introduction of the quite dangerous idea of

conception by the Holy Spirit. Early Christians were familiar with narratives about sexual intercourse between pagan gods and human
creatures, the virgin birth of some gods[10] and even about the sexual
encounter between the 'sons of god and the daughters of man-
kind' mentioned in the Scriptures.[11] The conception of the Christ
had to be distinguished from these indecent stories and therefore,
starting with the only two testimonies of the event from Matthew
(1.18–25) and Luke (1.26–38), the whole episode of conception in
both accounts is strongly asexual and directly related to God's
miraculous involvement. This Scriptural endorsement inspired
early Christian theologians to acknowledge the concept of *the Holy
Spirit's* great intervention, completely asexual, and in every way a-
somatic and divine. And the majority of early Christian literature
shows that the encounter between *the Holy Spirit* and *the Virgin Mary*
was free from any sexual context, while both participants were
acclaimed as necessary in the acts of incarnation. It is right to
conclude that the realism and historicity of incarnation depends
on co-operation between *the Holy Spirit* and *Mary*. To illustrate their
role we shall turn to some examples from early Christian
documents.

The nature of Christ's origin as both *divine* and *human* is boldly
declared by Ignatius of Antioch[12] in his epistles. The Bishop of
Antioch, who was attacking a tendency among his flock, which
denied that the Saviour had human flesh, reminded them that:

> For our God, Jesus the Christ, was conceived by Mary according
> to God's plan, both from the seed of David as of the Holy
> Spirit.[13]

Ignatius reveals[14] three mysteries or three stages of salvation:
Mary's virginity, her childbearing and Christ's death, concluding
that God's greatest secret is to reveal himself as a man/human.[15]
This bold pronouncement of Christ's simultaneous divinity and
humanity must have been provoked by some kind of Christology
known to Ignatius that disputed his concept of salvation. The
emphasis on the combination of both natures in Christ responded
to a Docetic theological challenge. This tendency in Christology
would, according to defenders of Christ's real humanity, undercut
the whole act of salvation accomplished by the Saviour's human
blood and death. Therefore to theologians like Ignatius the central
point of Christology was Christ's incarnation. For Ignatius, who
embodies the Catholic position, the reality of salvation and even
Jesus' existence depends on the reality of the manhood of Christ.
Thus, in Jesus Christ God reveals himself in a human way.[16]
Ultimately, from this proto-orthodox outlook God's revelation

could not happen without the collaboration of *Mary* with *the Holy Spirit*. Divine and human agents guaranteed that the Word became flesh at the annunciation.

The clear voice of the Bishop of Antioch finds its echo in other early Christian sources.[17] The idea is reflected in the writings of another Bishop, this time of Lyons, who also faced the challenge of Docetism[18] which, since it rejected a true and full incarnation, consequently undermined the value of Jesus' passion, death and resurrection. The logical result was the serious questioning of the idea of salvation. In response to this danger the Bishop of Lyons underlined Christ's birth of *the Virgin Mary* in many places in his writings. The *Proof of the Apostolic Preaching* contains full evidence of this approach.[19] A similar accent on the role of Mary[20], not only as a mother, but also as *the Virgin* is documented in his *Against Heresies*.[21] Like Ignatius, Irenaeus emphasised the physicality of Christ's body, but also intrepidly stated Christ's divinity through his divine origin. Once again Isaiah (the *LXX*) provided Scriptural arguments[22] showing the human and divine lineage of Jesus Christ. This interpretation defended Irenaeus' understanding of Jesus' birth of *the Virgin* against various alternative teachings.[23] From this polemic and in order to capture the imagination of his readers, Irenaeus devised the rhetorical model of Christ as a 'new Adam' and the Virgin Mary as 'the new Eve', pointing not only to Christ's full humanity but also to his divinity, holiness and moral perfection. The relationship of Christ with his divine Father, now under pressure from a theological reductionism, is extended to include his natural relationship with his mother. This new dimension of Christology developed by Ignatius and Irenaeus gained even more importance in later Patristic theology.[24]

Justin Martyr discussed the same issue on two different occasions. His two *Apologies* addressed a pagan audience that had some acquaintance with philosophy and with the religious concept of the birth of heroes based on ancient mythologies. Secondly, the theme of the virgin birth appeared during the debate with Justin's Jewish opponents. Both expositions of this Christian belief referred to the same crucial Scriptural source that is to Isaiah (7.14), which in Greek translation (the *LXX*) made an important amendment to the original Hebrew narrative. The passage in Justin's interpretation reads as follows:

> Behold, a virgin shall conceive and bring forth a son, and they shall say for his name: 'God with us'.[25]

The original Hebrew record of the same prophecy does not mention in those words 'a virgin' as the mother of the Messiah, but 'a young woman of a marriageable age' (Hebr. *ha-alma*). As Justin Martyr dedicated his *Apology* to the Emperor Antoninus Pius and his immediate circle, he did not attempt to convince them about the general possibility of the virgin birth of Christ, since they had heard about various Greek heroes born of a virgin. But to Jewish ears the same idea sounded very odd, and the Christian Apologist had to use a different argument speaking to Trypho. Justin explained then, having in mind a pagan reader, that Mary's virginity meant that she did not have intercourse with Joseph, her husband, but:

> She conceived of the Holy Spirit.[26]

As the whole event is incredible and simply impossible, Justin's persuasion referred to God's intervention so that even the pagan listeners might believe in it, as they had heard similar stories related to gods' capacities told in Greek and Roman mythologies. Thus, it seems to be a way of introducing to a pagan mind the idea of the virgin conception. The authority of Isaiah and other Hebrew prophets was compared by Justin with the role of ancient poets respected by the Romans. To Justin's way of thinking, even more esteem should be given to the biblical prophets and sages. Justin's *Apology* is a particularly intelligent construction of arguments for the virgin birth of Christ, as the Christian philosopher and convert, who knew the pagan mentality very well, refers to what is recognized by his audience as possible on the ground of their culture, and introduces a totally new element from Jewish-Christian revelation. This tactic was later remodelled when Justin addressed his Jewish opponent. Trypho had obviously read Isaiah, including the prophecy about the circumstances of the Messiah's birth. The first attempt to discuss the issue is made in Chapter 43 of the *Dialogue*, once again referring to Isaiah (7.14) in *the Septuagint* edition, and was designed to demonstrate to Trypho that nobody before Jesus of Nazareth had been born of a virgin. In Jesus, then, God's prophecy was fulfilled. However, Justin was aware of the fact that the Jews had already rejected the Christian claim, based on *the Septuagint*, about the virginity of the mother. So he came back to the argument from the Greek translation of Isaiah, later on quoting the context of the prophecy.[27] The Apologist proved Christ's virgin birth not just from one Scriptural sentence or a particular translation of the term, but rather from the whole context of that sentence, that to him, undoubtedly, pointed to Christ's life, and to Mary, his mother as virgin (Gr. *parthenos*).[28]

Tertullian's substantial contribution in the debate went alongside Ignatius' and Irenaeus' efforts to reject Docetism, although with a different geographical (North African) and cultural (Latin, Western Christian) flavour.[29] Tertullian loudly and persistently raised his voice against denunciations of Christ's human body and consequently his human existence. In his polemic against Marcion, he rejected the view that Christ's body was a sort of phantom and he criticises any deviations from the view that Christ was in the flesh.[30] In one of his most famous statements from this treatise, he contradicted Marcion with a characteristic sharpness of his wit:

> If, being the Son of man, he is of human birth, there is body derived from body (Lat. *corpus ex corpore*). Evidently you could more easily discover a man born without heart or brains, like Marcion, than without a body, like Marcion's Christ. Go and search then for the heart, or the brains, of that man of Pontus.[31]

This is just one example, among many from his polemic against Marcion, of how ardently Tertullian defended the real flesh of Christ. In addition to this work, he even wrote a separate treatise focused on the issue of Lord's body (*On the Flesh of Christ*) where he stated that the incarnation includes spirit and flesh, as he was born and begotten in the flesh.[32] Tertullian's powerful emphasis on Christ's humanity provoked by Marcion's Christology did not lead him to play down Christ's divinity. But it highlighted the role of *the Virgin Mary*, to whom references in his treatises are numerous. Tertullian, along with all the other proto-orthodox theologians of the period, accepted the virginity of *Mary* before she conceived, however, unlike later Latin theology, he rejected the theory of her virginity 'during' (Lat. *in partu*) and 'after' (Lat. *post partu*) the birth of Christ.[33] *The Virgin Mary* became, then, the essential assurance of the fact that Christ had real flesh and in Tertullian's polemic her role is not only irreplaceable, as would be logical, but also a unique theological signpost in Christology. According to Tertullian, *the Virgin Mary* and the virgin birth were a central part of God's plan of salvation, since without Christ's humanity his suffering, death, resurrection and ascension are insignificant.[34]

A Voice of the Opponents on Jesus' Incarnation

Tertullian's explanation of Christ's double origin was provoked by alternative views among Christians on Christ's birth. But can we trust the proto-orthodox apologists, bishops and orators? In this highly polemic, emotional and oratorical dispute all rhetorical skills used were the defenders of the mainstream stance. Certainly, some 'heretics' were closer if not openly in favour of 'Docetic'

Christology, others preferred an 'adoptionist'[35] solution to the problem. But the opposition against the teaching of the 'Church Fathers' contained a more complex composition of themes and interpretations, than just one or two theories. In the collection of documents from The Nag Hammadi Library we may find also a more balanced view on the crucial relation between *the Holy Spirit* and *the Virgin Mary*. These original insights into Gnostic imagery and mentality offer some response to the apologists of the Greater Church.

For various Gnostic theologies the issue of the entry of the Saviour into human reality was very highly problematic if not incomprehensible. The main problem was how the perfect spiritual and divine being, that is the Redeemer, could pollute himself by the direct contact with the material sphere and human flesh? Christian Gnostic were aware of the 'catholic Gospels' and other documents, but those controversial testimonies needed to be either interpreted in the light of the Gnostic paradigm, or replaced by more accurate, sound and convincing narratives about the Saviour. In addition, not all Gnostic theologians identified 'Christ' with the same person that is Jesus of Nazareth of the proto-orthodox, mainstream sources. According to some trends of Gnostic thoughts, 'Christ' was only a metaphor of the Gnostic soul, an example to the Gnostic disciples of possible self-salvation or becoming 'redeemed Redeemer' (Lat. *Salvator salvandus*).[36] The Nag Hammadi Library reveals substantial differences between the Gnostic narratives and the stories from the literature used by the orthodox Christianity. Gnostic theologies provide a particular version of the earthly birth of Christ. Above all, in *the Gospel of Philip*, Mary receives positive attention as one of the three close female companions of Jesus who were always with him.[37] She is openly called his 'virgin mother' (Gr. *parthenos*)[38] but immediately, as if in a polemical tone, it is added:

> Some said, 'Mary conceived by the holy spirit'. They are in error. They do not know what they are saying. When did a woman ever conceive by a woman? Mary is the virgin whom no power defiled.[39]

This passage reveals important characteristics of *the Holy Spirit* and *the Virgin Mary* as opposed to those presented above the main-stream, orthodox interpretation. First, referring to Syriac and other Semitic languages, the word 'spirit' had a feminine connotation, therefore the Gnostic author recalls this tradition and applies it to the nature of *the Holy Spirit*, as a divine feminine power.[40] It was then impossible for Mary to conceive by *the Holy Spirit*, as a woman cannot conceive by another woman and in the context of this passage *the Holy Spirit* is undoubtedly feminine. Secondly, among some followers of Valentinus[41] there was a common belief that Christ was conceived by the Holy Spirit, although Jesus' body had an ethereal nature. The *Gospel of Philip* underlines that Mary was a virgin, but the text offers a different meaning of her status. Instead of proto-orthodox concern about the sexual purity of Mary in relationship to Joseph, the Gnostic author stresses her freedom from defilement by demons.[42] Joseph is the natural father of Jesus, as the Gnostic Gospel argues in another place,[43] so it must have been another form of corruption, this time spiritual and caused by evil spirits, from which Mary was saved. But this statement about the human parentage of Christ does not mean that he was not divine. A more sophisticated Christology which emerged at the time presented Christ's body as a result of the union between 'the Father of all' and 'the *parthenos*-Sophia', which was one of the spiritual beings/aeons. Sophia was the divine Virgin and Christ's true mother.[44] It is possible to distinguish, according to this Gnostic source, a double birth of Christ. The first is in the domain of divinity, as a result of the union of his divine parents; the second here on earth as a result of union between Mary and Joseph, the carpenter. The first birth happened in eternity, and the second in history. The appearance of Christ in this world was confirmed by the event of his baptism in the river Jordan that was also a revelation of his divine origin.[45] Christ's anointing by John the Baptism was thus his spiritual birth, as his birth of Mary and Joseph was only a physical act. The second, true birth links Christ directly with his original, heavenly source, which was the union of his divine parents. The *Gospel of Philip* thus suggests two groups of parents: the heavenly and the earthly. This double origin points to Christ's double nature: divine and human.

Another Gnostic document, the *Testimony of Truth*[46] also argues for the double birth of Christ, here called the 'Son of Man', although the *Testimony* offers an alteration. The Saviour was born of 'a virgin by the Holy Spirit'.[47] This *virgin* is clearly identified with Mary,[48] and his birth is contrasted with John the Baptist's origin. John was born of an elderly married woman, Jesus of a virgin,[49] and in addition to that Mary was found to be a virgin again after giving birth to her son.[50] This is the first birth of Christ. The second birth happened when he was baptised by John the Baptist in the River Jordan.[51] But here, in the context of the whole document, Christ's baptism is not a revelation of his divinity or second birth, it is rather a symbol of the material powers/world through which the Saviour must have come without being defiled. Elisabeth's womb and the

River Jordan represent the same, negative realm of the material sphere and of sexual desires, while he, the Christ, came through a *virgin's womb* that did not know any sensual pleasure. This Gnostic interpretation is closer to the proto-orthodox theology in its assessment of the symbol of Mary's virginity. Thus, it is possible to conclude that the human nature of the Saviour, as it has nothing in common with carnal desires, passions and defilement since he 'passed through Virgin's womb', is closer to Docetic Christology.

Mary, the Virgin – an Example of the Apocrypha

As we already might see, a Jewish woman Mary was placed by Christian theologians in the centre of the battle about Christ's real incarnation. But this observation must be enlarged by yet another aspect of Mary's nature as a woman, which is her virginity or chastity. As it has been noted in the introduction to this chapter, the accent on Mary's virginity can be seen in the context of the Late Hellenistic view of human sexuality, where radical denial of bodily pleasures was a commonplace, and therefore not an exclusive characteristic of Christian religion.[52] Mary's chastity was a symbolic expression not only of her sexual purity, but also of her freedom from any pollution, sinful mark or imperfection. Peter Brown[53] points to another early Christian apocrypha, the *Protoevangelium of James*, where Mary is totally separated from any contact with *profanum*, by being enclosed in the holy space of the Temple. In the light of this document that reflects the larger phenomenon of early Christian Mariology, the virgin Mary was pure in her soul, mind and body, she was without any carnal desire, any smear of sin or her own will that would not harmonise with God's will. Brown illustrates this picture of Mary's perfection by referring to a noteworthy ancient Coptic testimony and symbolism:

> She was pure in her body and her soul, she never put her face outside the doors of the Temple, she never looked at a strange man, and she never moved herself to gaze upon the face of a young man. Her appeal was dainty. Her tunic came down over her seal; her headcloth came down over her eyes . . .
> She never craved for a large quantity of food, neither did she walk about in the market-place of her city . . .
> There was no limit to her beauty, and the Temple was wont to be filled with angels because of her sweet odour, and they used to come and visit her for the same of conversation.[54]

Mary surrounded and served by pure angels, a heroic and virtuous young girl freed from the common, daily and prosaic matters of the present world, Mary submerged in contemplation of the divine and life of prayer, this 'hidden from the world' Mary in retreat soon becomes Christ's mother. In this logic, Mary was predestined to rather than achieving perfection by her own ascetic effort. However she responded to her vocation by remaining focused on her mission and avoiding any defilement. Much later (19 CE), the Roman Catholic theology would develop the idea of Mary's exception from the current condition of this world in her freedom from 'original sin'.[55] According to this view, Mary was not marked by sin and its consequences because she was destined, by God's choice, to become Christ's mother. In another words, this doctrine supposes Mary's perfection, implicitly her deification, as she was not inclined to any form of evil, selfishness or defect. Again, the ancient motif from the *Protoevangelium of James* comes back as Mary is portrayed as an exceptional icon: the *Immaculata* detached from all other women, a virgin filled throughout with the divine inspiration and responding only to God's will, she is a pure channel of divine descent. Paradoxically, the Gnostic theme of 'channel'/ 'pipe' returns however this time to disconnect Mary from other women and their so crucial experience of the feminine. This over-spiritualised picture of Mary, who gave birth to the Saviour while retaining her virginity, has rather much more in common with the spiritual beings than with other women who painfully suffer during giving a birth. Mary, the ideal woman, the new Eve, unveils also that in the original historical and religious context, she has a number of characteristics shared with the contemporaneous 'mother goddess', she gives birth to the divine being and as the mother of the Saviour she becomes the mother of all.

*

Summarising the selected testimonies, it must be said that for these authors the particular involvement of *the Holy Spirit* and *the Virgin Mary* played an irreplaceable role in constructing their model of Christology. This brief pronouncement, as recorded by the Apostles' Creed, reaffirmed to the double origin of the Saviour. It promoted the essential idea of two natures, when Jesus' divinity and humanity encounter each other without reducing or undermining the value of the opposite. The statement encouraged the belief that the true, natural Son of God 'went among us' and human beings 'could see him in human flesh'. For the proto-orthodox theologians the axiom was that through Jesus, and only through him, humanity is able to reach divinity, while at the same time his humanity becomes the unique channel of God's self-revelation. Still, within this line of interpretation, as we have seen, there is room for moderate Gnostic amelioration. But even this explanation does not end our wonder about Mary's virginity. Whatever the modern reader thinks of Mary's chastity as a biological phenomenon, or even as a Christian myth it gives evidence of a historical concern to portray Jesus as a son of a woman who was committed to God, in an exclusive way.

CHAPTER 5

Suffered under Pontius Pilate, was Crucified, Dead and Buried

> I glorify Jesus Christ [. . .] truly nailed in the flesh for us under
> Pontius Pilate . . .
>
> Ignatius of Antioch, *the Epistle to the Smyrnaeans*, 1.1[1]

This section of the Creed is a continuation of the debate between emerging orthodox doctrine and other theologies that has already been noted in the previous part. As Christ's incarnation is related to the Holy Spirit and the Virgin Mary, so Christ's death refers to the Roman prefect of Judea. It is thus possible to see Mary's and Pontius Pilate's position in the Creed as two poles, which hold up a model of Christology based on real incarnation and then suffering and death. In this part of the Apostles' Creed these three stages of Jesus' life appear alongside secular history with Pontius Pilate linking the history of salvation with the history of the Roman Empire. But this is only one level of meaning. On another level this credal pronouncement about Pontius Pilate echoes the polemic against various interior and exterior opponents of early Christian proto-orthodox theology. Unlike the previous part, this section of the Creed is mainly concerned with Jesus' humanity and his real death.

Pontius Pilate and Early Christianity – an Intriguing Relationship

The connection between *Pontius Pilate*, the fifth Roman prefect[2] of Judea (26–37 CE) and Jesus of Nazareth appears to be the most coincidental in the context of the Creed. It must be said that Pilate's own ambivalent role in the drama leading up to Jesus' crucifixion, and his actions afterwards, have made him a character of great fascination ever since the period of Christian antiquity.

47

One of the New Testament *pseudepigrapha*,[3] the *Gospel of Nicodemus* contains, among others, sixteen chapters which later received the title *the Acts of Pilate*, relating how the main character became a Christian. In addition to that, in the Coptic and Syrian churches *Pilate* has been canonised.[4] Certainly the Scriptural detail that Jesus of Nazareth was executed under the rule of *Pontius Pilate* is one of the definite facts of Christianity. His role in early Christian apologetics and also in the creeds is to bring very important historical credence. The position of Pilate is at the centre of various Christological trajectories that originate in his appearance in the New Testament.

First, his function is to guarantee the factual execution of Jesus and to lead towards the next essential event that is Christ's resurrection. Secondly, *Pilate*'s position is linked with Christ's physicality as he *suffered under* him, and counters the already mentioned Docetic tendency among some Christians who believed that the Saviour did not have a human body. Thirdly, the same Roman prefect connects the stories about Jesus' life with a historical, verified period of time and pagan chronology marking Jesus' crucifixion. Moreover, this carries great weight against an accusation that Jesus was merely a mythological figure. Finally, against the Jewish critics, the same character of the Roman governor provides reassurance that what happened in Palestine with Jesus was a typical, brutal Roman execution of an innocent man who in fact was the blameless Messiah. All these theological trajectories come together at the junction that is *Pontius Pilate*.

Pontius Pilate and the Suffering Saviour – the Narrative of the Great Church

Chronologically, the first group of testimonies stem from Ignatius, the Bishop of Antioch who after his arrest was sent to Rome to be executed. On his way to Rome Ignatius wrote a number of letters to his fellow Christians in the cities which were close to his itinerary, probably as a response to their support and respect. It was Ignatius whose strong faith expressed in his correspondence, encouraged the local communities to remain faithful to their vocation and to the teaching that they received from the authentic Apostolic tradition.[5] One of Ignatius' greatest concerns was the presence of some 'false teachers' amongst Christians.[6] Those false tutors denied Jesus' incarnation, suffering and death. For example, in his *Epistle to the Trallians* Ignatius presented a short summary of Jesus' earthly life where Mary and Pontius Pilate are co-witnesses of Christ's real incarnation and crucifixion:

Be deaf therefore when anyone speaks to you apart from Jesus Christ, who was of the family of David, who was the son of Mary; who *really* [the emphasis – P.A-S] was born, who both ate and drank; who *really* was persecuted under Pontius Pilate, who *really* was crucified and died . . .[7]

Ignatius' frequent use of the adverb 'really' (Gr. *alethos*) emphasises that Christ's incarnation, crucifixion and death *under Pontius Pilate* truly happened as a fact or an event, and was not just a metaphor. This apparent accent had a bearing on other views which worried Ignatius. Those opinions understood the events from Jesus' life either allegorically or did not pay enough attention to the reality of the crucifixion. The same strong persuasion and almost idiomatic expression we find in another letter from Ignatius to a different Christian community.[8] Ignatius aimed to reassure them about Christ's physical, ultimate death, and he argued against a theology of salvation 'without the cross', which was current with at least some Christians from Asia Minor. This kind of erroneous opinion, from Ignatius' point of view, had started to spread among his fellow Christians, as the bishop raised his voice in order to deny those 'worthless opinions'.[9] Ignatius' theological opponents, who promoted those 'opinions', although belonging to the large Christian family, were seen by him as 'unbelievers' about whom he states:

For he [Christ – P.A-S] suffered all these things for our sake, in order that we be saved, and he *truly* [the emphasis – P.A-S] suffered even as he *truly* raised himself – not, as certain unbelievers say, that he suffered in appearance only [Gr. *to dokein*].[10]

The stubborn opponents are characterised by Ignatius as the 'unbelievers' who denied that Christ had real body. Those sceptics, unlike the representatives of the Great Church asserted that the Saviour's contact with this material reality was only illusory. 'Docetism' seemed to 'protect' purity and divinity against the tendency to bind it with humanity. The logical assumption of the second position is that as the divine cannot mix with the human, so holiness cannot participate in sinfulness. Unfortunately, the majority of ancient documents represent only one, orthodox, side of the dispute: the party that won the battle and finally, the war. Ignatius encountered this challenging Christology in Asia Minor, but our second proto-orthodox apologist, Irenaeus Bishop of Lyons, combated similar views in Gaul.[11] First, in the *Proof of the Apostolic Preaching* Irenaeus points to the direct link between Jesus Christ's crucifixion and *Pontius Pilate* as one of those who were directly

responsible for his death.[12] Secondly, in his other important
work, Irenaeus takes issue with different, mainly Docetic Gnostic
teaching in a number of passages. As various schools of Gnostic
theologians taught modified versions of the myth of the descent of
the Saviour, Irenaeus quotes the erroneous stories in detail in
order to confront them with his version that originates in his view
in 'the teaching of the Apostles' and to deny his opponents.[13] In all
his accounts *Pontius Pilate* is a recognisable evident sign of Christ's
time on earth.[14] To Irenaeus, as to Ignatius, the teaching about
Christ's suffering *under Pontius Pilate* is an important part of the
legacy of the Apostles, and therefore belief in it is also a characteristic of the true Church.[15] In some of Irenaeus' testimonies on the
role of Roman prefect it is possible to recognise a tune of empathy
with him, he who tried to defend Jesus against the Jews.[16] In
another passage from Irenaeus' work, the prefect is one of those
who by their crime fulfilled God's plan of salvation.[17] This plan has
its full expression in the doctrine of the cross: Christ's suffering,
death and burial represent the lowest point of Christ's humiliation,
so Christ's resurrection and ascension point to the climax. This
glory is both, according to Irenaeus, hidden and revealed in
Christ's suffering.[18] Now, in this process of humiliation/exaltation,
or paradoxically in Christ's revelation of majesty through ultimate
degradation, the figure of *Pontius Pilate* is irreplaceable as he is in
the centre of that transformation. The prefect sentencing Christ to
death initiates the crucial stage of the drama. From now on, the
King will reign from the cross, which is the most outrageous place
for the Lord of Glory.[19] In both Ignatius and Irenaeus, the role of
Pontius Pilate in Christian teaching highlights the crucial aspect of
the true Christian faith in the real character of the events from
Jesus' earthly life. Now, we should turn to their opponents. However, as it has been noted, our access to their theology is rather
limited to a few surviving documents.

'The Laughing Redeemer' *versus* 'Suffering Saviour'

The proto-orthodox Christology, although exemplified so far by
Ignatius and Irenaeus, unanimously emphasised the tragic, brutal
and bloody end of Jesus' life. This image and scenario is so deeply
rooted in our imagination that it seems to be the only possible
version of the events. However, the ancient apologists faced a
serious test, as other teachers presented a rather different interpretation of the crucial events. Christianity of the first two, even
three, centuries presented a great diversity of forms and shapes,
including a variety of narratives about Jesus' life and teaching. In

that colourful spectrum of theologies, especially among Gnostic Christians, we may find different accounts and interpretations of salvation. Some of these narratives prove to be Docetic, as they deny any real incarnation or death of the Redeemer, while other documents testify to Christ's real suffering and death.[20] However, generally the Gnostic treatises spent little time describing Christ's passion *under Pontius Pilate* in detail or even openly, as for instance, the *Second Treatise of the Great Seth* denied his physical death, suggesting that it was Simone (i.e. Simon of Cyrene, cf. Mt. 27.32) who was crucified.[21] This 'omission' came from the Gnostic paradigm: salvation can be achieved by an inner illumination, not by 'grace', 'deeds' or 'faith in Jesus'. This essential new stage of religious awareness, 'knowledge' (Gr. *gnosis*) and experience, comes from the correct understanding of the Redeemer's life and teaching, not by proto-orthodox literal exegesis of the Scriptures, and the effort to formalise that 'experience' of the living Lord in the set of dogmas or even through martyrdom so openly promoted by the authorities of the Great Church.[22] The Gnostic narratives, when they quote Jesus or refer to him, present him as 'a mystagogue'[23] who reveals the secrets of heaven and earth to his disciples, rather than a figure engaged in the matters of this world, including his death/resurrection so important to proto-orthodox Christians.[24] If there is a note of Christ's crucifixion in Gnostic sources, it refers to a *cosmic* event rather than to a *historical* execution.[25] From the Gnostic point of view, it was not crucifixion *under Pontius Pilate* that make the Redeemer suffer but rather his descent and entrance into a physical body, or the heavenly Christ's inhabiting of the body of the earthly Jesus of Nazareth. This distinction between 'the divine Seed', that is the Redeemer and physical Jesus, posed the question of whether or not the divine Redeemer was able to suffer in his human 'costume' of Jesus of Nazareth. According to some Gnostic narratives, because of the true, divine and hidden nature of the Redeemer which cannot be destroyed, he could not be killed or experience suffering. Therefore his image is presented as the *laughing Redeemer*, laughing because of the ignorance of those who believed that they could kill the divine one, as is shown explicitly in the *Apocalypse of Peter:*

> When he had said those things, I saw him seemingly being seized by them. And I said 'What do I see, O Lord?' That it is you yourself whom they take, and that you are grasping me? Or who is this one, glad and laughing on the tree? And is it another one whose feet and hands they are striking?
>
> The Saviour said to me, 'He whom you saw on the tree, glad

and laughing, this is the living Jesus. But this one into whose hands and feet they drive the nails is his fleshly part, which is the substitute being put to shame, the one who came into being in his likeness. But look at him and me.'[26]

It is evident that from the Gnostic perspective the 'catholic' eulogy of Christ as suffering Lord *under Pontius Pilate* revealed a great deal of immaturity or even very naïve reading of the Scriptures. The 'superficial' reading proclaimed as true, that which was only a metaphor of the more profound events, which were beyond the comprehension of the exegetes of the Great Church. For Gnostic commentators the interpretation of the Scriptures made by their opponents was not able to comprehend the true nature of events, not able to penetrate the surface and unveil the mystery beyond words. The 'catholic' or orthodox interpretative failure held to the plain and only apparent meaning of the biblical text and concluded that the Redeemer *suffer under Pontius Pilate*. Therefore according to the Christian Gnostic view, the 'shallow' or literal exegesis produces, as an outcome, a trivial model of Christology focused on bloody sacrifice safeguarded by the biblical character of the Roman governor, as on another occasion by the Virgin Mary. The dispute between these two internal Christian factions dominated a number of theological debates during the second century. But at this early stage of history the proto-orthodox, soon to be victorious stance, had to address yet another, this time external adversary, and as before, the role of *Pontius Pilate* in connection with Jesus' suffering and death was crucial.

Pontius Pilate – the Motif Used Against the Jewish and Pagan Critics

The dispute among Christians sketched earlier presented only one facet of the rhetorical battle, in which the figure of *Pontius Pilate*, like a military banner, gathered sympathisers of the Great Church. Another front was presented in the writings of Justin Martyr and Tertullian. In Justin's case the role of the Roman pontiff was explored in his polemic against the pagan intellectuals and the Jews, represented by here by a Jewish theologian, Trypho.

First, his two *Apologies* contain evidence of his effort to explain Christian faith to the pagan authorities and to change their attitude towards the religion of the 'vulgar mob' which was seen as 'a superstition'[27] or another form of atheism. Justin composes his response when he gives details of the Christian doctrine known to him, and uses his skills to present his belief in Christ in a way that can be understood by a pagan reader or audience. In the first

Apology, while addressing the pagan intellectuals, Justin presents the description of the Christian faith, with direct references to *Pontius Pilate* as the significant proof that Christianity was not yet another form of newly invented religious fantasy.[28] Against the charge of 'atheism' Justin connects Christian worship of God with Jesus Christ, the true teacher of that worship. Justin reminds his readers about the real existence of Jesus, by stressing the Scriptural, chronological framework of Jesus' life and references to 'Tiberius Caesar' and to *Pontius Pilate*. In this rhetoric Jesus is portrayed as an historical, not mythological, founder of the ultimate religion. *Pontius Pilate* is thus an important part of the argument, as the Roman governor gives credibility to its reasoning. In another passage of the same *Apology*, having his pagan audience in mind, Justin makes an even more substantial reference to *Pontius Pilate*, the Roman prefect from an apocryphal document the *Acts of Pontius Pilate*, as the apologist quotes him to prove fulfilment of Scriptural prophesies about the suffering and crucified Christ.[29] That reference to yet another document such as the *Acts* must add, in Justin's view, credibility to the Christian claim about Jesus' death as an historical event.

The polemic against Trypho requires a different argumentative strategy. Justin uses 'the case of' *Pilate* to emphasise not Christ's physical death or the historical fact itself, but to highlight the theological outcome of this event. For instance, as some Jews were interested in demonology, Justin states that it is thanks to Christ's crucifixion *under Pontius Pilate* that Christians are protected from evil spirits, who quail in front of the Saviour.[30] Those demons are now subdued under Christ. A review of the passages from the *Dialogue with Trypho* shows that Justin's main concern is to convince his Jewish interlocutors of Christ's rule over the demonic realm. The whole issue of demonology played a special role in Justin's polemic as Trypho recognised the supremacy of demons and also agrees with Justin that pagans worship the demons instead of the true God.[31] Thus, the Christian connects the Messiah's death *under Pontius Pilate* with his later triumph over death, and subsequently over the dominion of the evil spirits. The principal focus of Justin's persuasion is established in relation to Christ's death and victory over demons, which prevented people from recognising the Messiah in Jesus of Nazareth. This strategy is apparent when the apologist stresses the supremacy of new life in Christian faith,[32] which exorcises all evil spirits. For Justin, it is only Christ's name that empowers believers against evil spirits and makes their exorcisms efficient.[33] This argument also serves to show that there is no other name in the Old Testament that can perform the same miracles.

Christ's name expels, overcomes and subdues dark powers.[34] In Justin's examples *Pontius Pilate* appears to be linked with the death of Christ that changed, transformed and enhanced the human ability to resist evil, which can be achieved by no other means.

Finally, Tertullian's contribution to understanding *Pilate*'s role in God's plan of salvation added a new and stronger pro-Christian element to the character of the Roman governor. This amendment had an important function in the rivalry with the Jews. Among Tertullian's many treatises, *Apology* offers a very intriguing portrait of the *praefectus*, which is no doubt rather biased and rhetorically elaborated. The character of *Pontius* is openly contrasted with the Jews, as the Roman prefect is put under pressure by the Jewish establishment to crucify Christ.[35] Even more, Tertullian states that:

> This whole story of Christ was reported to Caesar (at this time it was Tiberius) by Pilate, himself in his secret heart already a Christian.[36]

This brief passage shows something more than a marginal gloss on 'Pilate's story' known from the Scriptures. Tertullian dares to suggest something significant. By citing the legendary idea that the Roman prefect was a hidden sympathiser with Jesus, the Christian apologist promotes a form of 'Christianisation' of *Pilate*, if not welcoming the Roman governor as one of Jesus' hidden supporters. This clear gesture made by a great orator hints at the possibility of reconciliation between the Church and the Roman Empire. Tertullian's admiration of Rome and his respect for its authority, including the emperor, is noticeable. The Latin orator went as far as to deny any tension between the institution of emperor and Christians even if history proved that there were different attitudes among emperors towards the new religion. To Tertullian, the emperor is the instrument of God who enforces the law[37] as well as guaranteeing the stability of the state. The emperor punishes crime[38] and protects the rights of his subjects. In some way, he represents God's law and order. *Pontius Pilate* thus in Tertullian's elaboration was a symbol of his appreciation of the Roman Empire, a *civitas* that may inspire a Christian understanding of society, structure and respect for tradition and order. *Pontius Pilate* was much more for Tertullian than a private person accidentally attached to the credal formula. His opinion constitutes the climax of the transition of *Pilate*'s status in early Christian literature. The position of Pontius Pilate changed dramatically alongside the development of Christian apologetics and in the search for a new political alliance with the Empire. *Pilate* began his role in the Christian literature as co-culprit with the Jews in the gravest crime. He was then portrayed as one of the crucial witnesses of Christ's real suffering and death. Then, in the last stage he is elevated to the status of a crypto-sympathiser of Christ, an opponent of the Jews,[39] almost a saint. It is not surprising that the Coptic and Syrian churches canonised him.[40]

*

In conclusion, I wish to highlight the fact that that early Christian literature, particularly the movement representing the mainstream Christian communities, including on this occasion Tertullian,[41] was very attached to, later even attracted to, the character known as *Pontius Pilate*. This attachment was neither nostalgic nor marginal, as the Roman governor provided proto-orthodox Christianity with great arguments against their Docetic, then Gnostic, Jewish and pagan opponents. Certainly *Pontius Pilate* in the Creeds, including the Apostles' Creed, remains as a sign of the ancient theological debate, which aimed to prove the real human nature of the Saviour, not laughing, but rather suffering Redeemer.

CHAPTER 6

... *He Descended into Hell; on the Third Day He Rose Again from the Dead* ...

And those who had died ran towards me; and they cried out and said, 'Son of God, have pity on us.

And deal with us according to your kindness, and bring us out from the bonds of darkness.

And open for us the door by which we may come out to you; for we perceive that our death does not touch you.

May we also be saved with you, because you are our Saviour'.

Then I heard their voice, and placed their faith in my heart.

And I placed my name upon their head, because they are free and they are mine.[1]

Odes of Solomon, 42.15–26

Christ's suffering, death and burial were incomplete without his resurrection. Understandably, the latter claim called for elucidation as resurrection as an event/miracle had no analogy in human experience. Although it was possible to find many colourful stories about life after death among ancient mythologies, Christianity did not want to be 'another mythology'. Faith in Christ's return to life opened an opportunity for theological insight into the mystery of life after death or into 'the underworld', as a symbolic dimension of the invisible world. Resurrection needed an interpretation in the light of faith in the Conqueror of all worlds, including the murky realm of *Hades/Sheol*.

It must be noted that the sentence about *descent into hell* is one of the most problematic in the whole Apostles' Creed. The difficulty of this declaration is related to its various metaphorical connotations. It could, for instance, allegorically represent the physical agony of Christ's death on the Cross. This kind of brutal death was hellish in its pain. But the same term 'hell' could also refer to the biblical notions of *Hades* or *Sheol*, and later *Gehenna*. The statement may also suggest that the Saviour carried the Good News of deliverance to the righteous departed who were presumed to be languishing in *Sheol*. Various early Christian communities adapted and developed this motif as important to their theology of salvation. For the mainstream, proto-orthodox tradition, it is interesting that the idea does not appear in the older form of Roman Creed, but its first appearance is quite late, in the Fourth Declaration of Sirmium in 359 and in the contemporary document published at Nicea and Constantinople.[2] Despite that weak credal reference, the motif of *descent* (Gr. *katabasis*) has significant theological meaning, reaffirming the principal postulate of Christ's redemption of the whole universe: visible and invisible, those who are alive and the departed. As the essential content of the statement introduces the notion of 'hell', it is necessary, although in a very limited way, to recall the basic biblical meaning of this term. This notion was later incorporated into Patristic theology and iconography and played an important part in Christian eschatology. The Scriptural evaluation and meaning of Sheol was commonly accepted by early Christian writers and therefore its biblical meaning is directly connected with the Apostles' Creed.

The Biblical and Apocryphal Folklore of 'Hell'

Early Christian theologians were first and foremost exegetes and commentators on the Scriptures. The biblical narrative was at the heart of Patristic reflection and theology.[3] Therefore our investigation into the Patristic assimilation of the notion must begin with a very brief outline of the Biblical concept of 'hell'. In the Old Testament and Hebrew theology, the existence of a realm called *Sheol* in Hebrew, which literally means 'the grave', is well documented.[4] Among the most characteristic features of *Sheol* is its strongly negative connotation. It is a 'place' of 'no return' (2 Sam. 12.23; Job 7.9), darkness and gloom (Ps. 88.7, 13; Ezek. 10.21–22), the land of forgetfulness (Eccl. 9.10), corruption of the body (Ps. 16.9–11; Isa. 14.11), the pit of destruction (Ps. 30; Isa. 38.17; Ezek. 28.8). There is also another element of this dark realm, which connects this sphere with the place of punishment of the unrighteous (Ps. 31.17). But in *Sheol* are also found faithful people (Ezek. 32.21, 27), whom God may one day deliver from it (Ps. 49.16).

The New Testament contains all these allusions, but also

introduces additional interpretations of *Sheol*. First, in the Greek
New Testament the Hebrew term is replaced by the Greek word
Gehenna, which originates from the name of the place, a burning
rubbish dump just outside of the walls of Jerusalem beyond the
Potsherd Gate (Jer. 19.2), that was called *Ge-Hinnom*, (Neh. 11.30;
Josh. 15.8) where once children had been sacrificed to the god
Moloch. The New Testament theology reflects the transformation
of the term from a physical, geographical 'valley of Hinnon' to a
sphere of God's judgment and the ultimate punishment. It is at this
time when the Hebrew notion of Sheol, interpreted in the light
of *Gehenna*, began to denote 'hell', that is an otherworldly place of
suffering (e.g. Mt. 5.22; 10.28; 23.33; Mk 9.43–47). It is the site of
punishment of those who are deprived of the vision of God (e.g.
Phil. 2:10; Acts 2:24; Rev. 1:18; Eph. 4:9). All these briefly
mentioned references present the Scriptural background for the
notion that appears in this part of the Creed.

However, the crucial statement, in the light of the Apostles'
Creed, is the very problematic declaration found in Peter's
theology as signalled in his Pentecostal sermon (Acts 2.24):

> But God raised him up to life, having freed him from death [Gr.
> 'the pains of death' or as some manuscripts read: 'the pains of
> Hades' – P.A-S].

In addition to that, the enigmatic concept of Christ's presence in
Hades that appears in Peter's speech is more clearly stated in two
passages from Peter's first letter (1 Pet. 3.18):

> He [Christ – P.A-S] was put to death in flesh, but made alive in
> the spirit, in which he went and made a proclamation to the
> spirits in prison.

And yet another passage (1 Pet. 4.6):

> For this is the reason the gospel was proclaimed even to the
> dead, so that, though they had been judged in the flesh as
> everyone is judged, they might live in the spirit as God does.

These important passages and imagery expressed the Jewish-
Christian belief in preaching deliverance to the departed. Also, the
same idea inspired early Patristic theologians as it highlighted the
universality of salvation in Christ.

But early Christians, whether the representatives of the Great
Church or 'heretics', also read literature that was later designated
as Jewish and Jewish-Christian apocrypha. Its evidence is equally
important to our investigation, therefore some examples need to
be briefly mentioned.

The *First Book of Enoch*[5] contains some ambiguous passages describing the time of repentance given to the sinners and the giants between the first judgment (the Flood) and the final judgment at the end of the world. It is to them that the name of the Son of the Man was revealed bringing joy and hope of salvation. A similar notion is presented by the *Ascension of Isaiah*, where the Word of the Lord descends through various levels of the universe, and ultimately enters the realm of *Sheol* to liberate the angels who are there. But, and this point must be underlined, it does not descend to the great abyss, the place of eternal imprisonment of evil angels.[6] Two parts of the underworld emerge from this description: one where some good angels are temporarily present, and one where evil angels are incarcerated. The first is visited by the Word and the angels there are 'saved'. The second sphere of the underworld is not penetrated by the Word, as it remains eternally closed after the Last Judgment. It is highly likely that Jewish-Christian theology was aware of this proposed structure of the underworld and that Peter may have referred to this theological heritage in his speech. In Peter's elaboration of the motif of descent, the Messiah proclaims the Good News about His act of salvation to the good angels or righteous spirits. In this way Christ affirms his authority over the entire world, an idea that finds its expression elsewhere in the New Testament.[7] The idea of the Lord's descent to the world of the dead, who are identified as 'the saints of the Old Testament', appears also in other apocryphal New Testament sources such as the *Gospel of Peter*.[8] With this widespread popularity, it is not surprising that the theme influences early Patristic theology.

The Diversity of Assimilation of the Motif in Proto-orthodox Literature

This part must begin with the crucial question: why did early Christians need the motif of Christ's descent to the underground at all? It seems like this motif responded to strong theological, but also emotional and psychological, needs. First, for those who converted from Judaism, Christ's descent brought reassurance that their ancestors were not forgotten. It is right to say that Christ's *descent to hell* had a great significance in Jewish-Christian theology. A good example of this kind of interpretation can be found in one of the most mysterious documents from the first century, which represents the Jewish-Christian outlook: Hermas' *Shepherd*.[9] In a visionary picture of the underworld, that is filled with water, a distinction is made between those who had been there a long time in a stage of sleep and those who entered this world recently to proclaim the 'name of Son of God'. The first group must describe the Jewish people, prophets and saints. The second group is easily identified by the opening sentence of the passage and these are the messengers of the Good News, not, as we would expect, Christ. Therefore the narrative of this passage offers a reinterpretation of the theology of *descent*. It is not just about the Saviour's visit to the departed, but is about the continuation of the Saviour's mission of evangelisation to the departed.[10] The most important, pedagogical significance of this line of interpretation, is to provide reassurance that the departed are not forgotten by the Saviour. Even if they lived before Christ's incarnation or even if they had never heard about the Saviour, they could still be converted or even baptised in the underworld.[11] The surprising idea of 'baptism of the departed' highlights belief in importance of this sacrament to salvation.

Secondly, while the previous connection with Jewish-Christianity points to the hope that all the faithful departed were embraced by Christ's salvation, the same motif was important to the proto-orthodox theologians, such as Irenaeus of Lyons, in their polemic against dualistic theology. For example, Marcion,[12] who was called 'first-born of Satan' by his theological opponents, was convinced that Christ went to Hades where he redeemed the wicked of the Old Testament such as Cain or the Sodomites. However, Marcion contended that Jesus did not save the Jewish ancestors as they were too bound to the Jewish Law and its evil Creator and were therefore not able to accept Christ's grace. In response, Irenaeus of Lyons provided reassurance that the departed of Israel were part of Christ's redemption.[13] Irenaeus also explored a new understanding of Christ's *descent*. According to Irenaeus, God's plan of salvation was focused on the imitation of Christ. In order to save humanity, Christ imitated the first man, Adam, although obviously the Son of God responded to God's will with perfect obedience. That is, Christ assimilated himself to man in his life and death.[14] Consequently, after Christ's death he also followed the path of Adam and all departed, and descended to Hades. This was a necessary stage of the Lord's mission and experience, as Adam became the example for Christ, and Christ – the example to all men. Irenaeus' thought leads to the conclusion that Christ fought for all humanity and won freedom for all. He liberated the captives from all forms of slavery, including eternal death in Hades, where the Saviour conquered its power, bringing salvation to the whole of creation.[15] Christ's death, burial, *descent to Hell* and his resurrection are sequences in the process of redemption which Irenaeus terms *recapitulatio*. This is the cosmic victory and all parts of the universe are invited by the Saviour to participate in it.

The Motif of Descent to the Underworld in Gnostic Documents

The Great Church had a particular pedagogical and theological interest, as has been noted earlier, in the promotion of this *leitmotif*. But the same theme attracted the imagination of those, who saw themselves as equally, if not more, faithful heirs of the Saviour's teaching and mission. The Gnostic documents from the Nag Hammadi Library provide us with an inspiring theological alternative to the one that we find in the works of the Fathers of the Church. So, again, we may ask: why did the Gnostics need the Redeemer to descend to Hades?

The Apocryphon of John mentions the descent of the Saviour into Hell in order to waken the one who is in deep sleep.[16] Here the Redeemer is identical with 'the light' that enters the realm of darkness and as we can see from the following passage, he descends to save or 'wake up from the sleep' those who belong to him:

> Again I returned for the second time, and I went about. [. . .] I entered into the midst of darkness and the inside of Hades, since I was seeking (to accomplish) my task. And the foundations of chaos shook, that they might fall down upon those who are in chaos and might destroy them. And again I ran up to my root of light, lest they be destroyed before the time.[17]

In contrast with the proto-orthodox or apocryphal documents, this passage does not mention any Old Testament figures. This argument suggests that the act of liberation in Hades reaches individuals who are able to receive salvation and *gnosis*, but it is not related to any particular 'righteous' characters from the time of the Old Covenant. In another words, the text does not continue the Scriptural connotation of Hades as the realm where the 'souls of saints' are imprisoned. Instead, it implies the liberation of those who already belong to the predestined race, whose names are called by the Saviour. In addition to that, Hades, or the place of darkness, appears not to be in some underworld, but inside of 'the prison of the body' (30.33–31.4). This reveals a totally different perspective from that of the Christian sources discussed previously.

The *Teaching of Silvanus*, although its Gnostic provenance is still disputed,[18] treats the same theme with special attention to the context of Christ's redemption. The divine Redeemer-Revealer gives his life for the believer, as a ransom for his sins and liberation from Hades/underworld:

> He descended to the Underworld. He released the children of

death. They were in travail, as the scripture of God has said. And
he sealed up the (very) heart of it (the Underworld). And he
broke its (the Underworld's) strong bows completely. And when
all the powers had seen him, they fled, so that he might bring
you, wretched one, up from the Abyss, and might die for you as a
ransom for your sin. He saved you from the strong hand of the
Underworld.[19]

The narrative stresses the role of Redeemer, who is the only Saviour
of the soul. He confronts the powers of the underworld and after
overcoming them, he frees the soul. In this interpretation, there is
was a fight between the Redeemer and the powers of Hades. As a
result of that confrontation, the victorious Saviour brings up the
soul from the Abyss to life. However, this act of redemption, unlike
in the *Apocryphon of John*, is presented as part of a struggle within
the cosmological structure of the universe, rather than as a liberation of the soul from a bodily existence. The *Teaching of Silvanus*
does not suggest any theory of predestination of the redeemed. It
also underlines the paradox shared with the 'orthodox' sources
that death of Christ has power to give life to those who are dead. All
these elements put the theological narrative of the treatise closer
to proto-orthodox theory of salvation than to the radical, dualistic
view of some Gnostic sources. It once more confirms that the motif
of *descent* continued to inspire Christian imagination during the
second and early third century.

The third example points to another aspect of the idea of the
descent. The theme of the Saviour's struggle with the powers of
darkness is further explored by the *Testimony of Truth*. The tractate
recounts the Son of Man's conquering of Hades and his victorious
works:

> For the Son of [Man] clothed himself with their first-fruits; he
> went down to Hades and performed many mighty works. He
> raised the dead therein; and the world-rulers of darkness
> became envious of him, for they did not find sin in him. But he
> also destroyed their works from among men, so that the lame,
> the blind, the paralytic, the dumb, (and) the demon-possessed
> were granted healing.[20]

In an earlier passage, the text narrates the Saviour's fight against
the dark spirits of Hades such as angels, demons and stars,[21] while
in another place the text names 'fathers of the world',[22] 'fathers of
baptism',[23] 'powers and demons'[24] and the 'powers of Sabaoth'[25] as
the opponents of the Redeemer. It looks like the Son of Man had
against him a whole range of spiritual adversaries, who inhabited

Hades or for whom the underworld was a natural milieu. In relation to the two documents presented previously, there is a question about the 'place' of Hades on the cosmological or anthropological scale. One possible interpretation is that the Gnostic notion of the descent to Hades encompassed the descent of the Redeemer to this material world. Therefore, the overall picture would present the idea of *descent* to Hades as symmetrical to the first descent to the earth, in the sense that it continues the Redeemer's mission in the underworld, creating a 'second stage' of redemption, this time among the dead and against the evil spirits of Hades.

As can be seen even through this brief reference to Gnostic documents from Nag Hammadi, the *leitmotif* of *descent* was the subject of rich theological elaboration in the early Patristic period. It fascinated various theologians and presented different modes of interaction of the Saviour with the structure of universe and its habitants. It appeared in the context of Christ's redemptive work, including incarnation, passion and death, and the ultimate descent to Hell. It called for the second stage: fulfilment in heaven or briefly: *ascension*. Between Christ's descent and ascension there was just one, essential point that required theological explanation: his resurrection.

Jesus' Resurrection on the Third Day[26]

Christ's resurrection *on the third day* is the central event of New Testament teaching. Jesus, a new 'Jonah' (Mt. 12.40; Lk. 11.30), emerged *on the third day* and showed himself to his chosen disciples, men and women. This appearance, or 'Easter experience' changed not only life of that first group of witnesses, but also the whole notion of time. Crucially, it also transformed the meaning of the relationship between life, death and life. In early Christian rhetoric the metaphor of *third day* reiterates the fulfilment and conclusion of Christ's task in the underworld before the risen Saviour appeared to his followers. In this rather overextended hermeneutics, the Scriptural symbol of *the third day* and secular, human notion of time and chronology are connected to bring a sense of reality to the event.

It must be said that Christ's resurrection was the ultimate miracle. It summed up the whole Christian hope and faith. It accredited Jesus of Nazareth with the authority of God's Messiah.[27] But, at the same time, Jesus' resurrection as presented by Christian teachers and missionaries sounded incomprehensible. Celsus, the second century pagan philosopher, directly attacked this belief by undermining the originality of the story about Jesus' resurrection, as well as making the important point that what Christ's followers said about his resurrection was not what really happened but what they wished had happened:

> After this the Jew [i.e. a Jewish adversary] says to his fellow-citizen who believe in Jesus: Come now, let us believe your view that he [i.e. Jesus – P.A-S] actually said this. [i.e. about his resurrection] How many others produce wonders like this to convince simple hearers whom they exploit by deceit? [. . .] Moreover, they say that Orpheus did this among the Odrysians, and Protesilaus in Thessaly, and Heracles at Taenarum, and Theseus. But we must examine the question whether anyone who really died ever rose again with the same body. Or do you think that the stories of these others really are the legends which they appear to be, and yet that the ending of your tragedy is to be regarded as noble and convincing – his cry from the cross when he expired, and the earthquake and the darkness? While he was alive he did not help himself, but after death he rose again and showed the marks of his punishment and how his hands had been pierced. But who saw this? A hysterical female, as you say, and perhaps some other one of those who were deluded by the same sorcery, who either dreamt in a certain state of mind and through wishful thinking had an hallucination due to some mistaken notion (an experience which has happened to thousands), or, which is more likely, wanted to impress the others by telling this fantastic tale, and so by this cock-and-bull story to provide a chance for other beggars.[28]

This kind of criticism was well known to theologians and therefore formed the background to the credal affirmation. A careful reading of Celsus' criticism shows that the pagan philosopher was aware of the Christian belief in the *bodily resurrection* of Jesus – that is, that he had not simply appeared to his followers as a 'phantom' or spirit. The 'marks of his punishment' point to the interpretation of Christ's resurrection taught by the Great Church. This is in contrast to the views of other early Christians who believed that the Lord's life after his 'death' was purely spiritual.[29] It is interesting that the Apostles' Creed does not elaborate on the bodily or carnal nature resurrection *on the third day* as it assumes this, not any alternative understanding of the pronouncement. It is clear from Celsus' comment that he had encountered Christians who believed that Christ was risen 'in the same body'. As a pagan intellectual, he found this idea laughable as it ran counter to the notion of reincarnation (in a different body) which was current among some philosophers such as the Platonists.[30]

Against pagan critiques such as that of Celsus and against a possible Docetic or Gnostic interpretations of Christ's resurrection, the early form of the credal statement appeared as a positive affirmation of faith. Naturally, as will be explored later in this book,[31] Christ's resurrection *on the third day* was a paradigm for the final resurrection of all (2 Cor. 4.14).[32] This direct connection between the archetype that is Christ's resurrection and its extension to all in eschatology was commonly accepted by early Christian theologians.

From the enormously rich evidence of early theological discussions about Christ's resurrection I wish to refer to a short passage from Irenaeus of Lyons' work. In his coherent theology this particular sequence is a part of the succession of events that brought salvation to all. In the *Proof of the Apostolic Preaching*, the author underlines Christ's resurrection in relation to God's perfect plan of salvation:

> Great, then, was the mercy of God the Father: He sent the creative Word, who, when He came to save us, put Himself in our position, and in the same situation in which we lost life; and he loosed the prison-bonds, and His light appeared and dispelled the darkness in the prison, and He sanctified our birth and abolished death, loosing those same bonds by which we were held. And he showed forth the resurrection, becoming Himself *the first-born from the dead* (Col. 1.18), and raised in Himself prostrate man, being lifted up to the heights of heaven, at the right hand of the glory of the Father, as God had promised through the prophet, saying: *I will raise up the tabernacle of David, that is fallen* (Amos 9.11; Acts 15.16), that is, the body sprung from David; and this was in truth accomplished by our Lord Jesus Christ, in the triumph of our redemption, that He raise us in truth, setting us free to the Father.[33]

In Irenaeus' view, Jesus' passion, death, descent into Hades and resurrection (later ascension), are sequences of God's plan, which include not only a spiritual element such as Christ's soul but also the material dimension of his body.[34] Both elements 'flesh' and 'soul' are important in the process of achieving salvation and both participate, according to Irenaeus, in Christ's resurrection. The latter is the prime example of Christian hope in life after death, but also it strengthens the important connection between the individual believer and the visible Great Church as Christ lives in his Church. This theological interpretation of Christ's resurrection is the foundation of the pronouncement from the Apostles' Creed.

*

With this pronouncement we have made an intriguing journey not only into the history of early Christian literature, its influence and diversity, but also on another level, towards the original Christian intentions which promoted this belief. This is the moment when the whole narrative of the Creed, from the original line of descent towards humanity, now turns towards ascent to the divine. This particular statement is thus at the centre of the Creed as a narrative and as a theological model. From now on, we shall climb to new stages and secrets of salvation as testified by early Christian documents.

CHAPTER 7

He Ascended into Heaven, and Sits at the Right Hand of God the Father Almighty

And I saw how he ascended into the seventh heaven, and all the righteous and all the angels praised him. And then I saw that he sat down at the right hand of that Great Glory, whose glory I told you I could not behold.

Ascension of Isaiah, 11.32–33[1]

This declaration of the Apostles' Creed contains both a direct reference to the Scriptures[2] and an indirect supposition about Christ's ultimate destiny.[3] The opening quotation brings together these two trajectories. As a credal statement, the idea of 'ascension' depends directly on a model of cosmology, which presented the universe as divided into the underworld, earth and a higher sphere of heaven or heavens. However, this distinction must be treated with a certain degree of criticism.[4] The theology of this proclamation is more complex and significant than just the poetic licence of the 'uplifting' Christ according to the popular Ptolemaic astronomy of the time. To illustrate the early Christian theological understanding of the statement we should refer to its three representative witnesses: the Jewish-Christian sources, the Greek apologists and some alternative interpretations of the motif. The last group of narratives supplements the proto-orthodox perspective and help us to understand better its stance.

Ascension, its Scriptural Origin and Controversy

In general terms, Christ's ascension reflects not only the conviction that after his mission Jesus was reunited with his Father. For early Christian theology, including Gnosticism, this particular belief summed up the whole process of redemption as Christ's descent (Gr. *katabasis*), and Jesus' ascension (Gr. *anabasis*), which presents two crucial stage of the plan of salvation. Christ's mission reaches its climax by his return to the divine realm and the symbol of ascension sums it up very well. The statement of the Creed applies, in a Christological context, the famous passage from Psalm (110.1) underlining the final glorification of the Davidic monarch:

> The Lord says to my lord,
> Sit at my right hand
> until I make your enemies your footstool.[5]

This specific passage served as a messianic metaphor that found common acceptance among Christian authors from the very beginning, and it was adopted and explored in the context of Christ's post-resurrection life. The number of New Testament references show that this motif was a popular theme of preaching in the very early Church.[6] The main line of Christian hermeneutics points to the Saviour's return to the 'heavens', or to the 'bosom of the Father', responding to the Hebrew idiom of 'sitting at God's right hand'.[7] It also underlines Christ's unquestionable domination over both the whole visible, and invisible creation. This is the theological core of the symbol of ascension, which was essential to an early Christian understanding of Christ's destiny.

It must be noted that the concept of 'ascension' is not an original theological invention of the Christian commentators. First, it appears in the Old Testament in relation to the end of Elijah's earthly life,[8] or as an idea in Isaiah's theology.[9] Secondly, although probably without direct connection, the theme of 'ascension' or elevation of a human element had many parallels among other religions and concepts of the time.[10] Therefore this aspect of the Christian faith did not sound original, or even peculiar and exceptional. This common religious pattern or rather a model of the final glorification of a hero portrayed as 'the eternal happiness in the realm of gods' provided some parallel to the Christian belief.

But still, there was a controversial aspect of the belief in assumption, which was known to early Christian commentators. The simple arithmetic shows that between Jesus' resurrection and his assumption is an enigmatic period of 'forty days' (Acts 1.3). The Scriptural narrative suggests that Jesus appeared at intervals to his disciples to convince them about his resurrection (1 Cor. 15.5–7) and to pass them the final instructions. In which sphere of reality was the Lord during that period? Not any more on earth, but not yet in heaven? Resurrected, but not ascended? While this question remained open,[11] another issue emerged in early Christian documents. Among some Christian Gnostics there was an opinion, that during the forty days the Risen Redeemer handed over to some of his Apostles an esoteric teaching, not included in other Christian literature, and later in the New Testament.[12] Other Christians may have been inclined to see, for example, the early document on church order, the *Didache* as a record of the direct teaching of the twelve Apostles by the Risen Lord.[13] As this example shows, the mystery of Christ's 'delay' with assumption, created an additional riddle which early Christians tried to comprehend.

The Evolution of the Motif in the Early Christian Literature

Among various early Christian communities, the Jewish Christians paid a great deal of theological attention to the motif of ascension. One of the modern scholars notes that Jewish Christianity understood that Christ achieved his full glory in his ascension, not in his resurrection.[14] It was the ascension more than the resurrection that revealed Christ's might, glory and splendour as the Son of God, and also as the Saviour of humanity. From this tradition we may list a number of documents which elaborate in detail the theme of ascension, for example: the *Epistle of the Apostles*, the *Ascension of Isaiah*, the *Gospel of Peter*, or the *Apocalypse of Peter*. This evidence reflected a certain ambiguity of the Scriptural notion as either an identification of resurrection with ascension, or as a distinction between Christ's resurrection and his ascension. The theologians of this period were still not certain whether Christ ascended to heaven while he was 'risen from the dead' (Gr. *anastasis*), or some time after his 'resurrection' (Gr. *anabasis*). At this time it was difficult to give a concluding answer, and so another metaphor of Jesus' ascension began to play an important role within the tradition of Jewish Christianity. The *Epistle of Barnabas* contains one of the earliest examples of a new theological interpretation, which links Jesus' ascension with the symbol of the 'eighth day':

> This is why we spend the eighth day in celebration, the day on which Jesus both arose from the dead and, after appearing again, ascended into heaven.[15]

This important symbol both to Jewish and Gnostic Christians[16] refers to the semantic of the seventh day, which is the day of Christ's resurrection, and therefore his ascension/glorification takes place on 'the next day', as 'the Lord's Day', which is the eighth.[17] The *Epistle of Barnabas* refers to this very important

metaphor of 'the Ogdoad'. Among many meanings, this symbol
denotes in the context of Jewish Christian apocalyptic 'the final
period of history', and 'the place of eternal rest'. *Sibylline Oracles*,
for instance, suggest that 'the Ogdoad' was 'the consummation of
the cosmic week'.[18] In relation to Christ's ascension, 'the Ogdoad'
symbolises the elevation of the Lord above all created levels of
reality, that is to 'the seven heaven'[19] or the hebdomad, to the
eighth heaven – 'the Ogdoad'. It is therefore an expression of
Christ's access to God's realm – that is to God's transcendence.
Some early theologians accepted this distinction and affirmed that
the invisible universe is composed of 'the seven heavens.'[20] In the
light of the early Christian documents, 'the eighth heaven', or 'the
Ogdoad', is thus the realm of God which transcends the seven
spheres created for spiritual beings. It is a 'sphere', but also 'a day',
an 'eternal rest' or 'time' that represents a new order of things.
This metaphorical language tries to express the Christian intuition
of Christ's post-resurrection access to the spiritual realm of God. It
is thus the same sphere that another metaphor: 'sits at the right
hand of God' will make more popular through the Credal formulation. A more careful look at some early sources supplies traces of
this understanding. For example, Justin Martyr in his *Dialogue with
Trypho* states that 'the eighth day', which is also the day after the
Sabbath, becomes for a Christian, the first, and the most important
day.[21] This statement, along with others from Justin's comments,
reveals the meaning of 'the day' as the time of salvation. According
to Justin, there is a connection between the first Day of creation
and the Eighth Day. In this way, the beginning of human history,
related to the creation of the universe, and is accomplished by
Christ's resurrection and ascension. This interpretation appears
during debate with a Jewish theologian, Thrypo, who knew the
Messianic passages of the Old Testament very well. Now, in Justin's
hermeneutics, as previously in Peter's speech at Pentecost, the
statement from the Hebrew Scripture is joined to the Christian
apologetic of Jesus as the Messiah. Justin follows this line of argument identifying 'my Lord' as Jesus Christ.[22] The plain exposition
of Justin's understanding of the crucial statement of Psalm 110 is
contained in his *1 Apology*, where the apologists state that Christ's
final triumph over evil will take place at the end of time.[23] In this
interpretation, Justin continues the popular Jewish-Christian motif
of Christ's ultimate struggle and victory with his 'spiritual enemies'.
As other early Christian testimonies of this tradition show, Justin
also underlines that the Risen Lord in his ascension overthrows the
evil powers of the invisible world, and therefore his ascent is a
triumphant procession of the Victor. This theological accent is a

very important characteristic of 'ascension', as it emphasizes total domination of Christ over every possible aspect of the universe and confirms his right to the title of 'the Lord'.

In another section of his *Dialogue*, Justin very originally, poetically and creatively merges Christ's incarnation/descent (Gr. *katabasis*) into His glorious return (Gr. *anabasis*) combining Psalm 110 and Psalm 23. The Saviour's entrance to the eternal Kingdom provokes amazement among 'the rulers of heaven', that is the angels, as they struggle to recognise their Lord with his human body. It is thus the Holy Spirit who helps them to recognise the eternal Logos coming back from his mission on earth.[24] In this way Justin indicates an explicit trajectory of the Christian proto-orthodox understanding of the ascension, where the 'ascension' includes Christ's physical body. The positive affirmation of the statement is not only directed against the Jewish failure to recognise in Jesus of Nazareth the promised Messiah, but also now in a new theological context, against some Christians who while believing in Christ as the Saviour, reject the idea of his physical resurrection, and equally his physical ascension. In this polemic, Justin finds strong allies in Irenaeus of Lyons and Tertullian.

First, it is possible to see in Irenaeus' account similar motives, language and images as in Justin's. His *Proof of the Apostolic Preaching* contains a highly imaginative picture of Christ's ascension composed of many symbols and references:

> And that when raised from the dead He was to be taken up into heaven, David says as follows: *The chariot of God is myriadfold, thousands of charioteers; the Lord among them in Sina, in the holy place, hath ascended on high, He hath led captivity captive. He hath taken, hath given gifts to men.* (Ps. 67.18) And 'captivity' refers to the destruction of the dominion of the rebels angels. And he announced also the place whence He was to mount to heaven from earth; for *the Lord*, he says, *in Sion hath ascended on high*. For it was on the mountain which is called that of Olives, over against Jerusalem, after His resurrection from the dead, that having assembled His disciples and having instructed them concerning the kingdom of heaven, He was lifted up in their sight, and they saw how the heavens opened and received Him.[25]

The scenery recreates some Scriptural and apocalyptic metaphors such as the fallen angels, the captive souls, and themes such as the triumph over evil, and the liberation of the departed. Irenaeus shares with Justin the same conviction that the full exaltation of the Saviour is unfinished until his last enemy is defeated. Although Christ won the battle with death, still after his resurrection there is

a final act in the plan of salvation.[26] Irenaeus pronounces quite
clearly that the resurrection and ascension of Christ will have its
accomplishment in the ultimate triumph over 'all enemies'. It is
not surprising that the Bishop of Lyons takes this opportunity to
show his rhetorical skill by equating the revolt of the angels, these
are evil spirits, with 'those who were found in apostasy', and also
those 'who despised the truth'. For Irenaeus, the angels took care
of the created world, and when some of them rebelled against God,
they influenced some people to follow their example. Those evil
people are the heretics, who are his adversaries.[27] Yet in another
section of his oeuvre,[28] he reaffirms previous statements about the
eschatological victory of the exalted Lord, it also highlights
redemption 'by His own blood' pointing to the Redeemer's passion, crucifixion and also of his physical nature. As already noted in
previous chapters, in Irenaeus' Christology, the element of Christ's
human flesh and his suffering on the Cross is absolutely essential.
Against various groups of Docetic Christians, Irenaeus proclaims
many times in his writings, that the suffering and death of Christ
was real and that his ultimate humiliation led towards his resurrection, ascension and the final judgment over his enemies – both
fallen angels and heretics. Irenaeus thus sees Christ's descent and
ascent as a part of the miraculous exchange between God and
human beings through Christ. It is therefore through Jesus Christ,
we underline once more the central motif of Irenaeus' theology of
salvation that God became human, and that it is also through
Christ that each one who accepts the true faith may become God.
Equally, Christ's humiliation and glorification are parts of the same
process. There is no division between the extreme humiliation of
the Saviour in flesh on the Cross, and his exaltation in glory. Passion, death, resurrection and ascension are to Irenaeus stages of
the same, interconnected and inseparable process of salvation.
Even more, the brutal, real and bloody death of Christ revealed the
triumph of life and truth, and also offers the gift of incorruption.[29]
This paradox of death that brought life in Irenaeus' theology is
also a sign for Christians to participate in Jesus' experience of
death as well as like him, aiming for final glorification.[30] While
Christ's resurrection shows the beginning of the new life, his
ascension has a cosmic dimension as it is his victory over the spiritual, evil powers of the universe.[31] Irenaeus accommodates the
notion of ascension within his whole model of the theology of
salvation and divine mission of Christ as recapitulation. The Ascension brings Christ back to the paradise from which Adam was
expelled. Jesus' work of repairing the damage caused by Adam's
disobedience achieves its purpose. The gates of heaven are once

more open to individual Christians. The reconciliation of God and man attained by Jesus Christ who put himself instead of man on the cross, so now in ascension places man back in God's realm. It is thus a proper consummation of history. In it Christ's flesh and blood play the crucial, irreplaceable role.

Tertullian's theology shows some parallels with Irenaeus' anti-Gnostic polemic stressing the reality of incarnation, but also it reveals an additional aspect of ascension. First, some examples of Tertullian's commentaries show how he guarded the full incarnation by reference to Christ's ascension. His treatise *On the Resurrection of the Body*, presents a strong rhetorical elaboration of the argument that Christ's celestial exaltation includes his body, or the material element of his nature.[32] In the context of Tertullian's theology of salvation, ascension confirms that Christ who 'assumed manhood'[33] also reconciled man to God.[34] Further, Christ's death and resurrection is thus his triumph over death, the 'last enemy'[35] and shows him as the *Christus Victor*. Christ's ascension is a glorious return of the victorious chief of the army from the greatest battle. This military imagery is very much characteristic of Tertullian's perception of the fulfilment of the plan of salvation. But Tertullian also addresses an additional danger which is coming with the theory of *modalism*,[36] this reduced the person of the Father and the Son to one, divine being. In the context of ascension, Tertullian attacks this view in his treatise *Against Praxeas*, which title names one of the founders of that theory. Against Praxeas' error, Tertullian states that it was not God the Father who was crucified but the Son, therefore also in this event of glory, it is not God the Father who returns to his realm, but the Son who 'sits at the right hand of the Father, not the Father at his own right hand'.[37] And again, Tertullian's lively wit makes clear what others have confused.

Christian Gnostic Adaptation of the Theme

The evident early Christian attraction to the theme of ascension was a feature of only one major or minor tradition. In the case of Gnostic Christians, particularly those who had a dualistic tendency, the main problem came out from the connection between the carnal and spiritual elements in the nature of the Saviour. Depending on a particular commentator's theological stance, different accounts of Christ's ascension were given. The parallel between various narratives of Christ's glorification was based on the principal that the Redeemer ended his life in this world after accomplishing his mission. Then the Lord handed over his secret teaching/message to those disciples who were able to comprehend it. This 'end' of Christ's earthly life is strongly connected with his return to the primordial realm. It seems that for the Gnostic type of eschatology Christ's 'visible', or 'physical' ascension, had no special significance. For example, *The Sophia of Jesus Christ* finishes with the characteristic laconic declaration:

> These are the things [the] blessed Saviour [said] [and he disappeared] from them.[38]

The disappearance of the Redeemer is thus related to the commissioning of his disciples with *gnosis*, and this is the main theological interest of many Gnostic documents. At the same time, these sources show a notable silence about any details of ascension, references to geography are missing, and no further information about chronology is given. It is as if these characteristics were not important to the main *corpus* of the Gnostic testimony and message. Also, the issue of measuring the chronological distance between resurrection and ascension is treated with liberty. The Scriptural, later canonical notion of 'forty days' does not play any significant role in Gnostic hermeneutics. On the contrary, while some Gnostic documents suggest that Christ's exaltation was immanent after his resurrection, others as recorded by Irenaeus believed in eighteen months (!). *The Apocryphon of James* proposes 'five hundred and fifty days' as the period which separates the Lord's resurrection and ascension.[39] Here we have another view on the length of Christ's sojourn after his resurrection, but whatever meaning is hidden behind the number,[40] it is certain that the final ascension did not take place immediately. During the dialogue with James and Peter, the Lord confesses that he has not returned to his original place 'as the Son is ascending as he should'[41] he still has a mission to accomplish. When the secret knowledge is finally passed on to James and Peter, they witness Christ's ascension.[42] Now, in the form of a vision, the two disciples are allowed to go after the Lord and see his glorious return to heaven.[43] This motif of celestial celebration shares imagery larger the Christian canvas in describing Christ's triumphant entrance to the heavens. The Lord predicts his glorious arrival and his place at the right hand of the Father:

> These are the things that I shall tell you so far; now, however, I shall ascend to the place from whence I came. But you, when I was eager to go, have cast me out, and instead of accompanying me, you have pursued me. But pay heed to the glory that awaits me, and, having opened your heart, listen to the hymns that await me up in the heavens; for today I must take (my place at)

the right hand of the Father. But I have said (my) last word to you, and I shall depart from you, for a chariot of spirit has borne me aloft, and from this moment on, I shall strip myself, that I may clothe myself. But give heed; blessed are they who have proclaimed the Son before his descent, that when I have come, I might ascend (again). Thrice blessed are they who were proclaimed by the Son before they came to be, that you might have a portion among them.[44]

Then, he introduced into Lord's *gnosis* Peter and James, who follow the ascended Redeemer with their minds:

> And when we had passed beyond that place, we sent our mind(s) farther upwards, and saw with our eyes and heard with our ears hymns, and angelic benedictions, and angelic rejoicing. And heavenly majesties were singing praise, and we, too, rejoiced.[45]

This closing act of imitation of the Redeemer and following him to the spiritual realm sets the role of the most important model to the Gnostic audience. This illuminating, simple and inspiring vision remains free from any further, local detail known from the canonical literature or its proto-orthodox interpretation.

*

Christ's elevation to the highest heaven ultimately finishes his mission on earth and concludes the drama of reconciliation between the divine and human beings. This is a common early Christian understanding of the meaning of ascension. Gnostic Christians added that at this stage salvation was given to all who were found worthy of *gnosis*, and while the majority of Gnostic stories stop at this point,[46] the narrative of the Great Church goes further, introducing the next couple of theological themes summarised in the creeds. The Creed finds its extension as new articles of faith are introduced. It is plausible to assume that theologians of the Great Church continued the elaboration of Christian doctrine with more details as they wanted to draw a clear, distinguishable line between the teaching of their Church, and the teaching of other centres of theology. Therefore those theologians could not finish the Creed with the article about Christ's ascension. Too many theological issues remained unfinished and too much room was left for error. The reaffirmation of faith must go on. The next pronouncement of the Apostles' Creed addresses yet another worry known to the early Church.

CHAPTER 8

. . . From Thence He shall Come to Judge the Living and the Dead

For the robber, or ruler, or tyrant, who has unjustly put to death myriads on myriads, could not by one death make restitution for these deeds; and the man who holds no true opinion concerning God, but lives in all outrage and blasphemy, despises divine things, breaks the laws, commits outrage against boys and women alike, razes cities unjustly, burns houses with their inhabitants, and devastates a country, and at the same time destroys inhabitants of cities and peoples, and even an entire nation – how in a mortal body could he endure a penalty adequate to these crimes, since death prevents the deserved punishment, and the mortal nature does not suffice for any single one of his deeds? It is proved, therefore, that neither in the present life is there a judgment according to men's deserts, nor after death.

Athenagoras of Athens, *On the Resurrection of the Dead*, 19[1]

The Saviour's return to heavens is the last Christological statement of the Apostles' Creed. Christ's ultimate 'judgment' of the visible and invisible worlds and 'the living and the dead' emphasises the end of the dramatic history of salvation. The belief in eschatological judgment is clearly proclaimed in the New Testament. It also had established a place in the Hebrew Bible and flourished in Jewish and Christian pseudephigrapha and apocalyptic literature of the period.[2] As we shall see, in the context of the Christian faith, the final judgment is logically and linearly related to the last two statements of the Creed on the *resurrection of the body* and *life everlasting*. But by its position within the structure of the Creed it remains separated from the two statements by some additional announcements about the Holy Spirit and the Church. Therefore, it may seem that the whole composition of the Creed suddenly extends, losing its rhetorical rhythm in a way which disrupts the smooth transition from one pronouncement to another, as from a premise to a conclusion. In the Creed, the current sentence concludes Christ's final victory over death and evil bringing eschatological peace by the separation of good from evil. This chapter sheds light on a very significant aspect of the whole plan of salvation that the Apostles' Creed aims to summarise.

The Creed begins with a strong emphasis on monotheism and introduces God as One and Almighty. Next comes the crucial Christological section which sums up the New Testament revelation. Christ's glorious ascension finishes this part with a triumphant conclusion, but God's might proved by Christ's resurrection and ascension calls for a last act of fulfilment. God's might needs to resolve the problem of evil and this solution will be sought in the form of God's justice. Christianity from its very beginning stressed the notion that human moral action in this visible, temporary world bears consequences in the world to come. The merits attained here will persist in God's kingdom, but equally, the wrongdoing will have a severe cost. This paradigm implicitly points to the issue of human freedom or freedom of human choice between good and evil, the role of consciousness and ultimately the direction of human life in the light of human destiny to eternal co-existence with God. Early Patristic pedagogy developed the Scriptural theme about God's judgment but it also stressed God's justice with which all human beings will be measured, restoring the balance in human society and individual lives disturbed by evil acts.

The Biblical Origin of the Last Judgment

As has been already noted, the Christian theologians from the Patristic period, including the first three centuries, were first and foremost commentators on the Scriptures. Their theology was primarily exegesis, which adapted some Scriptural and other selected contemporary ideas[3] to a new context and educational requirements and constructed as well as promoted a new Christian identity.[4] Therefore the concept of 'the judgment' was assimilated, not invented, to a new framework, as it was a part of both first Hebrew, then Jewish Christian literature and imagery. It is thus necessary briefly to explain its Scriptural background.

First, Jewish history provided concrete examples of God's judgment over all people. The archetypical events of God's judgments over Adam and Eve (Gen. 3.14–19), over humanity during the deluge (Gen. 6.13), His wrath over Sodom and Gomorrah

(Gen. 18.20; 19.13.), His judgment over Egypt that preceded the
Exodus (Gen. 15.14.), and His warning to Nineveh (Jon. 3.9.) provided models of divine judgment that had already happened in the
past or near present times. These stories exemplified very well the
profound faith that the whole world was dependent on YHWH and
that He is the ultimate Judge over it, and all its inhabitants pagans
as well as Jews, whole nations and individual beings. God's judgment reflects his ruling over the created universe, the whole and its
particular elements. YHWH's domination over events and history
stresses his supremacy.

Secondly, in the post-exilic Biblical literature, the understanding of God's judgment acquires an important new dimension.
The divine act of judgment appears in the eschatological perspective as *the last judgment* when all the nations will be gathered
together and the people hostile towards God and His Law will
receive just punishment. For instance, Third Isaiah proclaims in
many places God's judgment which is given the even more dramatic symbolism of execution of judgment by fire (Isa. 66.14–16).
Daniel, in the form of a visionary narrative, puts the event as the
closing stage of the old era and the opening of the new one of the
everlasting kingdom (Dan. 7.9–12, 26–27). God's judgment is
seen by those narratives as the conclusion and fulfilment of history
but at the same time as a new and eternal stage of humanity with
their God and Judge. Therefore the righteous, the poor and suffering find protection in God so they don't need to be afraid of 'the
solemn trial' (e.g. Ps. 75) while sinners have to be scared of the
might of God.

The New Testament, in its various theological traditions, takes
up both aspects of the Hebrew idea of *the last judgment*. All three
Synoptic narratives start with the opening episode about John the
Baptist's ministry openly proclaiming the present moment of
God's judgment and immediately add the role of baptism as a
means of deliverance from punishment (e.g. Mt. 3.1–12; Mk 1.2–6;
Lk. 3.1–20). For the New Testament sources, the coming of the
Saviour, Jesus Christ, is the 'moment', 'time' of judgment as Jesus
embodies the judgment over the world. His arrival opens the last
stage of history, so the trial has already begun, but Christ's glorious
return will accomplish it. Equally, the second aspect is emphasised
as many of Jesus' parables (e.g. Mt. 25.31–46) and the apocalyptic
literature in the New Testament (Rev. 20.11–15), underline the
ultimate, cosmological and inevitable event of the judgment of the
world and humanity. On one hand, the prospect for sinners is
extremely gloomy and terrifying (e.g. Heb. 10.27–31). On the
other hand, the faithful ones who put their trust in Jesus Christ

find consolation and hope on that day. The faithful people simply should not fear judgment as they are no longer condemned. The threat of divine retribution weighs only upon wicked men. This ultimate moment of truth shows Christ as the Judge of *the living and the dead* (Acts 10.42; 1 Pet. 4.5; 2 Tim. 4.1; Rom. 2.16; Rev. 19.11–16) providing later creeds with an idiomatic formula.

In summary, the motif of judgment was expounded in the Hebrew Scriptures in two different forms. One line of interpretation of this particular act of God saw it in the context of the present moment of Jewish history. The second theological outlook turned towards the eschatological point which introduces the perspective of the end of the world and the idea of waiting for God's justice. The New Testament reconciles these two lines of hermeneutics in a new way, but also, adds some new emphasises.

The Last Judgment – Rhetoric of Justification

For early Patristic theology, so substantially dependant on the Jewish-Christian symbolism, the last judgment was profoundly inspired by both sources: some poetic statements from the four Gospels about the Son of Man's return and horrifying apocalyptic imagery of *mysterium tremendum* of that judgment and its consequences. But psychologically and emotionally, faith in the last judgment offered a hope of the ultimate act of justice to the first generations of Christians who lived under the threat of persecution and even brutal death.[5] Ignatius of Antioch,[6] the *Epistle of Barnaba*[7] and the *Didache*[8] explicitly point to the last moment of history that now takes place. Hermas' *Shepherd* describes the current period of history and the Church using the symbolism of the tower under construction that is about to be finished, which, when it is accomplished, will herald the end of the world.[9] All these, along with numerous other documents, present the time of their composition as the ultimate opportunity in which Christians are called to give witness to their faith, and if necessary, to give their lives, as the Lord is coming and reward is near. The martyrs were not scared of human trial and consequently death, rather they were aware of the divine trial that would bring reward in the end.[10]

The last judgment is also commented on by the Christian Apologists such as Athenagoras of Athens and Justin Martyr. Both authors present the motif as one of the most certain and important events in the Christian history of salvation. Both apologists address a sophisticated pagan audience, and therefore make efforts to explain *the last judgment* as a natural, rational and welcome event that will re-establish definitive justice. Athenagoras as a

convert from paganism and a philosopher aimed to harmonise
Christ with Reason, and saw Christianity as a rational, coherent
'new philosophy'. His two treatises *Embassy for the Christians* and *On
the Resurrection of the Dead* present some logical arguments supporting Christian faith. Writing his *Embassy* to Marcus Aurelius, the
Emperor-philosopher, and to Lucius Aurelius Commodus, the
Christian apologist tries to introduce his religion as a comprehensible, sound and morally valuable tradition. Therefore his rhetoric
portrays Christian ethos as the true *via media* between two
extremes: a nihilistic rejection of the visible world and glorification
of earthly life. The Christian way of life, according to Athenagoras'
overview, is a sensible assessment of current existence in the light
of eschatology. The treatise *Embassy for the Christians* emphasises
God's judgment over the world and therefore explains the whole
Christian ethos of life as a way to respond to the truth about God,
who is the Creator and Ruler of the world. This theology also
means that God is the righteous Arbitrator whose providence governs reality. This kind of theodicy must have particularly appealed
to a Stoic philosopher, such as Marcus Aurelius. Athenagoras
underlines the Christian moderate, benevolent and peaceful style
of life, which is inspired by faith in *post-mortem* judgment bringing
either rewards for a virtuous existence or punishment for sinful
behaviour.[11] It is clear that the author stresses the value of a specific
Christian moral conduct in earthly life as the present style of life
has consequences at the ultimate trial. He argues that it is important to stress that the way people live their current life has a direct
influence on their forthcoming destiny. Athenagoras openly questioned hedonistic misuse of the present moment, expressed here
by an ancient aphorism 'let us eat and drink, for tomorrow we die'
which has nothing in common with Christian values or the
rational, philosophical existence.[12] Therefore awareness of the
eternal life should help, in Athenagoras' view, individuals to make
the right moral choices during the present conditions of life. It
should reflect faith in God revealed by Christ, which is the true
Christian wisdom or philosophy. Athenagoras' message can be
summed up as the idea that life on earth is a journey towards an
eschatological end and Christians are aware of their transcendent
aim.

Athenagoras' second treatise *On the Resurrection of the Dead*
returns to the issue of the eschatological trial as it discusses its main
theme, which is the Christian faith in resurrection of the body, but
this time we find a more reflective explanation of *the last judgment*.
The eighteenth chapter contains a whole section where the Apologist elucidates this particular view of Christian faith and doctrine.

His logic and argumentation lay alongside the reasoning and theology that each human life will be assessed by the divine and rewarded or punished according to the norms of justice. The ultimate act of justice comes from the common conviction, also shared by some pagans, that God, as the Creator of the universe, in His providence rules over its creatures.[13] An essential element of that divine governance is His *righteous judgment.*[14] The judgment will include both elements: the soul and the body, but this distinction is tangential to the main point that Athenagoras emphasises: eschatological trial and assessment.[15] The apologist clearly believes, and also addresses the same conviction among his pagan readers, in divine rule over the world, which is a philosophical and theological paradigm. From that paradigm he draws conclusions about divine justice that oversees all human beings and their acts. If so, the Christian faith in *the last judgment* is not a novelty or an irrational belief. On the contrary, it can also be accepted by those who see themselves as the sages. The opposite view, that is, rejection of divine judgment, leads to a nihilism that cannot be accepted by wise men.[16] In this life, the current existence does not provide any evidence of the unbiased assessment of human acts: good people are not rewarded and wicked ones are not punished. Therefore, the last word must belong to God. This appeal to the universal act of justice over the whole of humanity is the core of Athenagoras' argument.

Justin Martyr comments on the same theme of *the last judgment* on both occasions, first while writing an apology of his religion to the Roman authorities and secondly, during his theological debate with a Jewish theologian. Both circumstances give Justin different opportunities to underline the crucial statement about the just trial, punishment of wicked and eternal reward for the virtuous. His two *Apologies* are addressed to pagan readers, while his *Dialogue* has in mind a reader who is well acquainted with the Scriptures, Law and the teaching of the Prophets. Both narratives are given different emphases. Justin's exposition of Christian belief to the pagan audience contains all the main points of Christian teaching, where the resurrection of the body and the final judgment are interconnected.[17] Justin openly states that this ultimate trial will bring separation of people into two groups and those who were immoral in this life will face punishment in 'hell'.[18] And he adds more details about the place of retribution, using a rhetoric which contains some analogies with pagan poetry and philosophies supporting the Christian claim of judgment and punishment.[19] This particular point of Christian doctrine is thus not a new, unheard of teaching, but has, as Justin stresses, some references among noble ancient authorities. Justin makes an apparent link between this dramatic event and the freedom given to each individual by God. This point shows a new perspective in Christian theology which stresses the responsibility of all human beings for their acts during this life, as all, not only Christians, will stand the divine trial.[20] To Justin, *the last judgment* is not a horrifying trial based on God's accidental verdict, or any cosmological determinism, but on the contrary, it is an upright reprisal for good and bad deeds committed by rational creatures with free will. This aspect of freedom, which in Justin's philosophy should follow reason and faith, is openly spelt out to his pagan readers in order to give them an opportunity to exercise their free will and reason and end the persecution of Christians. If not, they, along with those noble Roman dignitaries who knew the Stoic doctrine of dissolution of the world into fire, will stand the same trial and eternal punishment by fire.[21] Justin candidly pronounces the forthcoming event of judgment that will concern all people, dead and alive as well as the invisible world of the spirits.[22] In his opinion, *the last judgment* will be not only a cosmological event, as the Stoics taught, but universal, as it includes the world of demons. Here the Christian apologist combines elements of Stoic philosophy with the Biblical narrative about the fallen, evil angels who will stand the same trial as the human beings.[23]

While his two volumes of *Apology* express the Christian belief in a manner accessible to a pagan intellectual acquainted with some philosophical ideas, Justin's polemic with Trypho offers elaboration of the same theme in a different, Christological perspective. Justin does not search for analogies between Christian belief in *the last judgment* and the Hebrew's views on God's act of retribution. Rather, his main effort this time focuses on Jesus Christ as the Judge and Arbiter.[24] The crucial Biblical evidence for Justin's hermeneutics comes from the Psalm 72, which in *Dialogue* is given as Christological interpretation. We can thus see that the emphasis in Justin's argument shifts from questions about the reality of the forthcoming event (the pagan readers), to the role of Christ.[25] For those who put their trust and faith in Him, 'the King of the glory',[26] He, Christ, will be the Saviour, but for those who did or do not accept Him as God's Messiah, He will become the Judge. In the section where Justin explains the possible salvation of patriarchs and all Jewish people who were faithful to the Law, he also makes a strong point about the central figure of the Saviour/Judge.[27] Justin's interpretation of this article of faith strengthens its inevitable reality but also stresses the role of faith in Christ as the crucial distinction that can save or condemn each human being. Both the pagans and the Jews are called to accept the Saviour as Jesus of Nazareth; and both are taught about the role of free choice in life that expresses faith in good deeds. However, neither Justin the Martyr nor Athenagoras distinguished between the judgment of each soul immediately after death and the universal judgment of all humanity, which follows the resurrection of the body. It seems that Athenagoras and Justin paid most attention to the universal event, which brings together all people, although each individual prepares himself or herself by personal choices.

It is with Tertullian's eschatology that the separation of both judgments is clarified.[28] According to his view, after death all the departed were subject to individual judgment, but, irrespective of the outcome of the judgment, with the exception of the martyrs were confined in *Sheol* until the last day. But after the *last judgment* all the righteous gained access to heaven along with the martyrs, while the evil-doers were condemned to eternal fire. Earlier, the letter from the Christians in Rome to their fellow believers in Corinth, commonly known as *1 Epistle of Clement*, hinted at individual judgment after death[29] as it spoke of Peter and Paul's presence in 'the place of glory' together with all other godly people. But generally *the last judgment* is seen as the event of the last day. In Tertullian's elaboration, the resurrection of the body and judgment are closely interconnected. The first makes possible the second as our present physical condition does not allow us to participate in the spiritual, eternal reality of heaven. The role of Christ's return as the Judge is also emphasised by Tertullian, but this time against his various Gnostic opponents, who undermined the meaning of the judgment.[30]

Irenaeus of Lyons' views on the subject of *the last judgment* have some connections with the theory of millenarianism.[31] But his main effort is to emphasise the reality of the eschatological judgment which will separate those who will enter God's glory as their reward for earthly life of faithfulness to God and those who will not participate in this communion. In Irenaeus' theology, this ultimate trial has an ecclesiological dimension. His ardent struggle against various groups of heretics and apostates also influenced this article of faith, for he believed that those enemies of the true Church would share severe punishment with other evildoers.[32] Irenaeus plainly states 'the eternal fire' as the destiny for such people.[33] It is possible to see in this Patristic theologian as the first who introduced the concept of eternal punishment for the enemies of the church.

The Last Judgment – Human Freedom and Responsibility

The issue of human freedom underlies the theological concept of *the last judgment*. In Justin Martyr, human free will finds its first champion among the Christian authors, as has been noted earlier. For Justin, amongst all creatures, only human beings and the angels have the power to choose. This potential is part of their glory but also shapes their destiny. Freedom of choice and responsibility are fundamental values stressed in his message to the Jews as well as to the pagan intellectual audience.[34] Writing to the Roman authorities, inclined to the Stoic philosophy with the essential belief in fate, Justin points out that his fellow Christians are very committed citizens of the Roman Empire promoting a life of peace, as they are aware of their freedom and the final judgment of God.[35] Individual free choice and responsibility is for him the ultimate cause of either eternal salvation or punishment.[36] God also gives time to humanity to make the right choices and this is the reason why the end of the present world is postponed.[37] Debating with Trypho, Justin uses examples from Hebrew history, such as the story about the tower of Babel, to illustrate the value of freedom given to all human beings.[38] But he also becomes more direct when he stresses that rejection of the truth taught by Christians leads to serious consequences.[39]

Irenaeus, whose sharp blade of rhetoric was pointed against a whole range of the erroneous doctrines, including pre-determinism, also paid special attention to human freedom as it was a very important battle ground. First, according to the Bishop of Lyons, freedom is God's gift to humanity from the beginning of its existence. God offered humanity free will, reason and autonomy as a part of His plan of salvation, leading man to his eternal purpose.[40] The gift of freedom is an essential aspect of a human being, who exists as 'God's image'[41] as God is free as well.[42] As the purpose of human life is to make the transformation from God's image to God's likeness,[43] there are three factors that make this transition possible: God's free will, man's free will and a call to live according to God's will.[44] This elementary human freedom has double meaning. It is a freedom from necessity[45] and the freedom to make the right choices that will reflect human resemblance to God. That original positive human potential, although misused by Adam, is renewed by 'the second Adam' – Jesus Christ or as Irenaeus calls him, 'the word of freedom'.[46] He then delivers humanity from the chains of slavery to sin and offers it a new, eternal life.[47] While life before incarnation of the Logos was marked by slavery to sin, His coming, death and resurrection changed the status of the human

being. Christ replaced slavery with freedom offering a new covenant. Those who follow Him reject acts of evil and live their life
based on that positive aspect of freedom. It must be also noted that
in Irenaeus' view nobody can be truly free or achieve God's likeness without God's support, that is His grace. Grace thus renovates
that with which man was made.[48] But human freedom is not total
and anarchic, it is still dependent on God's will and therefore as
long as fulfilment of God's will motives human acts, man is truly
free even being a servant of God.

Tertullian stands in the same line as both previous theologians,
emphasising that each person is free to commit good or evil acts.
The power of choice is given to man from the beginning of his
existence.[49] Like Irenaeus, this theologian also states that free will
was a part of human likeness to God and that man was free to
choose between good and evil or life and death. Free will is a
distinctive characteristic of man as the image of the divine Origin.
Against Marcion, Tertullian stresses that free will caused damage in
the original state of the universe.[50] Like Irenaeus who struggled
against Gnostic determinism and Justin's polemic with the
Stoic idea of Fate, Tertullian was also a passionate advocate of the
idea of human freedom to choose. This elementary freedom, in
Tertullian's view, has the positive potential to develop human
goodness with the support of God's grace. The crucial statement
for Tertullian's view is found in his treatise *Against Marcion.*[51] Freedom as a gift of God in the act of creation – here Tertullian's voice
is in tune with the whole early Patristic choir – enables human
beings to perform good deeds. Tertullian adds an additional note –
enables them to be performed spontaneously.

*

The belief in the *last judgment* has a long and complex history, and
that history is hidden behind the brief pronouncement in the
Apostles' Creed. As a belief, it originates in the context of Hebrew
theology and its assessment of the value of human life. But around
the Christian era, this belief received bright colours from the
Jewish and Christian apocalyptic literature where the vision of the
approaching Kingdom of God was painted as the *mysterium trem-
edum.* The early Christians were able to assimilate this idea, which
offered important comfort and security in the idea of ultimate
justice. In addition, some of the early Christian commentators
elaborated this belief in such a way that it became an opportunity
to highlight the reality, importance and value of human freedom.
Freedom thus expresses the original goodness of human nature. It

provides the space and inspiration to do good deeds, not just to avoid unnecessary evil. Ultimately this freedom is the basis of human accountability before God's tribunal. Thus, the notion of *the last judgment* is dependent on the idea of individual freedom, without which there can be no basis for judgment. In this way eschatology is directly related to anthropology and ethics as our future depends on our moral choices. Confessing the article of faith, Christians are encouraged to believe and experience much more than a specific hope; they are called by early theologians to take their freedom and responsibility for the visible world seriously.

CHAPTER 9

I Believe in the Holy Spirit

Faith in *the Holy Spirit*, as an acting divine power that accomplishes the Saviour's mission, was the essential part of the New Testament revelation. The Scriptural evidence of the existence, authority and activity of the Spirit of God is overwhelming, on one occasion I have already noticed the role of the Spirit at Christ's incarnation.[1] But the numerous Scriptural references to the Comforter (Gr. *Parakletos* – Jn 14.16) do not elaborate on his/her nature. Equally, the details of the relationship between *the Spirit of truth* (1 Jn 4.6) and the Son of God and God the Father are left rather ambiguous by the authors of proto-canonical documents (1 Pet. 1.2). *The eternal Spirit* (Heb. 9.14) remained the most mystifying 'part' of God to early, pre-Nicene Christian theology.[2] In this early period, faith in the divine Protector was a very strong, charismatic and overwhelming experience of the Spirit's gifts, while knowledge about the nature of the Spirit (Gr. *Pneuma*) was much less specific. Christian missionaries were called, using the Scriptural idiom, 'to baptise in the name of the Father, the Son and the Holy Spirit' (Mt. 28.19) and to proclaim forgiveness based on the power of *the Holy Spirit* (Jn 20.22–23) but those mighty actions needed more theological explanation, as evangelisation called for a positive catechesis. It was easier to say who the Spirit was not, than to define his or her status on the basis of the Scriptural evidence or even personal charismatic experience. However, the gradual growth in knowledge about the divine *Parakletos* took place in the context of a direct reflection on God as the Father, the Son and the Spirit in the course of early liturgical and baptismal expressions. The doctrine of the divine Spirit developed alongside Christology, the theology of salvation and the function of the Church, including the role of sacraments. It was thus natural that early Christian theologians saw the mystery of the Spirit closely connected with the whole economy of salvation, which started with the creation of the world and continued after Christ's ascension.

The Holy Spirit – His or Her Mystery

The beginning of Christian reflection on the nature of God's Spirit shows a slow but gradual emergence of a new comprehension of the Spirit from Jewish-Christian angelology, where his/her status was similar to that of the divine angels,[3] possibly with female characteristics[4] and moved towards more philosophical definition of *Parakletos*. For the earliest group of Christian theologians, such as the Apostolic Fathers, faith in *the Holy Spirit* was accepted on the basis of Christian revelation, and included the liturgical practice of baptism[5] or an oath,[6] but it was not a particular subject of theological investigation. The common belief shared by them was primarily that the Spirit inspired the prophets and was speaking through their writings.[7] This general conviction was the *leitmotiv* of many early Christian theologians that found its ultimate place in the credal formula. In Ignatius' theology, for example, *the Holy Spirit* participated in Christ's incarnation as the principle of His conception.[8] But Ignatius was also interested in underlining the role of the Spirit in confirming the Church's existing ministers.[9] Certainly in Ignatius' persuasion, the Spirit plays the role of reassurance that the ecclesiastical authority, including that of Ignatius himself, has the divine mandate and support in the struggle with the theological opponents.[10] Yet, among the Apostolic Fathers, the amount of attention that is focused on the Spirit in comparison with the divine Logos is not very great. Christ's role in creation and redemption played the main part, while the Spirit remained less discussed. For this source, although there is a distinction between the three divine persons after the incarnation, prior to it the person of the Logos was not discernible as distinct from the Spirit,[11] and also *the Holy Spirit* had the Christological title of 'the Son of God'.[12] At this early stage of the development of theology, a similar identification of the pre-existent Son of God with the Spirit can be found in many sources. It is therefore safe to say that even though at this stage Trinitarian terminology appeared in the documents, the status and the nature of the Spirit were still indecisive, which can be seen in the context of the previous pronouncements of the Creed. The main theological attention was elsewhere.

The Apologists, such as Athenagoras of Athens, openly

mentioned the divine Spirit and his role as a guide of the prophets.[13] The pagan audience had surely heard about their own oracles which some inspired holy men were commenting on, or translating to the mortals. Therefore, the Christian story about the Spirit as the inspiration to the prophets must have sounded familiar. Athenagoras adds another characteristic to previously noted descriptions of *the Holy Spirit*, writing that He is 'an affluence of God', which flows from God and returns to God 'like a beam of the sun'.[14] Here the important term 'an affluence', or 'an emanation' refers to the description of the divine Wisdom from the Book of Wisdom.[15] It does not specify any particular way of proceeding, but it rather poetically establishes the correlation between the Godhead of the whole reality and the Spirit/Wisdom that comes from it. Similar identification of the Spirit with Wisdom takes place in the work of Theophilus of Antioch.[16] Others, like Justin Martyr, mention 'the prophetic Spirit',[17] or 'the Holy Spirit',[18] but he does not go into details about the particular relationship between the Logos and the Spirit, merely accepting their differences as persons. The 'prophetic inspiration' is the main occasion for Justin, and later for his disciple Tatian,[19] to emphasise the activity of God's Spirit, who participated in the preparation of Christ's incarnation during the Old Testament period, acting through the prophets.[20] Introduction into the Christian mystery of faith revealed God as the Father, the Son and the Spirit. This distinction is well-known to Justin, but as in other cases of second century theology, Justin's idea of the nature of *the Holy Spirit* is rather blurred. Although there is enough evidence in his writings that he was aware of the special mission of the Spirit, terminology shows that Justin was not certain how the Spirit's activity could be distinguished from that of the Logos.[21] Confusion about terminology should not suggest that Justin mixed up the person of the Logos-Christ with the Spirit. He certainly believed in *the Holy Spirit* as a being that is different than the Logos-Christ. Justin obviously expressed his faith in God – that is the Father, the Son and *the Holy Spirit*,[22] although his lack of theological and terminological precision made him unable to explore further God's mystery as a Three-in-One being. Justin is silent about 'the origin' of God's Spirit, and of His unique relationship with the Father and the Son, and he remains satisfied with the notion that the divine Spirit is 'the power of God'.

So far, this proto-orthodox trajectory shows some coherent characteristic of *the Holy Spirit*, as a co-existent, eternal and active facilitator of God's salvation. With the documents representing Gnostic Christianity, the image, language and even the nature of the divine *Pneuma* changes dramatically. From the enormous dossier of material, we have to refer just to a number of selected documents, which present rather dissimilar conception of the Spirit. Additional difficulty arises from Gnostic fascination with cosmogony where the literal title 'the Holy Spirit' applies to the spiritual being, but in various traditions of Gnosticism it covers different semantics.[23]

Some Gnostic Christians believed that *the Holy Spirit* was the true Mother[24] of Jesus.[25] Among Gnostic treatises, the Spirit, sometimes identified with God's Wisdom/Sophia, constitutes a feminine aspect of the divine, or is even an autonomous divine being, a Mother and a Virgin at the same time. In the *Gospel of Philip*, which represents Valentinian theology, while Adam, the Hebrew child, had two virginal mothers, the Spirit and the earth,[26] a Christian Gnostic has the true 'father and mother', as the Logos and Spirit/ Sophia.[27] She, the Holy Ghost, is the spiritual Mother of her child. The Gnostic being born, through baptism, of divine parents,[28] receives a new status and even special protection from any form of evil,[29] as the female *Holy Spirit* governs over all powers of the universe:

> The holy spirit shepherds every one and rules [all] to powers, the 'tame' ones and the 'wild' ones, as well as those which are unique.[30]

It is possible to see that this Gnostic interpretation of the divine Spirit emphasises her characteristics as a protective, caring and compassionate Power, as the Mother and the Virgin, as the ultimate Wisdom/Sophia which governs the whole reality and leads it to its fulfilment. She is, in Valentinian theology, the Mother of all living, or rather the Source of spiritual life. Other Gnostic documents[31] proclaimed and honoured the feminine aspect of the divine being or even openly declared the androgenic character of the divine. It is evident from the Nag Hammadi library that Gnostic tradition represented a different approach from the proto-orthodox to the feminine as a feature of God revealed in the Christian revelation. That acceptance drew attention and criticism from proto-orthodox theologians, such as Irenaeus of Lyons[32] and later, Epiphanius of Salamis.[33]

Finally, a short reference must be made to an ancient intriguing Jewish/Christian document, the *Odes of Solomon*, which shares with the Gnostics an affirmation of the strong feminine characteristic of the Spirit. The *Odes* portray her in a very anthropomorphic, maternal way. One *Ode* in a central picture affirms the role of God's Spirit as the nourishing divine parent:

A cup of milk was offered to me, and I drank it in the sweetness of the Lord's kindness.

The Son is the cup, and the Father is he who was milked; and the Holy Spirit is she who milked him;

Because his breasts were full, and it was undesirable that his milk should be ineffectually released.

The Holy Spirit opened her bosom, and mixed the milk of the two breasts of the Father.

Then she gave the mixture to the generation without their knowing, and those who have received it are in the perfection of the right hand.[34]

According to this document, the role of the feminine Spirit was to facilitate salvation embodied in the Son of God, here hidden under the metaphor of 'milk', to those who were able to receive. In this way, the *Odes* elaborated the Johannine theme of ignorance of the present world (Jn 1.10) about the coming of its Saviour. Interestingly, this passage and theology shared with the mainstream Christianity the basic intuition on the crucial participation by the Spirit in the process of salvation, while unlike the proto-orthodox stance, it was openly unproblematic on the female nature of the divine mediator.

The Holy Spirit and the Abundance of Prophetic Ecstasy: Montanism

The already noted motif about the involvement of *the Holy Spirit* in prophesising found a specific expression in a controversial second century movement called 'Montanism'.[35] The 'New Prophecy' was a rapid outbreak of prophetic enthusiasm during the second century, which had some earlier examples in first-century charismatic phenomena (Acts 11.27; 15.32; 21.9; 10.1; 1 Cor. 11.4, 5; 12.10, 28; 14.3–4). This fervent apocalyptic movement within the Church looked for the immanent realisation of the pouring out of the Spirit in the last days (Joel 2.28–32; Acts 2.16–21), and although it started in Phrygia (Asia Minor), it soon reached Rome and North Africa. The movement originated from a prophet, Montanus, and his two female prophetesses, Maximilla and Priscilla. Montanus was, according to his followers, 'filled with the Spirit', inspired by Him and, when in the state of ecstasy was able to utter prophecies.[36] In Eusebius' record, a certain adversary of the movement describes the method of prophecy: first, the prophet appears 'distraught with horror'; next, he becomes 'quiet'; finally, he is seized by 'an uncontrollable madness'. This testimony shows the prophet in a spiritual trance that was a sign of being filled with the Spirit. Montanus described himself as possessed by God and claimed, according to his opponents:

I am the Lord God, the Almighty, dwelling in a man.[37]

The prophet identifies himself with the divine *Parakletos*, which meant a new form of 'incarnation', and that was, of course, a serious challenge for the Great Church. It is not surprising that the church fathers needed to explore more of the nature and role of the Spirit in relation to the Christian community, and to specify the circumstances when the Spirit of God was communicating the divine message to humankind. It was probably in those conditions when the orthodox perspective within the Church more and more loudly emphasised that God's Spirit 'spoke through'[38] the prophets, pointing at the Hebrew prophets, and also made the distinction between the prophets from the past and some charismatic, uncontrolled freelance leaders who claimed the same divine inspiration. Despite the rejection of the New Prophecy, and certainly some suspicion about prophetic occurrence, the theologians of mainstream Christianity believed in *the Holy Spirit's* participation in the economy of salvation. With Irenaeus of Lyons, this aspect of theology grows in significant relevance, but also thanks to this theologian, the Christian doctrine of the Spirit enters a new important stage.

The Holy Spirit as the Way to the Son

One of the major themes of Irenaeus' theology is God's economy of salvation, that is in the order of the divine government of the world's affairs which brings humanity back to its source. In this divine action through and in history, or through creation and redemption, God reveals the mystery of his intrinsic existence as the divine trinity. This self-disclosure of God calls for a response of faith from humankind. Irenaeus takes every opportunity to proclaim the faith of the Church in God as the Father, the Son and *the Holy Spirit*.[39] Now, the divine Logos and the Spirit are 'the hands' of the Father,[40] by which economy this idea reaches its purpose and climax. It is the Bishop of Lyons who describes the Spirit and His participation in the process of salvation in a most comprehensible way at this stage of the development of Christian doctrine.

Firstly, as Theophilus of Antioch, Irenaeus recognises that *the Holy Spirit* and God's Wisdom are the same, eternal being.[41] The divine Spirit as a distinct person in Himself spoke through the prophets, taught the patriarchs and guided righteous men.[42] It is He who has been poured on humanity in recent days,[43] and it is also He who is a gift to be received by the baptised.[44] He renews human beings,[45] and He is the 'Pledge of incorruption',[46] and as such He is helping Christians to be formed in the image and likeness of God.[47] It is through Him that people have access to God's life,[48] and it is through Him Christians can expect resurrection.[49] The Spirit is thus engaged in the process of salvation in a specific way. In Irenaeus' theology, the divine Spirit is surely a distinct person of the divine trinity. He has a different role, and he shares with the Godhead the fullness of existence,[50] as the Father, the Son and *the Holy Spirit* are united in creation and redemption.[51] Irenaeus gives other names to the Holy Spirit, which express His actions: 'Parakletos',[52] 'Gift',[53] 'Living water',[54] 'Dew of God'.[55]

Secondly, Irenaeus' theology of *the Holy Spirit* presents his special function as the one to self-disclose the nature of the Trinity. The divine Logos reveals His Father.[56] It is through Christ people can see the Absolute who otherwise remains beyond human knowledge.[57] Only through the Logos, and particularly through His incarnation, can people see for the first time in Christ's humanity the image of the invisible God. But it is through the Spirit, and thanks to Him that men and women can recognise in Christ the divine Logos, and by this act of faith receive from Christ the revelation of his Father. The Spirit plays the most essential role in God's self-disclosure as he leads Christians towards the Son, who is the fullest revelation of the ineffable God. This divine twofold disclosure, in which the believers recognise the Son through the Spirit, and through the Son, God the Father, is a vital part of the plan of salvation, starting with baptism and leading towards participation in the life of the Trinity:

> Therefore the baptism of our rebirth comes through these three articles[58] granting us rebirth unto God the Father, through His Son, by the Holy Spirit. For those who are bearers of the Spirit of God are led to the Word, that is to the Son; but the Son takes them and presents them to the Father; and the Father confers incorruptibility. So, without the Spirit there is no seeing the Word of God, and without the Son there is no approaching the Father; for the Son is knowledge of the Father, and knowledge of the Son is through the Holy Spirit.[59]

It is possible, therefore, to conclude that human sanctification is the work of the Spirit, who through baptism purifies Christians and guides them to fullness of communion with God.[60] The Spirit

inspires, supports and works with humanity in the life-long process
of transformation, from the earlier stage of being in the 'image of
God' in the act of creation, to 'become His likeness' by way of
sanctification. In the present life, through baptism, Christians
receive 'a portion', the divine Spirit, that allows them to grow, and
later to become 'bearers of God'.[61] It is right to conclude that
Irenaeus' exposition of the role of the Spirit leads his theology
towards a mature spirit-filled humanity. This trend is one of the
most original contributions of the Bishop of Lyons to the early
theology of the Spirit. Although Irenaeus does not explain in detail
the difference between the divine Logos and the Spirit in relation
to God the Father, his theory brings together theology, exegesis,
ethics and spirituality. Irenaeus is very interested in God's plan of
salvation of the world, but he does not forget about individual
human life which, while guided by *the Holy Spirit*, achieves its full
potential. The Spirit is thus in the centre of an economy that brings
all humanity, and each individual, in close relationship with God.

The Holy Spirit as the Divine Person

A new development of the ontological aspect of the doctrine of
God's Spirit comes with the theology of Hippolytus of Rome and
Tertullian. Both the second century theologians had to respond to
a particular challenge posed by the already discussed modalism,
which treated the three persons of the Trinity as 'modes' or repre-
sentations of one divine being.[62] But this time the tendency to deny
any real difference of persons within the divine nature included
the Spirit. Hippolytus of Rome, in a less elaborated fashion than
Tertullian, presents God's mystery in which he avoids the separation between the 'interior', eternal life of God in unity, and the
'exterior' manifestation of that existence as three persons. Against
his opponent, Noetus, Hippolytus reaffirms that both unity and
trinity co-exist in God in perfect harmony as always 'one', and also
'multiple'.[63] He openly states the existence of three divine persons[64] who later, that is in history, after the creation of the visible
world, revealed themselves as three individual beings.[65] In Hippolytus' view, both aspects of God's existence, 'interior' and 'exterior', are interconnected. Through revelation in Christ, human
beings may recognise that the eternal Son was engendered by His
Father and *the Holy Spirit*, who also co-exists with the Father and the
Son. While the world has been created through the Son, it is
through the Spirit that the same world is ordered and governed. It
is through the Spirit that it is possible to access this mystery of
divine co-existence. Hippolytus' whole theological and exegetical

effort is to show that through the history of salvation, Christians can recognise the activity of the different persons of the Trinity. Before this revelation, God has already existed in harmony as the Father, the Son and the Spirit. It is important to note that the biblical theme of begetting is applied only to the second person, that is to the Son, while the relationship of the Spirit with the Father and the Son is not specified.

With Tertullian the theology of *the Holy Spirit* reaches the next and higher level of clarification.[66] First, thanks to Tertullian, proto-orthodox theology finally adopts, without uncertainty, new terminology: 'trinity' (Lat. *trinitas*), 'person' (Lat. *persona*), and the third very important concept of the 'divine essence' (Lat. *substantia*).[67] Tertullian's polemic with various adversaries such as the Jews (monotheism), the Gnostics, such as Marcion (dualism), and the Christians, such as Praxeas (identification of God the Father, with the Son, as one and the same person), presented him with a unique theological challenge and opportunity. He needed to address God's mystery as unity, though confessed by the faith of the Church as the Father, the Son and *the Holy Spirit*. Thus for Tertullian, a certain way of elucidating the problem of the correlation between 'divine unity' and 'three persons', while avoiding falling into the Jewish comprehension of monotheism, Praxeas' error, or on other hand, into tritheism – called for a careful arrangement of strong belief in One God, at the same time recognised in the economy of salvation as three different persons. First and foremost, Tertullian strongly rejects the accusation that the distinction of the three individual persons within God suggests a division. It is possible, in Tertullian's view, to recognise three divine persons through their activity and at the same time hold the traditional monotheistic faith. From the very beginning, Tertullian makes the point that God the creator speaks in the plural (Gen. 1.26) and even responding to Adam's transgression against God (Gen. 3.22), God is revealing the existence of another divine witness of that tragic event in Eden.[68] Tertullian, the exegete, reads the story of the Fall as evidence of a plurality in God that later would be revealed as not three gods, but rather as a community of three members, which shares the same 'family propriety'.[69] *The Holy Spirit* emerges in Tertullian's elaboration as one of the three, who has the same substance, but is also different, as 'a person'. The last word is borrowed by Tertullian from the vocabulary of theatre as it means: 'a mask' or 'a face'. This notion originally denoted an individual character in the play, but in Tertullian's theology it emphasises the individuality of the Father, the Son and *the Holy Spirit*. In Tertullian's theology, this term receives a special function: it

denotes not only 'a specific actor or character', but rather 'a distinct individual existence', that is a precise divine individual, who is
known to humanity under the name of the Father, or the Son or *the
Holy Spirit.* Reaffirming God's unity of substance does not under-
mine the reality of three persons as the divine family.

Tertullian's important distinction of the one substance and
three persons rather 'adopted' than invented a terminology which
offers theology new tools that can precisely and rationally, though
still in accordance with the Scripture, explain the co-existence of
the three divine persons and their ontological unity. From now on,
it is hardly possible to confuse the Father with the Son, or with the
Spirit. The way in which the Spirit proceeds from the Father would
have to wait some time, until Augustine and the Cappadocians
(Gregory of Nyssa, Gregory Nazianzen, Basil of Caesarea) of the
fourth century to find satisfactory elaboration.[70] What emerges
from various passages of Tertullian's impressive theological oeuvre
is a specific hierarchy in God. At the top is the unbegotten Father.
Secondly, after Him, comes the Son/Logos, who is also identified
with the divine Wisdom, and who has been begotten before the
creation of the world.[71] The Spirit is the third.[72] Each one of these
divine persons takes a special role in the creation, redemption and
sustaining of the world, as they act together and in harmony.

*

Tertullian's contribution to the clarification of the inner existence
of God is irreplaceable for proto-orthodox theology. With his
explanation, *the Holy Spirit* appeared for the first time as a person,
as somebody who has an independent will and mind, as somebody
who exists in a family or community and acts in agreement with
other members of that unique household. The Christian 'history'
of *the Holy Spirit* shows a trajectory of gradual appearance from an
intuition and belief in his/her existence, towards a more rational
and philosophical comprehension of the nature of that existence.
Early Christian theologians had much more to say about what *the
Holy Spirit* 'does' or 'did' than 'who' he/she is. While the early
creeds, including the Apostles' Creed, reassured that this basic
intuition is correct, Christianity had to wait until the fourth century
to receive a theological icon of the Spirit, which as an icon, has its
place in all Christian churches to the present day. Still, knowing
more about God's Spirit only reaffirms that the third person of the
Trinity remains the most mysterious.

CHAPTER 10

. . . The Holy Catholic Church [The Communion of Saints]¹

Lord, remember your Church,
to deliver her from all evil
and perfect her in your love;
and gather her, the sanctified one, from the
four winds into your kingdom,
which you have prepared for her.

The Didache, 10.5²

You cannot have God as your Father if you no longer have the Church for your mother.

Cyprian of Carthage, *On the Unity of the Church*, 6³

The article proclaiming faith in *the holy Catholic Church* appears in the structure of the Creed just after the pronouncement of faith in 'the Holy Spirit', and before the last two statements on the 'resurrection of the body' and the 'life everlasting'. The composition clearly indicates at least two intentions of the authors. First, it stresses the direct connection between faith in *the holy Catholic Church* and the previous affirmation of belief in the Holy Spirit. Secondly, it reasserts the nature of the visible Church, emerging in its institutional form as *holy*, that is sanctified by God as his sanctuary, as acting on his authority. As in the previous cases, the formulation of this pronouncement reflects an encounter between Christian self-understanding and the given historical framework, including some theological challenges and a doctrinal response. Therefore its identification of that context is necessary in order to establish the intention of the theologians who included faith in *the holy Catholic Church* as a distinct feature of Christian faith.

The Opening Paradigm

To early Christians, but only to them, it was a paradigm that the Holy Spirit continued Christ's mission in the visible world, and thus that the divine Spirit was working 'in' and 'through' the Church (Gr. *ekklesia*).[4] This view appeared alongside a conviction that the same Spirit dwells not only in the individual Christian after baptism, but also in the midst of the local Christian community, sanctifying it by his grace. Therefore the mark of *the holiness* of the Church was seen as an extension of the life of the Spirit in the community. Reading the ancient documents it becomes clear that early Christians loved their Church with enormous passion. Their love was fervent, strong and openly emotional. There is little evidence of analytical reflection over the nature or structure of the Church; instead, the early Christian narratives appear to be full of affectionate words and prayers for the Church, full of vivid, poetic images and metaphors. They contain very personal confessions of commitment as well as various forms of encouragement to ultimate faithfulness to the Church. The Church was their source of inspiration and the object of esteem. This kind of rhetoric shows that the early theology of the Church was much more an issue of close personal attachment than a subject of a biased, realistic description. Idealisation of the Church, now the 'new Jerusalem' (Rev 21.2, 9–10), provided early Christians with a new identity and self-understanding. From the very beginning of patristic theology, there was a clear and strong awareness that the Church was not a mere organisation founded by human beings for other human beings. The Church had its origin in the Holy Spirit, had 'a divine architect' and was filled with the divine presence. For the early Christians their Church was 'a new Israel', the holy nation that had replaced the Jews as openly proclaimed by, for example, the apologist Justin Martyr in his dialogue with Trypho.[5] As during the Old Covenant, the Christians argued, God remained in the midst of Israel, so now His Holy Spirit was present in His Church. Through various metaphors denoting the Church, the sense of the new, mysterious reality of the Church comes into view: there is a particular bond between the Church and the Holy Spirit. Therefore the statement of the Creed is to be reaffirmed by all Christians.

The Holy Catholic Church – Her Mystery, Graceful Nature and Noble Age

Again, the main inspiration for early Christian ecclesiology stemmed from the New Testament, where the term 'holy' (Gr.

hagios) appears in direct connection with various Christian local communities. In Paul's theology, this designation refers to the all-faithful disciples who follow the original teaching of Christ (Rom. 16.2; 2 Cor 1.1, 13.12). Paul often used the adjective 'holy' in referring to the Christian communities of the local cities to whom he wrote his letters. Its semantics pointed to 'consecration', 'purity', or 'becoming God's sanctuary'. It also suggested a state of separation from what was seen as 'unholy', that is any form of idolatry or error. This important term was directly related to the Holy Spirit, as the 'holiness' or 'sanctification' of the individual as well as the local community by the might and presence of God's Spirit, which begins with baptism. This connection of the human and the divine, through the Holy Spirit, is then the essential context to the *holiness* of the Church. The Church is 'holy' as it is composed of members who have been spiritually cleansed, sanctified and dedicated to God through the specific ritual/liturgical act of baptism, when the Holy Spirit begins the process of 'regeneration'.[6] It is through baptism that remission and forgiveness of sins takes place and the Holy Spirit enters into the life of the newborn Christian.[7] As it is possible to observe, this particular article of the Creed implicitly contains a strong connection with baptism as the 'sacrament' by which human beings become 'holy', or consecrated to God, or predestined to immortality.[8] Tertullian in his polemic against Marcion names four spiritual gifts that come upon the newly baptised: remission of sins, deliverance from death, regeneration and the gift of the Holy Spirit.[9] All these various forms of sanctification express a shared common belief among the early Christian theologians that the newly baptised person is separated from his or her previous sinful existence, 'washed from sins', and is now rooted in God's life; or in other words, that he or she becomes 'holy'. It is in this context that *holiness*, as a mark of the Church, starts to play not only a very important theological, but also a political role. It confirms that only in the Church can this process of regeneration take place, and in an apologetic context. It also undermines other Christian groups such as schismatics and heretics whose life is outside this particular 'channel of grace', that is the Church. As Irenaeus', Tertullian's and Cyprian's theologies show, *holiness* is directly related to the uniqueness of the Church, its truth that is proclaimed and expressed by the succession of bishops that helps to set it apart from many other religious sects. It is not surprising that excitement and fascination with the nature of the Church inspired some of the early authors to endow the Church with epithets such as 'Church of life', 'the spiritual Church'[10] or, as in the case of Ignatius of Antioch, with an eulogy to her beauty:

'to the Church at Ephesus in Asia, blessed with greatness through the fullness of God the Father, predestined before the ages for lasting and unchangeable glory forever, united and elect through genuine suffering by the will of the Father and of Jesus Christ our God, a Church most worthy of blessing . . .'[11]

Ignatius' highly perfected image of the Church as not newly invented, but pre-existent, finds its analogy in rhetoric of Hermas' narrative, which shows the Church as 'the Elderly Woman'. During a dialogue with Hermas, God's angel reveals the true nature of the mysterious female figure as the Church.[12] From these examples it is clear that the Church has priority over the whole creation, and it is God's most original and perfect work. In another place the Church is openly called 'holy' and is said to hold a special place among all creatures of the God of hosts.[13] The holy Catholic Church comes into being in the context of the very beginning of the creation of the world, as depicted in the opening passages of the Book of Genesis, but Hermas modernises the original text, emphasising the primordial character of 'the holy Catholic Church/Elderly Woman'. The holiness of the Church as a mark of her special connection with God reaffirms her privileged place as a channel of God's communication with humanity.[14]

The Beginning of Ecclesiology – from the Language of Poetry to a Comprehensive Theology

The next phase of early theology progressed towards more systematic elaboration of the Church, although a strong poetic and oratorical element is still noticeable. With the works of Irenaeus the Church gains its rationale as it is recognised as the vital, irreplaceable mediator of salvation and the centre of communication between God and humanity. His persuasive theory had to counterbalance the attractiveness of Gnostic ecclesiologies, which emphasised more of the spiritual than the visible or institutional nature of the *ekklesia*. In Irenaeus' response, the (Catholic) holy Church was united with the Holy Spirit and held the central position as only through it did Christians receive 'every kind of grace',[15] including sanctification. Irenaeus' model of the Church aimed to bring together two dimensions or the same ecclesiological reality. It reaffirmed its divine origin and spiritual character as his opponents did, but against them it highlighted its visible worldwide structure and unity. Irenaeus' interpretation identified four characteristics of the true Church, which helped to distinguish, at least as guidance, heretical, schismatic, local sects from the original and holy *ekklesia.*

First, in opposition to the pluralism of the Gnostic schools centred on lone exegetes, Irenaeus underlined his belief in the *one Church*, or the *unity of the Church* that had its historical and direct connection with the Saviour, and therefore also with God. There is only one 'bridge' between God and humanity: the incarnate Son of God, Jesus Christ, whose teaching about his Father was conferred to the Apostles and then through the Scriptures. These testimonies of Jesus' teaching are correctly interpreted and guarded only in and through the Catholic Church. Therefore, if guided by *the one Church*, the believer can find *truth* about the One God. The second aspect of the Church, its foundation in *truth*, distinguishes it from the error that is heresy. Irenaeus related his ecclesiology to a more biblical than philosophical concept of *truth*, which denoted correct, that is orthodox faith in God revealed in Jesus Christ. The first witnesses, the Apostles, handed on this *truth* to the Church and it is still held by their successors, the Catholic bishops. Correct preaching and teaching was heard only in the *true Church*. This kind of catechesis offered sound knowledge about God as the Father, the Son and the Holy Spirit. In this way the Church is *united* by *truth* and is spreading it through the whole world.[16] Thirdly, the integrity of the Church was protected in another essential element of Irenaeus' ecclesiology: the succession. It is a very characteristic feature of Irenaeus' ecclesiology that he took into account the very historical, almost 'empirical' aspect of the institutional *ekklesia.* The one, true Church is supported not only by the Holy Spirit, but also by the specific chains of succession which authorises its status, nature, and claim. This kind of association guarantees the direct connection with Christ and therefore with God. Consequently, as there is only one truth, there is also only one line of continuous succession that protects the integrity of the Church, which descends through the Apostles to their successors and finally to the local Catholic bishop, such as Irenaeus. The fourth element is the *catholic* or *universal* dimension of the Church. The *catholicity* of the Church supported Irenaeus' effort to point at the visible community as both the spiritual and historical sphere of God's salvation. In every part of the world there was the same, one, Catholic *ekklesia.* In Irenaeus' view, all local Catholic churches share the same faith, doctrine and gifts of the same Holy Spirit. Again, the union between the Holy Spirit and the Church is boldly reaffirmed. For Irenaeus all these characteristics are held in the *holiness* of the Church, in a way that confessing faith in *the holy Catholic Church* leads to acceptance of its

nature and union with the Holy Spirit as presented by the Bishop
of Lyons.[17]

Can Sanctity be Mixed with Sinfulness?

The holiness of the Church became a serious bone of contention
between Hippolytus of Rome and Callistus (d. *c.* 223 CE), a colourful character and Bishop of Rome (the pope Callistus I). Callistus
was harshly attacked by both Hippolytus and Tertullian, now a
Montanist, among other things for his laxity, for example, in
readmitting to communion those guilty of adultery.[18] This erroneous practice, in Tertullian's and Hippolytus' view, undermined
belief in the *holiness* of the Church, as it became more and more a
community of sinners. The radical difference of opinions between
Callistus and both these rigorists seemed to concern not only the
role of penance, but even more profoundly the nature of the
Church. Hippolytus and Tertullian represented a supposedly traditional custom of the Church, and Callistus by decreeing a relax-
ation was regarded as the promoter of a new, 'liberal', unorthodox
and highly damaging law. To Hippolytus and Tertullian, Callistus'
relaxed attitude towards sinners caused enormous scandal and
disrepute. Instead of excommunication, Callistus' willingness to
accept sinners as a part of the Church undermined its holiness.
Thus Callistus' practice was seen as a profanation of that holiness, by allowing 'unclean' sinners to mix with the saints, the
inclusion of the wicked in 'the assembly of the righteous'. It is
possible to suppose that Callistus' ecclesiology comprehended
the nature of the Church as a mixing of those more and less
perfect in faith, or more or less advanced in sanctity. In this
view the *holiness* of the Church would refer to the divine act of
forgiveness and mercy, rather than to the moral purity of its
members.

Tertullian remained a key contributor to the emerging early
ecclesiology despite his defection or conversion to the Montanist
movement later in his life. Interestingly, his views on the *holiness* of
the Church, its discipline and morals remained largely unchanged
when he became a schismatic or non-Catholic. He upheld the radical view of the distinction not only between the Church (minority)
and the world (majority), but also within the Church he
emphasised the role and value of those who are 'pure', and 'faithful', and the 'separated', and the 'spiritual/pneumatic followers of
the Spirit'. The symbolism of Noah's ark served perfectly Tertullian's rhetoric as he underlined the fact that true Christians are
saved from annihilation[19] in 'the Ark', which symbolises the

Church, and they are also protected from impurity.[20] Between those true believers and the rest of the world there was no room for any form of compromise. In quite militaristic language he describes his Church as the camp of 'light', whilst outside of it there is the pagan army of darkness.[21] The Church is superior to any human institution, religion or school of philosophy.[22] The Church is also 'the Bride' of Christ who remains 'blameless',[23] 'sinless'[24] and a 'holy' Virgin.[25] These descriptions and symbols of the Church show Tertullian's strong conviction that the nature of the Church is utterly different to the rest of the natural world which is marked by sin and vice. From these metaphors emerges a common ecclesiological base that presents the Church as *holy* but also as *apostolic* and possessing an unquestionable *unity*. It is possible to observe that Tertullian's idea of the Church responds to his very personal comprehension of sanctity as a stage of perfection, which is achieved by only few. Therefore it is not surprising that this kind of Church is exclusive, small and composed of Christians as a spiritual elite, separated from the mass. Tertullian represented a dichotomist view of the reality of the visible world, culture, and the Christian ethos which is separated from it. On one side there is the *ekklesia*, the assembly of morally mature believers, on the other: the rest of people. Those members of the Church who were found unworthy because of their sins had to be excluded from this *holy* community.[26] Having such high expectations of his fellow Christians, Tertullian did not postulate a pro-Gnostic type of 'spiritual Church' different from the visible community; instead he emphasised the fact that the historical, local Church had to uphold the highest standards if it wished to be a Church at all. Therefore the *holiness* of the Church was always at the centre of his ecclesiology. The Church was *holy* not only because it was indwelled by the Holy Spirit, but also because it demanded a moral quality of its members. This quite radical expectation of *holiness*, although presented by a theologian who ended up *extra ecclesiam*, nevertheless left a mark on ecclesiology for centuries to come.

The Holy Mother Church and Her Limits

The next significant contribution towards the clarification of the term *holiness* in the pre-Nicene period came from Cyprian of Carthage, to whom Tertullian was 'the theological master'.[27] As the events of secular history prompted theologians to revise their teaching about the *holiness* of the Church, a brief historical sketch may be helpful. During Cyprian's lifetime, Western Christian theology was challenged on two fronts, and both had potentially

serious consequences for the doctrine of the Church, including its
mark of *holiness*. When Decius became the emperor (249 CE), one
of the aims of his political thinking was the restoration of traditional values and religion in Roman society. The newly elected
emperor embarked upon a programme of reinstatement of classical principles in order to become popular with the Roman aris-
tocracy, as well as with the legions which helped him gain power.
Soon, in January 250, he issued an edict requiring every inhabitant
of the empire to offer sacrifice to the pagan gods, and to obtain an
official 'certificate' confirming their participation in the cult.[28]
The common view is that this was a directly anti-Christian act,
aiming to annihilate the local communities and their leadership.
Some weaker Christians succumbed to the edict; others received a
'certificate' from bribed officials. Many members of the Church,
on the other hand, openly refused to sacrifice, and in consequence
were persecuted and executed. Decius' edict caused the first general persecution of Christians in the Roman Empire, provoking a
sharp crisis within the Church for years to come. In the North
African city of Carthage, Cyprian, the local bishop, fled from persecution, leaving his flock and going into hiding, while many of his
fellow Christians committed apostasy. As in other places, some
Christians did not offer sacrifice, but bought 'certificates' confirming that they had participated in the pagan cult of the emperor.
Others, having been tortured, became martyrs; those who survived
torture were called 'confessors', or 'witnesses', and gained growing
authority in the Church. Among the lapsed, some humbly
searched for forgiveness, others did not repent, yet other groups
joined the heretics. The whole situation caused even more confusion. In Carthage a group of confessors, including lay people,
emerged with a very significant role in authorising the return of
the 'lapsed' to the Church. They began to issue a 'certificate of
reconciliation' asking the clergy's permission to reinstate the apostates into full communion with the Church. Although just a year
later the persecution was halted by Decius' death, this tragic situation called for a new pastoral response. There was the following
dilemma: should the Church receive back 'lapsed' fellow-
Christians? Should the Church re-baptise those who were originally baptised by heretics, and now converted to the Catholic
Church? The controversy seriously challenged the unity of Latin
Christianity. But how were these issues related to belief in the
holiness of the Church? Again, Cyprian of Carthage is our crucial
narrator.

Cyprian's correspondence expressed his clear view on ecclesiastical policy towards those who were guilty of apostasy.[29] What

appears from his epistolary correspondence, and particularly from his treatise *On the Lapsed*, can be summarised as a new understanding of the *holiness* of the Church. First and foremost, Cyprian underlined the authority of the bishops and their loyal clergy, and emphasised their role in reconciliation. For him, only the bishops were in a position to restore the apostates to the Church.[30] Cyprian's apologetic work *The Unity of the Church* was the first, proper treatise on the nature and role of the Church. It presents a zealous eulogy of episcopate and emphasises the role, dignity and significance of the local bishops. It is the unity of the bishops which reflects the unity of the Church. It is their ministry which provides faithful Christians with the fullness of grace and with access to salvation. Cyprian restated the proto-orthodox doctrine that although the Catholic Church is one, it contains numberless local 'branches' always centred around a Catholic bishop. From Cyprian's theology, the idea of the Church was more than just an assembly of faithful Christians united by the Holy Spirit. The Church was described in strong institutional terms. Cyprian's apologetic model pictured the Church as a community with a visible, hierarchical structure: first, all faithful believers, then the ascetics and virgins, next, martyrs and confessors and the various grades of clergy, and finally, its leader, that is the bishop. That community/body exists in internal unity and allegiance to its leader, the 'head', as well as in external harmony with other Churches, creating the one, universal, holy Church. This Church is the mediator of all salvation. This kind of rhetoric clearly addressed the issue of heresy, division and disorder as an outcome of dogmatic, pastoral and sacramental disarray. In one of his letters Cyprian wrote:

> The spouse of Christ [i.e. the Church – P.A-S] cannot be defiled [i.e. coexists with heretics – P.A-S], she is inviolate and chaste; she knows one home alone, in all modesty she keeps faithfully to one chamber. It is she who preserves us for God, she who seals for the kingdom the sons whom she has borne. Whosoever breaks with the Church, and enters on an adulterous union, cuts himself off from the promises made to the Church and he who turns his back on the Church of Christ will not come to the rewards of Christ: he is an alien, a worldling, an enemy. You cannot have God for your Father if you no longer have the Church for your mother.[31] If there was any escape for one who was outside the ark of Noah, there will be as much for one who is found to be outside of the Church.[32]

This famous declaration had enormous impact on ecclesiology, including re-valuing the Church's *holiness* as well as its uniqueness as the way of salvation. From now on, two crucial idioms shaped the understanding of the Catholic Church. First, faithfulness to the Church includes obedience to the local Catholic bishop. Secondly, without the Church, or plainly 'outside of it', there is no salvation (Lat. *salus extra ecclesiam non est*).[33] Cyprian's ecclesiology stressed the authority of the hierarchy, which decides all spiritual and administrative matters to do with the flock, including reconciliation of sinners. This position had a significant effect. The *holiness* of the Church included members who were not, as Tertullian would have had it, a 'spiritual elite', but who were at a stage of penance. Although Tertullian was Cyprian's theological authority, he now diverged from his great teacher. The metaphor of Noah's ark shows a new line of interpretation, as 'the Ark', that is the Church, now contains 'clean and unclean animals'; but both groups must be compliant to their pastors: presbyters and bishops. According to this interpretation, the earthly Church is *already* pure or *holy*, as the sanctuary of the Holy Spirit, but at the same time this purity or *holiness* is not *yet* fully achieved by its members, who commit transgressions. The Church seems to be in a process of transition from sinfulness to *holiness*. Cyprian's ecclesiology is less concerned with the mystery of the Church, its pre-existence or eschatological fulfilment. It is rather a realistic, empirical, sacral-political and sacral-juristic project, with an emphasis on its administrative function, but also sacramental efficiency. The second feature came out during Cyprian's serious argument with Stephen, the Bishop of Rome. Although their difference of opinion was over baptism, it was really about salvation. Cyprian, against Stephen, held the traditional opinion, similar to his 'master' Tertullian, and also some ecclesiastical laws, that baptism performed by heretics and apostates was both null and invalid.[34] As a pastoral outcome, those believers baptised by heretics were treated as non-Christians and were to be sent for catechesis and baptism in the Catholic Church. Cyprian's argument was quite simple: baptism is a sacrament of the Catholic Church offering the means of salvation, and only those who are connected with the visible, institutional Catholic Church can validly baptise. The man who by the act of apostasy proves himself unworthy of his office has lost also his spiritual authority and capacity to provide other people with God's sanctification. Therefore baptism performed by heretics and apostates was not valid. This was Cyprian's controversial point which was later found to be erroneous and rejected at the Council of Trent.[35] As to Cyprian's life, on

14 September 258 he went to his death as a Christian; this time he did not avoid martyrdom.

*

As can be seen from this brief reconstruction, belief in *the holy Catholic Church* has a number of very specific aspects formulated in early Christian history. They all came into being through various controversies. This chapter has drawn attention to only some of those early debates, in order to contextualise the statement of the Creed. Belief in the *holiness* of the Church was for Christians a part of the conviction in their particular vocation and self-understanding. Although those cultural and historical circum-stances determined a substantial part of the construction of the Christian identity, they did not overcome the original intuition that the institutional Church, involved in both good and bad polit-ics, was more than just a human construction. The Church of the martyrs, virgins and confessors, was at the same time a community of villains and other lapsed and sinful characters. This paradox suggested that the *holiness* of the Church meant that this historical and 'limited' reality possessed all the means and resources to administer God's unlimited grace. It was this Church, and only this Church, according to those early theologians, that could proclaim *forgiveness of sins.*

CHAPTER 11

The Forgiveness of Sins

The disciples explain that the Five Loaves of the miraculous feeding are symbol of our Christian belief, that is

in the Father
and in Jesus Christ
and in the Holy Spirit
and in the Holy Church
and in the forgiveness of sins.

The Epistle of the Apostles, 5[1]

This article is closely related to the previous belief in the holiness of the Church, and the place of *forgiveness of sins* in the structure of the Apostles' Creed suggests that crucial connection. The statement emphasises the authority of the ('Catholic') Church in the administration of absolution and assumes the role of the institutional and visible *ekklesia* as the mediator of God's grace. In its simplicity, the present belief affirms the realism of any sin as a part of human, religious and spiritual experience. For early Christians, the sinful act meant separation from God and the Church community, therefore each sin was against God and the Church.[2] But the core of this belief points to actual liberation from that negative experience of alienation. For early Christian theology this statement produced a firm foundation of hope that achievement of reconciliation with God is also possible in the current life – not in a secret, private 'do-it-yourself way', but publicly, through the ministry of the other members of the Church. Christians received baptism with the intention not to sin again. Baptism meant the beginning of a new life with Christ and rejection of previous wickedness and ignorance. But, as people were baptised and later

committed post-baptismal sins, there was an evident pastoral need
of an act of reconciliation. Under pressure of new circumstances,
the Church was called to revise its theology, pastoral policy and
accommodate it to a new context of Christian life. But as the
conflict between Hippolytus and Callistus shows, lay and ordained
Christians were divided about the conditions of *remission of sins*. In
the third century Rome, already introduced to our readers, Hippolytus attacked his former rival in the See of Rome on the
grounds that he, Callistus, now the Bishop of Rome, too easily
admitted sinners into his Church, or rather from Hippolytus'
point of view 'a school', by the promise of forgiveness of their
sins. According to Hippolytus' bitter attack, his opponent
accepted continuation of episcopal ministry by men guilty of
moral sins.[3] Callistus was criticised by his opponents for accepting
Ministry as deacons, priests and bishops by men who were already
divorced and remarried. Also, in one case, he did not raise an
objection, when a certain man who was already ordained got married.[4] Finally, the gravest misconduct of Callistus as a bishop was to
promote the idea that 'sins are forgiven by everyone by himself.[5]
These and other errors against the 'correct' or 'catholic' order and
discipline, disqualified Callistus, made him a heretic and ultimately
enrolled him on Hippolytus' list of villains. This example especially
illustrates that the extension of the ecclesiastical authority over
remission of sins was not at all clear. The Universal Church, especially the Western Latin Christianity, needed a more systematic
reflection on the nature of the Church and its spiritual power to
forgive sins. This present chapter summarises some important
phases in the development of that self-understanding. Alongside
this development was also the notion of the 'original sin'[6] and
other transgressions appeared more clarified in post-Apostolic literature. As early theologians based their teaching on the evidence
of the Scriptures, a short reminder of that evidence opens our
investigation.

The Scriptural Meaning of 'the Sins' and the Call for Repentance

The Hebrew symbolism of 'sin' which played an important role in
the New Testament and then in early Christian literature unveils
rather compound meaning.[7] Although the Hebrew Bible does not
possess one abstract term which covers all semantics of what
latterly became 'the sin' it is possible to distinguish three main
images based on its meaning that try to explain the experience of
'sin'. One of the most frequent refers to the idea of 'missing the

target' or 'missing the mark' of an action; another notion denotes
'a winding road', 'iniquity'; the third concept points to an intention of somebody to commit an evil act or breaching of the law.
The first and the second terms were later translated into Greek as
hamartema and into Latin as *peccatum.* Both expressed the concept
of departing from some order, rules and direction of, for instance,
a journey. The third concept, sometimes translated into Greek as
hybris, entails a freewill insult based on arrogance, an initiative of
committing mistreatment, or means 'to sin against somebody'. Sin,
in its metaphorical representation, was presented as 'a blemish', or
at other times as 'a burden' or, as 'swerving from the path'. All
these images arising from ancient semantics shows an existential
situation of trespass of an established order, lawlessness, iniquity as
a result of a conscious choice and action, ultimately a situation of
being lost in a journey. These characteristics receive the final theological interpretation when in relation to the Creator, they stress
that 'sin' is a rebellion against God and his commandments. 'Sin'
received more positive interpretation, particularly in the time of
prophets, as Israel is taught about conditions of forgiveness that
include confession, conversion, expiation and the ultimate deed of
God: redemption by the Messiah. With the last element comes the
New Testament message about Jesus from Nazareth who 'takes
away the sin of the world' (Jn 1.29). In the Christian perspective,
the Hebrew focus on the sin found its ultimate answer in Christ the
Lord, who redeemed his people, who called for repentance and
reconciled humanity with the Creator. The call for repentance, but
also following it, *forgiveness of sins* is one of the main *leitmotivs* of the
whole New Testament.[8] It is one of the chief themes of Jesus' teaching and as such it plays an important role in theology of salvation,
as illustrated for example, by Peter's call to repentance and promise of forgiveness of sins (Acts, 2.38; 3.19; 5.31; 8.22; 13.38; 15.9;
26.18). Paul's theology underlined understanding of sin as 'transgression', 'fault' and 'disobedience' already noted in Hebrew
thought but proclaimed *forgiveness of sins* as well (Rom. 3.25; 5.14;
7.9; Eph. 1.7; 4.32; Col. 1.14; 2.13; 3.13). Paul's exegesis
emphasises the motif of the archetype of all sins, that is the sin of
Adam (e.g. Rom. 5.12–19), but also he pays a lot of attention to
particular sinful behaviour that may be found in the current life of
the believers.[9] In relation to baptism, Paul's rhetoric uses the
imagery of 'washing from the sins' (1 Cor. 6.11) which refers to the
Hebrew symbolism of 'sin/blemish' or 'stain'. This very attractive
image significantly inspired early Christian language and
imagination.

The Motif of Repentance/Forgiveness in Early Christian Literature

Along with the spread of Christianity the concept of sin also spread widely in the world of the first and second century of the Common Era. The notion of 'sin' was a powerful ally of mainstream Christianity.[10] Its catechesis did not end up with a pessimistic observation of the failure of human nature. The same religion promoted and offered a remedy. The faith in real, absolute and merciful *remission of sins* was one of the axioms of Christianity. For the Jewish Christian, this notion expressed the hope of being reunited with God in a way that previous, Jewish penitential rites only foretold in symbols and rituals. For the converts from paganism, *forgiveness of sins* appeared to be an entrance to a new stage of life, as never before, dedicated to one Lord and Saviour. As a religious theme, forgiveness of sins offered an attractive motif which moved the hearts and imagination of ancient neighbours.

First, a good example of Jewish Christian uses of this powerful theme can be found in the *Epistle of Barnabas* which is saturated with Jewish motifs, but at the same time presents strong anti-Jewish rhetoric.[11] It explores the traditional symbols, adding to them the new Christian meaning:

> But let us inquire whether the Lord took care to foreshadow the water and the cross. Now concerning the water, it is written with reference to Israel that they would never accept the baptism that brings forgiveness of sins, but would create a substitute for themselves.[12]

The author contrasted the deficiency of 'Israel' with Christianity's fulfilment and perfection. The latter is identified with the act of baptism that is a full reconciliation with God and *remission of sins*. The 'new Israel', that is the Church, is able to receive God's gift in Jesus Christ. Barnabas, the anonymous theologian, explains further the meaning and consequences of the Christian baptism as the transformation from one sinful stage of life to another, purified and spiritually regenerated.[13] Again, in the centre of that transformation is baptism, here 'washing from the sins' with Christ's passion that is prefigured in the well-known Hebrew metaphor of the scarified Paschal lamb, whose blood saved the lives of the chosen nation (Exod. 12.1–19). Christ, in this interpretation is the focus of salvation, therefore his role, mediation in baptism, is emphasised in all aspects of baptism. Therefore three elements are united as three aspects of the same process of salvation: Christ's incarnation – Christian baptism – forgiveness of sins.[14]

The evident emphasis is put on the analogy between the sacrifice of 'the Paschal Lamb' and the death of Christ, including the important metaphor of blood, which 'washed iniquity of people' and foretold the meaning of baptism as forgiveness. In the light of this Jewish-Christian theology, baptism was associated with 'new creation'[15] that includes *remission of sins* and the new beginning of Christian life. The similar line of interpretation of the insufficiencies of Jewish practices and the value of baptism appeared in other Christian apologetic treatises.[16]

The connection between baptism and *remission of sins* was reaffirmed again, this time in defence of Christian faith against pagan critics. Justin's *First Apology* explains the significance of baptism as an act of being 'regenerated' or 'reborn', including God's forgiveness of previous evil acts.[17] Prayer for *remission of sins* precedes baptism, but the actual effect of remission comes with the act of being baptised. This is the ritual that washes the sins committed in the previous stage of life and marks the new 'era' coming into existence. It must be noted that the traditional Scriptural metaphors of this spiritual transformation, such as 'washing' or 'cleansing', are found in Justin's elaboration as well as the additional image of 'illumination'[18] at the end of the transition from the realm of 'darkness' to the realm of 'light'. Justin uses the symbol of 'illumination' as a synonym of 'washing the sins'.[19] It is thus clear that for Justin, and the Christian tradition that he represents, the pre-baptismal preparation, including catechesis, prayers and fasting, are necessary induction into the mystery of regeneration.[20] This period also brings up the awareness of sins and teaches about their evil but also shows the source of reconciliation with God and community. Baptism culminates in this process of recollection and conversion. In Justin's theology repentance, forgiveness and baptism are parts of the same process of spiritual regeneration. This transition is under direct inspiration from the Holy Spirit. The very significant concept of 'illumination' denotes this new life directed by the divine power and leads towards new existence.[21]

Very soon, if not immediately, the rhetorical promotion of the high ideal of life after baptism faced human weakness and fall. In documents of the early Church, the moral standards to the catechumens as well as to the baptised were set extremely high. Theologians and pastors/bishops agreed that baptism 'washes out' the iniquities committed before being reborn, but the urgent question emerged about the sins in later Christian life such as adultery or apostasy during persecution. Those serious crimes were punished by excommunication.[22] Excommunication as the last resort was imposed for sins related against either Christian faith or practice.

However in relation to the post-baptismal sin the theology of the early Church was indecisive for some time. The ancient homily called the *2 Clement* suggests fasting, prayer and almsgiving as the forms of penance for those who committed sin after their baptism. It was also around this very early time, when the distinction between 'minor' and 'grave' transgression appears in the theology of Christian morality. Ignatius of Antioch[23] and Polycarp of Smyrna[24] argue for reconciliation between the sinner and the Church with the mediation of the ecclesiastical authority which had power to readmit the penitent back to Christian community. Therefore they accept some form of *forgiveness of sins* after baptism. However the essential document to the early Christian history of penance: Hermas' treatise the *Shepherd* points out that there should be no fall into sin after baptism, surly picturing the ideal situation, and consequently no need for post-baptismal *remission*. In a passage that is quite difficult to interpret, in *Mandate* he states:

> 'Sir', I said, 'I would like to ask a further question.' 'Speak', he said. 'Sir', I said, 'I have heard from certain teachers that there is no other repentance beyond that which occurred when we descend into the water and received forgiveness of our previous sins'.[25]

No doubt Hermas refers to an ecclesiastical tradition ('certain teachers') already existing on baptism as the only means of forgiveness of sins. This doctrine is confirmed in the next sentence. However, what became evident in the next section of this document is a possibility of the second and ultimate repentance and following it *forgiveness of sins*.[26] The text with warning gives clear indication that although some pastoral reasons may allow second forgiveness of sins after baptism, no further encouragement to fall into temptation must be given by the teaching about endless circle of sins and forgiveness. It is possible to see in this significant testimony an emerging new practice of penance and therefore questioning the already established ideal model/tradition. This second repentance and public penitence is understood as the last resource and final hope. No encouragement of sins must be offered to the catechumens, by teaching about further possibility of remission. However, if they commit new sins, there must be a pastoral response from the Church that would address and heal those wounds that came into being even after baptism. It seems thus that *forgiveness of sins* was suggested according to the status of the sinners. In the light of this document, the effectiveness of *forgiveness* extends to all sins[27] including apostasy and adultery.[28] The only one obstacle lies on the side of the sinner and it is a result of his or her lack of repentance.

Sin and Forgiveness – the Gnostic Valentinian Remedy

With Christian Gnostic literature, we are about to enter into a radically different framework of understanding of 'sin', 'forgiveness' or even 'baptism'. The emerging practice of the Great Church based on the bishops' authority of remission did not have analogy in the Gnostic communities. Sociologically, some of them were based on some sort of 'hierarchy', but equally common was just the model: a teacher – a student, or a spiritual instructor – a catechumen. Some of the Gnostic texts, such as the *Gospel of Thomas*, do not suggest any 'institutional catechesis' other than the direct spiritual contact with the Saviour.[29] In addition the Gnostic understanding of a 'sin' differed radically from the 'catholic'. 'A sin' was less a moral act, intimate thought or desire against God's commandments, but rather a lack of *gnosis*, life submerged in ignorance, 'fall into sleep' or the stage of 'intoxication',[30] possible penance for the sins in the previous incarnation.[31] A 'sinful person' was the one who acted and lived without the spiritual illumination, 'a somatic' character focused on his bodily, vegetative needs. Or even, 'sinful' was an act of obedience to the Decalogue, as taught by Marcion,[32] because this set of rules was given by the evil God of the Jews. These and other discrepancies, but first and foremost the very complex nature of Christian Gnosticism, require that in order to exemplify an alternative opinion to the 'catholic' one I would like to refer to just one Gnostic school and theology originating in Valentinus' teaching.

In the early second century Valentinus' status as a leader, teacher and exegete of the Scriptures was established enough among Christians to make him a candidate to become the Bishop of Rome.[33] It seems that Valentinus in a quite 'catholic' way proclaimed that baptism brings forgiveness of sins, and ultimately redemption. According to Irenaeus' testimony, the followers of Valentinus, saw a parallel between the baptism of Jesus and the Gnostic.[34] While in Jesus' baptism in the Jordan the Spirit of Christ the Saviour descend on human Jesus, so in a similar way during baptism of a Gnostic Christian he or she receives the spirit of immortality, forgiveness of sins and redemption. The baptism of the Gnostic Christian makes him or her 'spiritual', allows him or her to enter into the community of 'pneumatics' (Gr. *pneuma* – 'a spirit'), and in future, participate in the eternal life of the spiritual /real Church. According to Valentinus, in Irenaeus' interpretation, the remission of sins is granted as yet another outcome of a spiritual baptism and it looks like with this view Valentinus was still within 'catholic' or proto-orthodox theology. However, in Valentinian theology, all events that happen in this realm reflect their origin or fulfilment in the spiritual reality. In a similar way baptism 'here' represents the eschatological baptism, when the Gnostic will enter the realm of glory in the eternal World.[35] The teaching about 'the second baptism' was not particularly shocking to the apologists, as they describe martyrdom as the baptism in blood.[36] So it was not the visible difference between Valentinian and 'catholic' theology of baptism and *remission of sins* that worried the proto-orthodox theologians, but rather the similarity, which suggests that there was a common ground between the heretics and the fellow-believers of the true Church.

Tertullian's Controversial Legacy

In the early Christian debate that clarified understanding of the *forgiveness of sins* a special place belongs to Tertullian. The treatise *On Penitence* offers an important insight into Tertullian's view of remission of sins when the author was in the 'catholic' phase of his life.[37] In this work the skilful orator argued for the forgiveness of the gravest sins and possibility of readmission of the sinners after their penance was completed.[38] In his view, 'the gate of forgiveness' was open to the catechumen, but was closed to the Christian who committed a sin after baptism, therefore Tertullian suggested the opening of these gates once more, and only once more, to those who complete penance. The idea of 'the second repentance' echoes the motif known from Hermas and shows that the early Christian theology took into account common experience of fall into sin after baptism. Later, in Tertullian's more rigorist phase, he accused the 'catholics' of an incoherent policy of readmission of all sorts of sinners to the Church.[39] The claim reflects further development of pastoral ministry in the 'catholic' Church that opened the 'gate' to sinners wider than Tertullian expected. Certainly, sins after baptism find a pastoral response in the forms of 'reconciliation' with God *via* the Church. This introductory aspect of remission of sins was not just private, secret and interior, but also was public visible confession, often leading to some form of humiliation: such as 'prostration in sackcloth and ashes'.[40] The public act was a necessary step towards reconciliation with God and the community; therefore it was essential introduction to the *forgiveness of sins*. Tertullian reaffirmed that the final act of reconciliation was performed by the bishop.

During the second phase of his life, Tertullian as a Montanist recognised two categories of sins: 'remissible' and 'irremissible'.[41] The first group contained 'lesser' offences of 'moderate'[42] and 'lighter'[43] character. These can be forgiven after 'a reprimand'. The second group of sins received other descriptions such as 'capital',[44] 'mortal',[45] 'greater'[46] and for those there is only 'condemnation'. Those sins were punished by excommunication from the Church. Tertullian's views on *forgiveness of sins* reflected his transition from 'catholic' to Montanist theology. During the first 'catholic' period, he did not mention any cases of unforgivable sins, however later he made a case arguing for the impossibility of forgiveness of some of the sins, which also include, as we can see in the treatise *On Modesty*,[47] God's forgiveness. As the Montanist he became more rigorous about *remission of sins* and stated that 'mortal sins' such as murder, idolatry, adultery, false witness or fraud cannot be forgiven. Although Tertullian's view develops alongside his transition from a 'catholic' to the Montanist position, there is still coherence in his theology as to the role of the Church in *forgiveness of sins*. Unlike the 'catholics', he assumed that 'the lighter sins' committed after baptism can be forgiven through the mediation of the congregation. The prayer of the local church is Christ's intercession for the sinner and it contains hope of reconciliation with the Father. In Tertullian's opinion, the spiritual power of the prayer over the sinner had some kind of divine efficacy. As Christ's prayer for people is always heard by his Father, the Church has the power/authority to grant *forgiveness of sins* as a part of Christ's own mediation. Tertullian, the Montanist, changes only one important aspect of this theology: while as 'catholic' he proclaimed the power of the Church to forgive all sins, including the serious crimes against God and men, as the Montanist he limited to efficacy of forgiveness to the lighter offences. Under pressure from the 'catholics', Tertullian addresses another important aspect of forgiveness. The bone of contention between him and the 'catholics' is the author of proclamation. Is it a local bishop? Is it the Church? Or maybe only the bishop of Rome, on the basis of commissioning from Christ, has the power of the 'keys' (Mt. 16.18–19)?[48]

Tertullian, the Montanist seemed to have some doubts about the exact source of that proclamation. He writes a special, exegetical chapter in his treatise *On Modesty* in order to address this issue. First, he suggested that the power of absolution was conferred only to Peter the Apostle, and not to the Church.[49] But this position was theologically indefensible as *forgiveness of sin* has been proclaimed by all and within all Christian communities. Tertullian thus readjusted his position and stated that the power of reconciliation had been given to 'the Church of the Spirit' and by this he makes a clear distinction between the Montanist ecclesiology which emphasised the priority of the charismatic gifts and authority, and the 'catholic' stance which was based on the authority of bishops. Using his eloquence, intelligence and wit, Tertullian summarised the difference, highlighting that the only Church that is able to forgive sins is the Church endowed with the power of the Holy Spirit, not the Church which consists of a number of bishops. It is God who forgives not a human being.[50]

Tertullian's famous distinction between 'spiritual' and 'institutional' Church drastically narrowed down the source of forgiveness only to those its members who are endowed with the power of the Spirit, not that of bevies of bishops.[51] The strong emphasis is laid on the authority of pneumatic Christians and not on the bishops and priests. The latter represent an institutional Church corrupted by mild and sloppy rules, which dissolve true Christian, at least for Tertullian, zeal and commitment. Although neither Tertullian nor Montanist were hostile to the institutional Church, they wish that any form of the ministry be associated with the manifestation of the Spirit such as prophetic abilities, which they value. For the 'catholic' party, the nature of the clerical office had different significance than the exclusively 'pneumatic' character of the minister. The 'catholics' were concerned about the mass-scale, universal organisation with visible degree and signs of unity. Tertullian, representing here the voice of Montanism, promotes the idea of the *ecclesia*, small in number but first and foremost 'spiritual' if not sinless. In this moment Tertullian's own theological journey reaches its end, as he attaches the authority of *forgiveness of sin* to the few selected, small number of pneumatic Christians who are able to forgive only lesser sins. This extreme vision of God's mercy over humanity did not disappear altogether with Tertullian's death. It would appear to many more radical Christians in the centuries to come.

*

With this stage of theological development the *forgiveness of sins* already achieves its full meaning and function. It is inseparable from the nature of the Church, particularly as a mediator of salvation, an exclusive spiritual and at the same time institutional communion. In this context, *forgiveness of sins* was understood as an act of God's grace over a sinner that took visible shape during the liturgical celebration. It restores spiritual life in the offender, and therefore appears as a sacrament of reconciliation. But it also opened the door to the communion with fellow-Christians. The *forgiveness of sins* had to be administered according those ancient sources within the 'catholic' Church as outside of it there was only doom. No other group, sect and alternative community had the power to proclaim the forgiveness. Tertullian's interesting case and his liaison with Montanism, only emphasise the extreme axiom of that opinion. The *forgiveness* was performed by the Church's authentic minister, that is the bishops, who have the power to restore unity between the individual and God and the *ecclesia*. This core of the early Western theological interpretation found its way to the Creeds and was reaffirmed by later Latin scholastic theologians.

CHAPTER 12

The Resurrection of the Flesh

It may come as a surprise to the modern reader that the divisive article on *the resurrection of the flesh* was one of the crucial pillars sustaining the construction of proto-orthodox doctrine. The number of documents affirming the value and significance of this statement is very extensive and revealing.[1] Clearly, the issue of physical/bodily resurrection was defended passionately by pre-orthodox theologians using every possible argument, philosophical as well as theological. This was a response to the acute questioning of this belief by pagan and Jewish critics. It also addressed the serious doubts raised by other Christians. At its core, this statement of belief reveals that from its beginning, faith, especially in its Catholic form, took seriously the physical dimension of human nature which was to participate in salvation equally with the soul. The belief in the life of the soul after death was commonly accepted by Christians, while faith in resurrection of the flesh was far more controversial.

In the structure of the Creed, the statement under discussion is linked with faith in Christ's resurrection (*on the third day He rose again from the dead*),[2] the last judgment (*from thence He shall come to judge the living and the dead*)[3] and predicts the next and final statement (*everlasting life*).[4] The place of this article in the architecture of the Apostles' Creed exemplifies very well its role as a passage between two stages of eschatology:[5] the final judgment and eternal rest. Between these two phases, there was a room for an affirmation that the human body would be included in future glory or punishment.

As noted in the previous chapters, we must remember that the early theology which laid the foundation of the Apostles' Creed was part of a colourful tapestry composed of at least three kinds of cultural thread. There were pagan critics to whom a variety of apologies of Christian faith were dedicated. Those listeners or readers, among whom some were educated in various Hellenistic-Roman philosophies such as Stoicism, Middle Platonism, Scepticism or even 'atheistic' Epicureanism, had already encountered the idea of the immortality of the human soul in classical mythologies and Greek mysteries. Nonetheless, *resurrection of the flesh* was for them a bizarre, Christian *novum*. This belief was seen by pagan intellectuals as part of a naïve Christian folklore and an evident example of the superstitious character of the 'new cult'.

The second thread represents the closest relatives of the Christians – the Jews. Jewish theology or rather various traditions of Jewish theologies of the first and second century contained a whole spectrum of beliefs, including various views about the ultimate destiny of a human being in the afterlife. The concept of resurrection within Hellenistic Judaism was exemplified by various kinds of theological literature. First, documents such as the Book of Daniel pointed to the resurrection as the climax of history (Dan. 12.2) and provided the Jewish apocalypses with convenient imagery.[6] Secondly in a comparable way, other forms of Jewish literature from the second century BC also hinted at a new turn in Jewish understanding of the life after death, which included full restoration of the body. This background set a natural context for the Christian claim about *resurrection of the flesh*.

The third thread that played a vital role in the original proclamation of this belief was the growing number of Docetic and Gnostic theologies which proto-orthodox theologians felt needed to be confronted urgently. As has been observed, the anti-Gnostic response stimulated the production of a great deal of apologetic literature. Mainstream Christianity aimed to reject 'false' teaching and promote the 'correct' understanding of eternal life. Against that pressure, the alternative interpretations aimed to revalue the connection between body and spirit, with a strong emphasis on the priority of the latter. These three aspects provide the context of this examination, which again, must begin with a brief reference to the Scriptural testimony and imagery.

The Scriptural Legacy – Resurrection of the Flesh

The concept of Sheol[7] is at the centre of the understanding of the afterlife found in the Hebrew Scriptures. In this post-mortal condition there was no clear distinction between the fate of the just and the unjust. As in many other cases, the theological concept of

Sheol and afterlife was shaped by the various tragic events faced by the Jews. In particular after the exile (6 BCE), a stronger accent was placed on the individual's survival after death, a view which also assumed personal responsibility for the conduct of earthly life (e.g. Ezek 18).[8] In this new ethical and eschatological framework the concept of Sheol also received further clarification. It was seen not just as 'a place of shadows', an 'underworld' forgotten by God, but rather as a realm of death, still under God's control, from which one day, the departed would be called to life. One particular passage, the famous resurrection of the dry bones from Ezekiel (37.1– 6) illustrates very well this new theology of physical resurrection of dead. Although this passage might have multiple layers of meanings such as reinstitution of Israel, return from exile, it also hints at a strong conviction that physical resurrection is an essential part of God's governance over his creatures. It is not surprising that this imaginative story inspired Christians too. This theological intuition received even further clarification in the Hellenistic period during the Maccabean revolt (2 BCE), when faith in the final resurrection found its new, Scriptural affirmation (the *LXX*: 2 Macc. 7.9 and 7.23).[9] However at this stage of Hebrew theology, resurrection of the dead was seen as a reward only to the just, while sinners and apostates had no hope of a future life (2 Macc. 7.9). Resurrection in the body began to be seen as God's gift to his faithful: only some will participate in eternal life, while God's judgment will apply to all. This development in Hebrew thought did not convince all Jewish theologians. The open conflict between the Sadducees and the Pharisees (e.g. Lk. 20.27–40) shows the pluralism of opinions on the final destiny of the human being after death.

Paul's apostolic authority among the early Christians was unquestionable. His theology of resurrection from the 1 Letter to the Corinthians (15.1–34)[10] had an enormous impact on the early Patristic visualisation of that mysterious event. However, Paul's theology emphasises *the resurrection of the dead*, not on the *resurrection of the flesh* as formulated by the Creed. Paul's exposition of the theme must have been provoked by views of some Christians from Corinth who denied the belief in resurrection of the dead (1 Cor. 15.12b). Nonetheless, in general terms his affirmation of the *resurrection of the dead* seems to be synonymous with his view on the *resurrection of the flesh*.[11] To Paul, Jesus' resurrection prefigured the resurrection of all, but at the same time, Jesus' resurrection required affirmation of resurrection in general.

The fourth Gospel and Johannine letters contain a more ambiguous treatment of the whole theme. Although there is a clear declaration that the risen Lord had a body, as shown by the case of

Thomas' post-Easter experience (Jn 20.26–29), at the same time the body of Christ was not straightforwardly identifiable (Jn 20.14; 21.4–6). John's theology of Christ's risen body is more concerned with other issues than with the physical dimension of life after death. Although concern about what was seen as erroneous Docetic teaching on Christ's incarnation can be noted in Johannine Christology (1 Jn 1.1), this tradition is focused more on the spiritual nature of Christ's resurrection than on its physical dimension and the consequences of this for the notion of resurrection.

This collection of the essential insights into the mystery of resurrection was the frame within which the next generation of Christians developed their ideas. In the early Patristic literature the idea developed a life of its own, including Gnostic offshoots.

Proclamation of the Incredible Against the Pagans

Athenagoras of Athens, as a Christian philosopher, took on a massive intellectual task. The dedication of his *Embassy for the Christians*[12] reveals what kind of readers he had in mind while presenting the foundations of Christian faith. It is quite sound to assume that a similar, if not identical, audience was addressed by Athenagoras in his second treatise *On the Resurrection of the Dead* in which he introduced the Christian rationale of the belief. Athenagoras' effort can be seen as the first serious endeavour to engage with philosophy or the first attempt to give Christian faith a critical and rational defence. The work's title, *On the Resurrection of the Dead*, reveals the chief theme and the main intention of the apologist. In this document, the author tries to prove as plausible the possibility and necessity of resurrection by referring only to rational arguments and the philosophical authorities of Plato and Aristotle. Athenagoras points out that Almighty God, the Creator of the universe, is not limited by anything, either human or natural obstacles. To illustrate this point, the philosopher presents graphic examples of the total destruction of the human body which do not interfere with God's ability to restore it. This famous example of 'chain of consumption' reveals some practical questions about the 'physical' aspect of the risen body that might have been asked by Athenagoras' opponents:

> These persons, to wit, say that many bodies of those who have come to an unhappy death in shipwrecks and rivers have become food for fishes, and many of those who perish in war, or who from some other sad cause or state of things are deprived of burial, lie exposed to become the food of any animals which

may chance to light upon them. Since, then, bodies are thus consumed, and the members and parts composing them are broken up and distributed among a great multitude of animals, and by means of nutrition become incorporated with the bodies of those that are nourished by them, in the first place, they say, their separation from these is impossible; and besides this, in the second place, they adduce another circumstance more difficult still.[13]

Athenagoras' response to this mockery is temperate and logically coherent. After death, whatever the cause of death, the human body is decomposed into the smallest elements which still can be gathered by God and used to create the identical body of the dead person.[14] All arguments for *the resurrection of the flesh* used by the Christian philosopher can be qualified into three categories. First, *the resurrection of the flesh* is possible because of God's unlimited Might. Eternal life, which is human destiny, includes existence in the body, as a part of God's creation. The human body is not unworthy of God,[15] so resurrection is plausible.[16] To Athenagoras, the *resurrection of the flesh* is not a newly invented Christian fantasy which provides fellow-believers with an immature hope. Rather, it originates in the Creator's will as he provided each human being with an immortal soul and set his destiny as eternal contemplation.[17] The body is included in God's prospect of immortality. The ultimate survival of man, not just as a soul, but also as a body, suits this divine purpose.

Secondly, because of the universal rule of justice, each human being must receive reward or punishment for his deeds during life. This point was particularly close to the Stoic philosophers. Therefore, for Athenagoras nobody can escape this judgment. This final act of justice will take place at the end of time and recompense or punishment will be eternal. The view that only the soul can be rewarded or punished is unfair, as the body also contributed to the ultimate situation of the human being. Therefore the body will also participate in the just form of retribution.[18]

Finally, as the purpose of the human being is eternal contemplation of God, which is a very Platonic view, resurrection is necessary to fulfil this fortune. Death cannot be the last stage of existence. On the contrary, human destiny exceeds it.[19] The treatise shows how Athenagoras tries to accommodate some philosophical assumptions in order to shield and explain this difficult Christian belief. Whatever we think of his effort, it must be noted that the apologist saw his faith as intelligible and communicable to what he saw as an atheistic audience. His effort thus remains an

example of the remarkable, positive dialogue with pagan contemporaries as well as a model of affirmative assessment of human
nature. Against the dominant Platonic tendency to underestimate
the material element and overvalue the spiritual one, Athenagoras
presents a realistic anthropology which harmoniously combines
anthropology and theology, current history and eschatology.

Explanation of the Credible to the Jews

Justin's *Dialogue with Trypho* introduces another response to a different adversary, which this time it shares much common ground
with the Hebrew Scriptures. Justin Martyr thus expounds a
different aspect of the *resurrection of the flesh*. First, a central role is
given to the risen Christ with whom all saints will be in communion
at that eschatological moment. Here, the typology of the Old Covenant with the central idea of entering and possessing 'the promised land' is revised in the light of Justin's theology of resurrection.[20] There is no doubt that the long expected entry into the
'Holy Land', so well known to the Jewish listeners, was chosen by
Justin to forward his rhetorical purpose to underline the role of
'the new Joshua', that is Jesus.[21] Jesus/Joshua leads his nation, the
'new Israel' to the promised Land or homeland. Only with Jesus
and by him, it is possible to reach this final destination, and all
previous Jewish leaders were but prototypes of him. This is the
primary emphasis of Justin's interpretation. It can be noted that
Justin does not explore, like Athenagoras, any anthropological
complications of the phenomenon of resurrection, as for him and
the Jewish theologians God's omnipotence does not have any
restrictions.[22] The human body can be raised by the Holy One, who
performed many other miracles in the history of Israel. Therefore,
this aspect of resurrection is taken for granted as Justin focuses on
the outcome of Jesus' resurrection[23] which was the climax of the
first 'advent'. To Justin 'the second advent' will close the current
stage of history and open another one, which will take a thousand
years.[24] Appealing to Paul's imaginative picture of the second coming, Justin also assumed that Christ and his angels will appear on
clouds.[25] Resurrection will be a universal event and the souls of the
risen will be then reunited with their bodies. Then, the judgment
of the nations will take place and after it the era of thousand years
of Christ's reign.[26] This eschatological period, the time of blessed
happiness, harmony and peace under Christ's rule includes life in
bodily form, which will not cease to exist. Justin seems to be convinced that at the end of historical time, Jerusalem will be rebuilt
not just as a metaphor of God's city, but literarily.[27] It is difficult to

assess properly the analogy of Jerusalem/human flesh, but these two realities perform a parallel function in Justin's rhetorical elaboration. Both may represent God's place of dwelling and their restoration expresses the accomplishment of God's project: salvation. As a theological project, Justin's scenario contains some discrepancies,[28] but nonetheless its main line remains unshaken: *resurrection of the flesh* is an integral part of the second coming of the Lord, his judgment and either the reward or punishment of all people.

Gnostic Glossy to the Early Christian Assertion

Although defence of *resurrection of the flesh* against pagan scepticism and Jewish suspicion significantly shaped the early clarification of the belief, the main challenge came from the Christian opposition of the Gnostics. Our crucial, though somewhat biased, witness, Irenaeus of Lyons, recorded a Gnostic opinion that the body was not disposed to eternal salvation.[29] Among early Latin theologians Tertullian defended participation of flesh in everlasting life in his treatise *On the Resurrection of the flesh*.[30] Both Irenaeus and Tertullian saw themselves as heirs of Paul's teaching on the resurrection, but their opponents were also certain that they represented Paul's thought in its most genuine, spiritual form. This was perhaps because Paul's teaching contained ambiguities. On one occasion, for example, Paul expressed his conviction that 'flesh and blood' could not inherit the kingdom of God (1 Cor. 15.50).

It is not surprising the diversity in early Christian views on this theme arose from the exegesis of various rather unclear Scriptural passages, which included the Gospels' accounts of a number of meetings with the risen Lord and his 'body'. The issue of resurrection of the flesh was controversial among Christians themselves. Among the first generation of Christ's followers there was a discrepancy about the nature of resurrection, as some thought that it would happen at the end of time, while others assumed that it had already taken place (2 Tim. 2.18). The radical evaluation of the present time interpreted 'resurrection' as a form of 'liberation' of the soul from the rulers/demons of the visible world which is achievable in the current life. This suggests that a very early pro-Gnostic stage of theology had developed among some Christians encountered by the Apostle Paul. With the paradigm of Gnostic interpretation *resurrection of the flesh/of the dead* was yet another metaphor of 'freedom of the soul' or 'liberation of the divine spark' from the bondage of the material element through spiritual illumination/knowledge. According to Epiphanius, some Gnostics claimed that there was no resurrection of the flesh, but only of the soul.[31] Hippolytus of Rome, whom we have encountered on many occasions, records, this time as an adversary of Gnostic Christians, that for a particular sect (the Naassenes) resurrection meant awakening of the spiritual man from his sepulchre, which is the body.[32] In that large spectrum of opinions, one example can illustrate the teaching of the Valentinian school. The Gnostic document, the *Treatise on the Resurrection*, distinguishes the three kinds of resurrection that reflect the archetypal resurrection of the Saviour:

> The Saviour swallowed up death – (of this) you are not reckoned as being ignorant – for he put aside the world which is perishing. He transformed [himself] into an imperishable Aeon and raised himself up, having swallowed the visible by the invisible, and he gave us the way of our immortality. Then, indeed, as the Apostle said, 'We suffered with him, and we arose with him, and we went to heaven with him'. Now if we are manifest in this world wearing him, we are that one's beams, and we are embraced by him until our setting, that is to say, our death in this life. We are drawn to heaven by him, like beams by the sun, not being restrained by anything. This is the spiritual resurrection which swallows up the psychic in the same way as the fleshly.[33]

The text places the Saviour and his ascent to the spiritual realm after conquering – here 'swallowing' – death in the centre. Gnostic resurrection is an imitation or extension of the Saviour's example. After physical death, there is an ascension of the Gnostic soul, but with its spiritual cover/flesh towards the higher region where the Saviour dwells. This theory accepts an existence after death not only of the soul or the spirit but also some sort of pneumatic body, as we can see in the case of Elijah and Moses.[34] Resurrection is then a metaphor of transformation from one stage to another (cf. 1 Cor. 15.51–52), and this transition into the spiritual realm provides the Gnostic with a new imperishable form or 'garment' (cf. 2 Cor. 5.1–4).

This example of the Gnostic perspective shows how easy it was to hold the view about necessary transformation from one kind of life (somatic) into another (spiritual), which offered a different form of eternal existence to that proposed by Catholic catechesis. At least this aspect could be understood as a pedagogical, useful metaphor of something more substantial and relevant. It is therefore not surprising that for theologians who saw themselves as representing Catholic doctrine, *the resurrection of the flesh* was one of the marks distinguishing and separating the true Church from the sects of dissident Christians.

Apologetic for the Belief

Confronting this kind of interpretation, Tertullian's treatise *On the Resurrection* fulfils several purposes: polemical, doctrinal, pedagogical and persuasive. The author also aims to confront those pagan philosophers who deny life after death.[35] He wants to deal with the danger of a certain kind of Gnostic theology, which, although accepting the immortal nature of the soul, rejected the resurrection of the flesh.[36] He confronts Valentinian's 'realised eschatology' which, as in the previous Gnostic document, suggested that resurrection had already occurred. Against that view, he underlines a future resurrection which is different from a 'pneumatic' conversion. Tertullian's opposition is unveiled by a more careful examination of his work.

In the first part, in order to attack his Christian opponents, Tertullian applies both rational investigation into the relation between the soul and body and the witness of the Scriptures. Tertullian's anthropology, although it contains many complex features, remains basically twofold: soul/spirit and body which must be distinguished[37] but not separated.[38] He underlines the value of the body as 'the tabernacle of the flesh',[39] as more than just a tool of the soul. Rather, it is an integral part of man. The dignity of the human body, although it is 'clay', is ultimately confirmed by God's Son's incarnation into a human body.[40] Incarnation provides us with the definitive affirmation that flesh is not contemptible, but must be respected and cared for, as God himself did by sending his Son to experience it. Christology with the central idea of Christ's flesh provides Tertullian with the strongest inspiration to defend the dignity of human flesh and its participation in a future life. He does not see any discrepancy between the soul or spiritual element in a human being and the material aspect of his composition. To Tertullian, both elements coexist during earthly life and through the material element the spiritual can flourish. In another rhetorical statement, the author eulogises this union:

> To such a degree is the flesh the pivot of salvation, that since by it the soul becomes linked with God, it is the flesh which makes possible the soul's election by God. For example, the flesh is washed that the soul may be made spotless: the flesh is anointed that the soul may be consecrated: the flesh is signed <with the cross> that the soul too may be protected: the flesh is overshadowed by the imposition of the hand that the soul may be illumined by the Spirit: the flesh feeds on the Body and Blood of Christ so that the soul also may be replete with God.[41]

The body takes part in the effort of achieving salvation and is necessary to its fulfilment. Therefore it must be seen as an important
part of that sanctification. The body also influences moral life; at
the end of time both elements, not just soul, must face the consequences of choices made during earthly life as divine justice will
be satisfied.[42] This judgment is seen as the reason for resurrection
of the flesh[43] and is linked with the coming of the Son of man on
the clouds of heaven.[44]

Thus, there are three kinds of arguments that Tertullian uses to
support his thesis on *the resurrection of the flesh*. First, that the dignity
of the body as 'the sister of Christ' will survive death.[45] Second,
belief in bodily resurrection expresses faith in God's omnipotence.[46] Thirdly, because of the unity between soul and body, they
both must continue to exist after Christ's judgment.[47] In the second and third parts of his treatise Tertullian becomes an exegete of
the Scriptures and uses them to reaffirm his main points about the
dignity of the body, the divine ability to raise up it again, and the
fact that the ultimate judgment will include the human body, not
just the soul. According to Tertullian, the Hebrew Bible with the
voice of prophets, the Gospels and the apostolic teaching, provide
unanimous evidence of the *resurrection of the flesh*. It is interesting to
see how Tertullian responds to the difficulty arising from Paul's
already quoted passage from Paul's letter (1 Cor. 15.50) about the
alleged exclusion of the flesh from participation in eternal life.
This passage in the Valentinian elaboration seems to be the hermeneutical starting-point of their eschatology. Against their interpretation, Tertullian, explains that the 'flesh and blood', which
cannot inherit the eternal life, refer to the evil acts performed by
the sinners.[48] These acts will be judged by God at the last
resurrection.

Finally the Latin orator considers the status of risen bodies and
their condition in the life without end.[49] It must be noted that the
whole treatise is an impressive tribute to the human body in a
period when flesh and its functions were under severe scrutiny not
only by the dualistic Gnostic Christians, but in the larger intellectual and spiritual/religious context. Tertullian reiterates in a
very original way the value of the body, combining the Scriptural
evidence with philosophical arguments. Under Gnostic pressure,
he defends the positive assessment of the body during life as well
in the future, post-mortal existence. His acclamation of the body,
however, does not encourage his readers to fall into another trap,
this time of hedonistic, uncontrolled euphoria. At the end of the
day, God's judgment will assess the coexistence of the soul and
body in this life. This inventive theological treatise provides many

arguments which defend human integrity and directly value human corporality. The work certainly inspired some further theological elaboration of its central theme, which for Tertullian was an excellent excuse to pay tribute to the reality of God's creation.

*

In summary, the Apostles' Creed, rather than clarifying the value of the *resurrection of body*, provokes further questions about the idea of the individual's survival after death inherited from the Hebrew and Christian revelation. In spite of the diversity of early Christian theology and inner-Christian disputes, a coherent understanding of this belief emerges from different documents. This belief, although strongly dependent on the idea of justice, retribution and reward, also contains an appreciation of the link between the spiritual and material dimension of human being. Of course, this positive evaluation of human flesh was the outcome of a specific Christology, which stressed Christ's real flesh, real death and real resurrection in body. There was a direct link between Christ's resurrection and the Christian hope of life after death. Naturally, the present pronouncement of the Apostles' Creed foreshadows the final article, faith in *the life everlasting*.

CHAPTER 13

. . . *And Eternal Life. Amen*

Then I saw an immense garden, and in it a grey-haired man sat
in shepherd's garb; tall he was, and milking sheep. And standing
around him were many thousands of people clad in white gar-
ments. He raised his head, looked at me, and said: 'I am glad
you have come, my child'. He called me over to him and gave
me, as it were, a mouthful of the milk he was drawing; and I took
it into my cupped hands and consumed it. And all those who
stood around me said: 'Amen'.

Martyrdom of Saint Perpetua and Felicitas, 4[1]

The *Grande Finale* of the Apostles' Creed, the promise of *eternal life,*
comes in a natural way within the structure of the whole theological *opus.* It confirms that after the reunion of soul and body at
the last judgment, some of the risen will attain eternal joy in God's
kingdom, others will face punishment. The present article is
related to 'life without end', which as a metaphor tries to express
the ineffable experience of the eschatological communion with
God. This union will be the climax of personal love, maturity and at
the same time the fulfilment of God's plan of salvation. Early theologians representing various ecclesiastical associations agreed that
the eschatological event has been already inaugurated. For some,
in Christ's resurrection and ascension, for others the eschatological event is anticipated in current choices, acts of faith, faithfulness or betrayal, acceptance of 'illumination and knowledge' or by
remaining in ignorance. Salvation 'already given' calls for its full
realisation in an event and phase yet to come.

I wish to note that within the theological frame of the
Apostles' Creed, this article is directly connected with the previous

one,[2] but also it is based on belief in 'the judgment', which has been discussed in Chapter 8. It is then helpful to assess the early Christian doctrine on *eternal life* against the background of these two affirmations.

'Life with God Without End' as the Scriptural Motif

A brief survey of the Scriptural symbolism that was assimilated by the early Christian interpretation of *everlasting life* must emphasise its three primordial aspects.[3] First, Scriptural documents give witness to life after resurrection that we may call 'personal' or 'individual' life, not just existence under the genetic term of 'humanity' or by the 'dissolving' of the human element into the divine. Secondly, eternal co-existence with God was perceived as life 'in perfect love' or as the continuation of an already existing 'life with Christ' here, during earthly existence. Particularly in the Pauline context, it is a sort of present life united with Christ, though 'hidden', that at the end of time will be fully revealed. Thirdly, the early Christian view of eternal life, particularly influenced by Jewish and early Christian apocalyptic literature, put bold emphasis on the necessary and forthcoming time of tribulation, a sort of cosmological crisis, which will lead to the appearance of the Saviour and then, to the return to his kingdom. In the light of this tradition, the post-mortal life is shown as common worship, adoration and praise together with other spiritual beings, such as angels, archangels, powers and principalities. All these chief aspects of *everlasting life* call for more accurate identification.

First, individual resurrection is one of the outstanding characteristics of, for example, Paul's theology. His famous statement on seeing God 'face-to-face' (1 Cor. 13.12) presents the eschatological communion with God as a very personal, intimate encounter. Secondly, this eschatological life with God will be as perfect as love is. Again, the end of Paul's eulogy of Christian life (1 Cor. 13.1–13), provides a hint of this understanding. Love (Gr. *agape*) is much more than a moral virtue, or a transitory quality of Christian life. It is for Paul, as well as for the Johannine tradition, a specific form of participation in God with and through Jesus Christ. This strong Christ-centred context of the divine love is shown by another important intuition of Paul's about 'life with Christ' (e.g. Phil. 1.23; 1 Thess. 4.17; 5.10; 2 Cor. 4.14; 13.4) which begins now and will be accomplished in *everlasting life*. The present union with Christ, so crucial to Paul's and Johannine theologies, will be fully realised in the age to come. The third aspect of everlasting life is well illustrated by Johannine symbolism and theology. It is about the ultimate common worship, joy and celebration. Heaven or the *ever-lasting life* is presented not as a static image, but rather as a dynamic liturgy focused on the eternal worship of God and his Lamb (Rev. 19.1–10). This is a vision of the perfect feast and banquet in 'New Jerusalem' (Rev. 7.15–17; 21.1–2, 9–10) which is full of enjoyment, blessedness and rest (Rev. 21.3–4). The concept of 'the heavenly City' inspired also Paul's understanding of eschatology (Gal. 4.26) which promoted the idea of 'citizenship' (Phil. 3.20) as anticipation of the future life and glory. These images of the *everlasting life* have influenced Christian imagery and literature over the following centuries.

Everlasting Life – a Hope Confirmed by the Christian Apocrypha

The New Testament documents were not the only sources which provided some models for the early Christian concept of *everlasting life*. Another crucial inspiration came from apocryphal literature, which showed great interest in painting vivid images of the context of the eschatological union with God. In Christian apocrypha the hope of eternal life was connected to the final period of terrifying events, abnormalities, and tribulation that would foretell the imminent end of this world and the coming of eternal life. According to these documents, the world will be at its final stage of painful agony. At that time wonderful and terrible signs will appear in its political and moral state, mirrored even in physical forms. One of the most characteristics examples of this petrifying eschatological dawn is preserved in *Sibylline Oracles*.[4] This eschatological *mysterium tremendum* will astonish the whole of humanity and nature, but it will be also a sign of the end of this world and the coming forthcoming appearance of the Lord. His judgment is inevitable as well as its consequences: hell or paradise. At his appearance the dead will be released.[5] Then the stern judgment will take place and the righteous will enjoy *everlasting life* and the sinners suffer eternal death. A good example of this dramatic scenario can be found in a document called *the Greek Apocalypse of Ezra*.[6] This kind of visualisation show some fondness for the horror of the final judgment, often related to purification by fire.[7] It builds up tension and provides a sharp contrast as the next phase promises peaceful, undistributed harmony of the community of saints with their God.[8] At this point, the Hebrew motif of 'the messianic banquet' with God (Isa. 25.6–8; Mt. 8.11; 22.1–11; Lk. 14.15) returns now with Christian colours, as the image of a shared meal. Again, the *Sibylline Oracles* provide us with a colourful example of the *eternal life* or feast with God:

And then, indeed, he will raise up a kingdom for all ages among men, he who once gave the holy Law to the pious, to all of whom he promised to open the earth and the world and the gates of the blessed and all joys and immortal intellect and eternal cheer. From every land they will bring incense and gifts to the house of the great God There will be no other house among men, even for the future generations to know, except the one which God gave to faithful men to honour (for mortals will invoke the sons of the great God). And all the paths of the plain and rugged cliffs, lofty mountains, and wild waves of the sea will be easy to climb or sail in those days, for all peace will come upon the land of the good. Prophets of the great God will take away the sword for they themselves are judges of men and righteous kings. There will also be a wealth among men for this is the judgment and dominion of the great God. Rejoice, maiden, and be glad, for to you the one who created heaven and earth has given the joy of the age. He will dwell in you. You will have immortal light. Wolves and lambs will eat grass together in the mountains. Leopards will feed together with kids. Roving bears will spend the night with calves. The flesh-eating lion will eat husks at the manger like an ox, and mere infant children will lead them with ropes. For he will make the beasts on earth harmless. Serpents and asps will sleep with babies and will not harm them, for the hand of God will be upon them.[9]

As it is possible to see infinite joy, harmony, peace and unity will be the 'endless day'.[10] In its literary construction, 'the end' mirrors its beginning in the original Paradise. The perfect climax will reflect the perfect genesis of humanity, its stage of innocence, equality and freedom from any worries, needs, hungers or distinctions. The new order, the new creation will accomplish the history of the old one. Now this perfection will not be challenged by any external or internal factor, as evil will finally be conquered and destroyed.

The Prospect of Eternal Life and its Richness of Expressions

Among the post-apostolic documents the theme of *everlasting life* sprang up in a variety of theological interpretations. For example, the *Epistle of Barnabas* presents *eternal life* as the rest of the saints on the 'eighth day'. However, as in many other narratives of this period, the blessed end is contrasted with the current moment of history and its tragic events. The *Epistle*, as it represents Jewish-Christian tradition, is sturdily dependent on Jewish and Christian apocalyptic and it reflects an expectation of the imminent end of

this world, final judgment and punishment.[11] The destruction of
Jerusalem (70 CE)[12] seems to give the first sign of the end, but also
of the beginning of the new 'Day'. The author states that the
present moment is overshadowed by the evil power,[13] however
Christians who are liberated by the Lord from this evil dominion
can await future glory only by remaining faithful. In the same way
as in *1 Clement*,[14] the *Epistle* also highlights the forthcoming judgment[15] and proclaims the 'new Sabbath' to come.[16] In this interpretation, the last phase of history will reflect its beginning, but this
time 'the reflection' of the original status will not have any imperfection. As God created the world in six days, and on the seventh
he rested, so after six thousand years everything will be perfected,
then the Creator will judge the whole of humanity, while resting on
the seventh day. The proposed analogy of 'the paradise' – 'the new
heaven' denoted for those original Jewish-Christians, the fulfilment of the promise made from the very first phase of the world,
which was for a life without end in God's paradise. However, the
Epistle does not provide any characteristics of that eternal bliss. For
these details we can turn to another document of the same
tradition the *Odes of Solomon*.

The *Odes* reveal more about *the eternal life*, as the author claims
the privilege of a mystical vision[17] of that ultimate happiness. Then
a 'change of garment takes place' and the previous corruptible of
the skin is taken off,[18] while a new one, the garment of 'incorruption'[19] or the garment of 'light'[20] is put on. In addition to this
heavenly gift, also justification, salvation and freedom are given to
the saint. The *Odes* also refer to the symbol of 'the crown' that
symbolises the new stage of life in New Jerusalem.[21] Finally, this co-
existence with the Lord is represented as the ultimate assimilation
to Christ:

> He became like me, that I might receive him.
> In form he was considered like me, that I might put him on.
>
> (. . .) Like my nature he became, that I might understand him,
> and like my form, that I might not turn away from him.[22]

It is worth highlighting that with this mystical narrative, the theme
of *everlasting life* receives a rather new and unexpected meaning. It
represents union with the Beloved. It is about an intimate relationship between lovers. As the Lord possesses the perfect important
life, so the lover, who is united with him, will also be offered the gift
of eternal life and incorruptibility.[23] The poet and the mystic who
wrote these lyrics expressed his hope of that everlasting union with
the Lord will assure immortality and rest for ever.[24]

With Justin Martyr, we enter a new ground. The saints will enjoy their happiness in two phases. First, they will create the early kingdom of renewed Jerusalem and they will reign there with Christ through a thousand years.[25] After the resurrection, the saints will be rewarded with the possession of 'the heavenly Land'.[26] Then they will receive immortality[27] and fellowship with God.[28] For the sinners and demons, Justin predicts eternal punishment by fire.[29] It looks as if Justin's attention is centred on the theme of the period between the second coming of Christ and the ultimate conflagration of the world. With some interest about the fate of the wicked, where their punishment depends on the proportion of their evil acts, his positive eschatology (i.e. 'the Heavens') is relatively less developed. Justin sees the *eternal life* as a reward and its lack, as a form of punishment. Those who accepted Jesus as their Saviour and lived a virtuous life will receive the ultimate prize. Others must expect punishment. With Justin and another document, the so-called *2 Clement*,[30] more emphasis is given to the idea of reward for proper moral conduct.

Yet another example, Theophilus' apologetic treatise *To Autolycus*, elaborates the motif of union with God. Theophilus describes the *everlasting life* as the climax of the ethical and spiritual maturing of a human being or the ascent to heaven.[31] In Theophilus' view, during early life, the Christian has the potential of assimilation to God through the divine gift of immortality and being obedient to God's commandments. The gift of immortality allows Christians to participate in the divine life, that is, everlasting. This is the highest apotheosis of the human being who has the potential to achieve immortality as a reward for a virtuous, noble life on earth. The final splendour and proximity to God reaffirm this positive anthropology. These selected examples of early Christian adaptations of the motif show various intentions behind their interest in *the eternal life*. For some, this attractive notion is primarily related to the present struggle with various forms of evil such as persecution, rejection and mockery. For others, the same theme represents the ultimate level of perfection as the response to God's call. For all, *the eternal life* was a part of God's justice. Yet, turning to some Gnostic documents provides another insight into the early Christian understanding of this motif.

Eternal Glory – the Shape of the Gnostic Hope

Everlasting life was for the Gnostic the accomplishment of the whole cosmic drama which began with the pre-historical catastrophe within the sphere of the spiritual world. That cataclysm caused by some evil powers, caused the fall of the spiritual into the material, which includes the fall of perfect elements (souls) into bodies. Therefore the end of the material world, which includes human beings, will take a form of 'restoration' of the most mature Christians, the regaining by them of their original status. This motif in its Valentinian expression can be noted in many documents of the Nag Hammadi library.[32] One of them, the *Treatise on the Resurrection*, presents the eschatological goal of the Saviour's task as the reinstallation of the primordial order in 'the eternal realm', into 'divine fullness' (Gr. *pleroma*). The act of returning back to the Pleroma is understood as the accomplishment of the history of the world and as in the case of early mainstream Christian theology, it begins now. It is defined as 'realised eschatology'. The Gnostic Christian, to some extent in the same way as his or her 'catholic' counterpart, is already 'dead' with Christ (Rom. 6.5–8)[33] but also he or she is already resurrected and participates in the eschatological rest.[34] The Gnostics are dead to this world-prison, the level of reality marked by corruption, matter and decay. However, in a spiritual way, particularly by *gnosis*, they already take part in the future life in the realm of peace. The Gnostics receive 'rest', which also means the state of freedom from any anxiety about suffering, persecution and death. Eschatology thus, in many variations of Gnostic theologies, is accessible 'now', is 'already' here. However it also contains some 'unfinished' aspect, therefore it is 'unrealized'. The Gnostic paradox echoes the rather common Christian struggle with two aspects of eschatology: the one that is achieved, such as salvation, and the second which needs to be accomplished, such as resurrection and eternal life. Even the Gnostic has to die as 'already raised'. This knowledge contributes to the nature of Christian *gnosis*. Some documents suggest that eschatology begins at the very moment of receiving the saving *gnosis*; other treatises unite this future age with the current through a particular sacrament, such as baptism.

The *Gospel of Philip* develops the particular imagery of eschatological marriage and nuptial consummation between the Gnostic, his or her soul and the divine Bride in a 'bridal chamber'.[35] In this spiritual heavenly space, the Gnostic and the Saviour are reunited as equal to each other. The purified human element achieves its final union with the divine in an analogical way, as a married couple, male and female, communicate their love in the intimacy of their union.[36] Eternal life becomes unending celebration of that unique love, passion, but also it reunites what previously was divided by the very fact of existence in the material world. Although the richness and complexity of Gnostic eschatology escapes from a simply summary, it is safe to conclude that these theologies of 'the last things' present a common paradigm. It is a poetical call to return from the current exile to our true origin, our true self. It is a spiritual voyage in which the Gnostics are called to imitate Jesus, who himself escaped from this current world of corruption to the higher world by knowledge about his unique relationship with the Father. This example and its application offers reassurance that although in the current world we are still far from the homeland, yet, already we have begun our journey home – the final consummation of our history.

It must be also noted that in the contrast with 'catholic' or orthodox eschatology, the existing Gnostic literature is less interested in the description of the punishment of the wicked or those who did not reach their perfection. In one document, the sinners are pictured as those who will receive punishment by fire[37] and torture in the depth of Tartaros.[38] These frightening images of eternal retribution in the underworld, as in the other Christian documents, played the pedagogical role of a warning sign to those fellow-believers who did not pay enough attention to the improvement of their lives in the current circumstances.

Life Eternal as Accomplishment

Irenaeus of Lyons' vision of the eternal glory, although it appeared in opposition to the Gnostic theory of eschatology, also contained a very original, positive elaboration of the theme of *everlasting life*. In the context of his overall theological and historical perspective, the glorious 'the end' summarises God's whole project of salvation, which aims to bring human beings even closer to God. Irenaeus' project of theology is based on his crucial notion of participation in God, in God's life and in God's perfection. Between God and humanity there is a relationship, as Irenaeus saw it, when both partners try to attain the best possible stage of communion, union and fellowship. This is God's 'plan of salvation' which planned and ordered all events: the creation of the world, paradise, men and women, providence over humanity during the time of the deluge, giving the Law, inspiring the prophets, sending Christ and the Apostles, finally, establishing the church.[39] The last episode of that history is God's judgment and its two consequences: communion with God or eternal damnation in fire.[40] Those faithful who spent their life in obedience to God's commandments will be rewarded with everlasting communion, while the sinners will be excluded from light.[41] The blessed, faithful disciples of Christ will be rewarded by the highest price: as they already possess the 'image' of God by the very act of creation, now through God's Son, they

will be restored to the divine likeness. Irenaeus' optimistic anthropology culminates in his concept of eschatological perfection.
There, in the age to come, humanity will reach its climax, each and
everyone who was obedient to God.

In the light of Irenaeus' understanding of the divine plan of
salvation human beings are called to grow in understanding of the
direction and purpose of their existence. This direction and aim is
in immortality or full, unlimited participation in God's life. This
idea of progress to perfection receives its form in Irenaeus' project
of progress from 'lost innocence' towards 'achieved maturity',
from being 'an image' to achievement of 'likeness to God' (Gen.
1.27).[42] The recapitulation of all in God, or the resemblance of
humanity to its Creator offers a vision of God[43] and the knowledge
of God.[44] This specific 'understanding of God' is not only about his
plan of salvation but mainly about God's self-revelation in Jesus
Christ and the mission of the Holy Spirit who provided the Church
with the gift of freedom from death and corruption.[45] Under the
pressure of his Gnostic adversaries Irenaeus' vision of the eternal
destiny includes the human body[46] and transcends the current
moment of history. After the resurrection of the bodies, which is
one of the axioms of Irenaeus' theology, as previously of Justin
Martyr and Tertullian, Irenaeus also believes in a thousand years of
prosperity in this visible, material reality. This is the true, new
Israel,[47] a necessary period to become familiar with human destiny
which is a form of participation in the divine nature. But this
irreplaceable phase in the history of salvation pays tribute to the
value of the material world held so much in contempt by some of
Irenaeus' adversaries. After a thousand years the final judgment
will take place while the dead will be raised and the unjust will be
punished. At this stage, eternal reality will be created for the faithful ones.[48] It must be noted that Irenaeus of Lyons is one of the first
theologians who distinguishes the grades of perfection among the
saints and an appropriate reward with beatitude according to each
one's merits. In his view, the most holy will be taken to heaven, the
less worthy to Paradise, then even the less perfect will receive the
splendour of the city.[49] But on this hierarchical, heavenly scale it is
possible to make a progress towards its peak which contains ultimately full union with God,[50] saturation with a vision full of light,[51]
seeing God face to face,[52] and restoration of the image for the
saint.[53] Irenaeus' understanding of *everlasting life* culminates in his
entire theory of creation, fall and salvation, which as events, are
inseparable parts of human growth in spiritual maturity, a transition under the divine guidance from 'childhood' to 'adulthood',
from 'an image' to the 'likeness'.

Tertullian's elaboration of *everlasting life* has much in common with his personal background as a lawyer. This article of faith is for him an essential part of the settling of accounts between God and humanity.[54] When God will deliver his verdict over all humanity and each individual, there will be no conflict between God's justice and goodness.[55] As a Father and Judge,[56] God is the universal arbitrator who will reward as well as punish his subjects. Tertullian forecasts a thousand years of God's direct rule on this earth when different saints will raise either sooner or later in accordance with their deeds.[57] Finally the visible world will be destroyed by a cosmological fire[58] and the saints' bodies will be changed into spiritual substances, then they will enter into the eternal kingdom. Tertullian's presents an *everlasting life* with many metaphors. First and foremost, the saints, now 'like the angels',[59] will live in the kingdom of God[60] where as victors,[61] particularly the martyrs, they will gain the everlasting crown.[62] This spectacular vision of eternal joy has some characteristics of the receiving the palm of victory at the end of Olympic games, when the best athletes gain their reward[63] with the applause of the whole audience, here the angels. Then the victorious heroes will meet with God the Father as well as with their Lord, Jesus Christ. In the atmosphere of eternal triumph they will celebrate their success. Tertullian seems to make a distinction between those Christian champions. Some, who struggled harder, will receive greater rewards. He also predicts different eternal accommodations for the saints which will depend on individual merits.[64] Heaven, the eternal banquet of winners, will resound with the voices of the community of saints, while 'losers', that is the sinners and the heretics, will suffer punishment with eternal fire.[65]

*

Early Christian documents show the great variety of understanding that lies behind the credal article of belief in *everlasting life*. Some theologians saw *everlasting life* as a relief from the present time of tribulation. They were waiting for God's intervention, punishment and reward, as only by this divine involvement justice could be done. For others, eschatology was already present, realised as they achieved the perfect knowledge about the value and meaning of visible reality. Some documents stress the imminent approach of the new era, others emphasize the importance of the current time as a patient preparation for final rest and reward. In many cases literature was substantially dependent on apocalyptic scenarios. Was it because of psychological unrest or political and existential uncertainty? I believe that these factors played an important role in

shaping early Christian eschatology. Nonetheless, the visible pluralism of interpretations of *eternal life* gives evidence to the main
Christian hope of an (imminent) end which will also be the beginning of the new era. No doubt, the individual soul, possibly the
body, will survive the very existential experience of death or the
cataclysm of fire. Early Christians were unanimous in their basic
hope: there is a life after this existence and people are turning
towards their destiny now in this limited life but open to the future.

Conclusion

Having reflected on the content and context of the Apostles'
Creed, we are now faced with a number of questions: how can we
understand and assimilate these ancient creedal statements?
Which among these articles of faith are still valuable to our faith
today, all of them, maybe just some of them, or perhaps – none? To
what extent do these articles of faith constrain our personal belief,
our intellectual inquisitiveness about God and salvation in the
present day? How can we cope with the inevitable limitations of
these pronouncements?

There are some important reasons why some Christians might
conclude that the Apostles' Creed does not have much to offer.
Let's identify the main arguments against relevance of this Creed.
First, readers who have embraced the post-modern ethos with its
suspicion of any established authority may rebel against the certainty of the Creed. Such a hermeneutics of suspicion turns against
any meta-theory. This often leads to a rejection of all religious
belief, but in its weaker form, which is widely diffused in contemporary Western culture, categorical statements of particular
beliefs are viewed as authoritarian, divisive and dangerous. The
Creed, from this perspective, is a signpost leading nowhere, or
rather nowhere closer to the divine.

Secondly, the Apostles' Creed may be viewed as an irrelevant
relic, an incomprehensible linguistic and theological fossil, which
fails to reflect modern concerns. Furthermore, all the creeds are
products of an obviously male-orientated theology, based on
mainly a Platonic/dualistic theory of the world and ancient
cosmology and anthropology. Given this, it is not surprising that
the Apostles' Creed has little, if anything, to say about modern

141

preoccupations such as those relating to global ethics, political and social justice, solidarity with the poor and unprivileged, and the questions arising from liberation theology. It is likewise silent on issues such as inter-faith dialogue, ecology and gender equality. It does not engage with modern dilemmas such as those posed by the tragic experience of the holocaust(s), and the progress of scientific discovery. It does not have a mystical character which could serve as a unifying form of spirituality for people from different religious traditions. Thus, from a modern liberal perspective, the creed looks seriously deficient. It sounds exclusive and divisive; it does not address the current cultural challenges to theology and spirituality. It could therefore be argued that any effort to understand the early Christian origin of the Creed is a purely academic exercise. Christians can do without the Apostles' Creed; it should be rewritten *de novo*.

There are three possible responses to these kinds of criticisms. The first, a traditionalist approach, is to deny that there is any problem with the creeds. The Creeds reflect the holy Christian faith, and stand apart from profane, fashionable and temporary 'philosophies'. The minority status of such belief in modern society is irrelevant: the core-Christian believers remain uncompromised heirs of the early Christian martyrs, Church Fathers and the defenders of orthodoxy through the centuries of Christianity. The Creeds from this perspective are unmistaken, perfect, unalterable, eternally valid axioms, even pillars of theology, which we should learn by heart and proclaim publicly, just as 'our forefathers did'. There is no need to engage with them critically.

But by approaching the early patristic legacy on its knees, this traditional approach falls prey to a number of perils. The statements of the creeds, which are only humanly created signposts towards the divine, are treated as divine in themselves, incensed and put on the highest altar. That is, this approach turns articles of faith into idols. But the Creeds are only icons; they only reflect and point to a mystery of God who is beyond 'a picture' or 'grammatical phrase' and theological jargon. If God can be constrained within human, historical and linguistic expression, then this expression becomes divine. In this case, God becomes as a product of a specific language (Greek or Latin) or theological system (Platonism, Aristotelism or Thomism, for example). Not only does this view treat the Church as an ivory tower alienated from the historical and social context, it is also arrogant, as it assumes that the truth can be possessed as an object. It correspondingly treats other people only as potential converts, but never as genuine partners in dialogue or in the search for truth. For these reasons, I consider the traditionalist answer to be a theological *cul-du-sac*.

A second possible answer to the dilemmas posed by the apparent insufficiency of the classical Creeds in relation to modern theological, ethical and ecclesiastical problems would be to reject such creeds altogether. In consequence, modern understandings of the divine could be liberated from their dependence on these archaic images and models. This would immediately deal with the problems mentioned above such as the patriarchal conception of God, and the exclusivity and the divisiveness of the formulations of the traditional creeds.

But while this radical response appears on the surface to solve the problems posed by the creeds, further examination reveals this 'solution' to be illusory. It is impossible to communicate about salvation in Jesus without a set of theological axioms. It is impossible, even for 'post-modern' Christians, to avoid some sort of 'creed'. Christian faith, as long as it aims to communicate in a comprehensive way its values and understanding of God and salvation, requires some sort of 'declaration of consensus' or 'core-values'. Christianity is not an 'exclusively Scriptural', 'merely ethical', or 'purely spiritual' religion. On the contrary, in its essence it is a form of a positive engagement with history and culture. In order to makes its voice heard, Christianity needs some rules of self-identification, it needs a 'symbol' that is part of a greater background. The creed cannot be simply a modern message regarding ethics or ecology.

It is impossible to escape the theological questions which gave rise to the Classical creeds. Questions regarding Jesus, his nature and his mission recur constantly. Despite the modern aversion to 'institutional religion' and 'declared revelation with its creed', we are witnessing a boom of ... alternative creeds. The mysteries surrounding Jesus have proved fertile territory for contemporary cinema and literature, as can be seen in works such as *The Last Temptation of Christ*, first a novel written by Nikos Kazantzakis, then a movie directed by Martin Scorsese (1988); more recently *The Passion of Christ*, directed by Mel Gibson (2004) and Dan Brown's best-selling novel *The Da Vinci Code* (2003). Meanwhile, *The Gospel of Judas*, published by the *National Geographic Magazine* in May 2006, caused a sensation. All these narratives presume a specific understanding of Christology, salvation and even God. The unquestionable popularity of these interpretations poses questions not only for theologians related to the institutional forms of Christianity, but also for critics and philosophers of culture about the source of that popularity. Whatever else, it shows that ancient questions, such as 'who was Jesus of Nazareth?', 'what are the conditions of salvation?', 'should I trust the teaching of the institutional churches' or even 'how do we understand our sexuality in the light of Revelation?' – are returning with a new vitality. However, this is far from a reason to dispense with the existing creeds. All these 'new' interpretations of Jesus' life are modern re-workings of ancient debates. That being the case, any modern Christian creed would run a major risk of reinventing the wheel.

This leads to the third response to the criticisms of the creeds with which this chapter began, which is to endeavour to understand the context and debates which gave rise to the Apostles' Creed. This is the approach I have adopted in this book. I have argued that it is essential to locate early Christian documents in their historical, philosophical and social framework, learning and discerning all the important ingredients which influenced their formulation. As we learn more about the emergence of Christian identity, about the early Christian break from Judaism and the assimilation of philosophical ideas into Christianity, we will need to review the trajectories of the early Christian doctrine reflected by the Creeds. This revision will have to take into account the vital tension between 'proto-orthodoxy' and other alternative Christian theologies, including the polyphony of Gnosticism. For example, the rejection of Gnosticism and elaboration of a doctrinal answer to its claims are interconnected in the theological frame of the early Christianity. We need to know more about the context of the Apostles' Creed and other crucial documents which constructed the early Christian, and later orthodox, identity.

But my approach is also open to criticism. A central problem with an historical analysis of the Creed is that a statement of faith, which is supposed to be eternal, is revealed to be time-bound, influenced by its context. Specifically, the Apostles' Creed has been shown to have been shaped by the catechetical needs of the Church, the philosophical and exegetical climate in which it was conceived, and the spiritual and emotional attitude of the audience of the time at which it was written. It is not the fault of the ancient theologians who wrote it that they were children of their time – this is an inevitable condition of all human agents. Indeed, this reveals the difficulty of producing a new creed – just like the ancients, we are unable to stand outside history, and our interpretation will be equally marked by our context. So if we stick with the creed bequeathed to us by history, what is the answer to the question of its relevance?

I would like to suggest a particular solution: we should treat the Apostles' Creed as 'an icon', not 'an idol'. In order to explain the difference, I wish to share with readers a very helpful observation which can be found in a comment of later Patristic theologian, St. John of Damascus (*c.* 675–749). During his lifetime there was a crisis of Eastern Christianity related to the importance of icons used in Christian worship. While some promoted the idea of iconoclasm – the policy of suppressing the use of images in Christian devotional practices – others, like John of Damascus, argued for the irreplaceable function of pictures in worship. In his treatise *Apologia against those who attack Holy Images,* John states that images are important, as:

> Since the creation of the world the invisible things of God are clearly seen by means of images.[1]

According to John, it is through the incarnation of the divine Logos that the invisible God, who is beyond any image, can be seen in a visible way by material means. The mystery, but also reality, of incarnation provides the ultimate justification for the human effort of representing divine reality with artistic tools. A concept or being who is incomprehensible by his very nature can be expressed in a representation. John of Damascus explains his assumption as follows:

> In former times God, who is without form or body, could never be depicted. But now when God is seen in the flesh conversing with men, I make an image of God whom I see. I do not worship matter, I worship the Creator of matter who become matter for my sake ... Never will I cease honouring the matter which wrought my salvation! I honour it, but not as God.[2]

In the context of this book these observations provide us with a new outlook on the whole theological narrative of this and other Creeds. The divine Son of God took on not only the nature of human being and the conditions of human life, but also, as the divine Son of God, entered into human language with its historicity, limitations and other imperfections. God, who was, is and always will be beyond any narrative, became the Word who can be seen in icons, heard through the Gospels and also, to some extent, described by human testimony. Therefore it is important, as John of Damascus points out, not to worship 'matter', that here is represented by theological notions and metaphysical concepts, but to reverence the Creator of language: the divine Word/Logos himself. Our attention should take into account the concepts and the network of notions which describe Indescribable, but we should never treat these notions as if they were divine in themselves.

In some ways, like an icon, the Apostles' Creed connects the invisible with the visible, the reality that is beyond words with discourse, not by defining it or even representing it, but an act of directing human consciousness to this impenetrable mystery. The Creeds are both limited and open, and pose an endless challenge to all generations of Christians. However, the Creeds are also the historical products of specific theological challenges, and when cut off from this background, they lose not only their brightness as 'icons', but also their intellectual framework and rhetorical function. Treating the creed as an icon means that it becomes an object of contemplation and this can involve understanding its context, revisiting the old debates and pondering the mystery of the statement as we have received it. I hope this book will assist this process.

Glossary of Theologians, Early Christian Documents and Theological Terms Cited in the Book

Adoptionism: The Christological view, later qualified as heretical, that Jesus of Nazareth was adopted by God at some point, for instance during his baptism/Epiphany, as his 'Son', therefore Jesus was a man who only possessed divine powers.

Apologists: Christian writers of the 2 CE who defended and tried to explain Christian faith to their Jewish and pagan opponents. The Apologists aimed to present Christianity as a religion superior to Judaism and paganism. Among Apologists were, for example, Aristides of Athens, Justin Martyr, Tatian, Athenagoras of Athens, Theophilus of Antioch, Melito of Sardis, the author of the *Epistole to Diognetus*, Hermas and Tertullian.

Apostolic Fathers: The Christian writers immediately following the New Testament authors, namely: Clement of Rome, Ignatius of Antioch, Hermas, Polycarp of Smyrna, Papias of Hierapolis and the anonymous authors of *the Epistle of Barnabas, 2 Epistle of Clement* and the *Didache*.

The Apostolic Tradition (3 CE): A liturgical document which some historians attribute to Hippolytus of Rome. It contains a detailed description of religious rites used during the Eucharist and at the ordination of various ministers. It also prescribes ways of accepting new members into the Christian community as well as discussing some details of Christian practice.

Aristides of Athens (2 CE): One of the Apologists. In extant fragments of his works, particularly of his *Apology*, he defends the

Christian faith as much more advanced than the beliefs of the barbarians, Greeks and Jews. Only Christians, in his view, possess a true concept of God.

Arius (*c.* 250–336): Alexandrian presbyter who refused to accept the divinity of Jesus of Nazareth. Little is known of his life and writings. His views are preserved in the writings of his theological opponents such as Athanasius of Alexandria (*c.* 296–373). Arius saw Jesus Christ as the embodiment of Wisdom that was the first created being, but not divine by nature or consubstantial with God. Arius and his followers were condemned by the first Synod at Alexandrian (*c.* 320), then by the first Oecumenical Council of Nicaea (325).

Arianism: The major early Christian theological movement and an ecclesiastical party which originated in the 4 CE. In the Arian view Jesus was God's supreme creature but not equal or co-eternal with God. He differs from all other creatures, as he was created directly by God and chronologically first (i.e. before creation of the world). However, as God's creation, he was not perfect and disposed to change.

Athenagoras of Athens (2 CE): One of the Apologists. He was the author of the *Embassy for the Christians*, addressed to the Emperor Marcus Aurelius and his son and aimed at defending Christianity from the charge of 'atheism'. Possibly his *On the Resurrection of the Dead* presented Christian understanding of the end of the present world.

Basilides (2 CE): Christian theologian, who taught in Alexandria, was a representative of Gnostic Christianity. His doctrine apparently held that the supreme God, incomprehensible to the human mind, was separated from the world by the hierarchy of spiritual beings, including the god of this world or 'the god of the Jews'. The highest God, the Father, sent his mind, that is his Son, to redeem humanity, but the Saviour appeared only to be human.

Cappadocian Fathers: Title given to three outstanding Greek theologians of the 4 CE: Basil of Caesarea, Gregory of Nazianzus and Gregory of Nyssa who lived in 'Cappadocia' (a part of present Turkey). Their theology, particularly their doctrine of the Trinity, contributed to the development of the orthodox understanding of the three divine persons who share one and the same divine nature. Among their chief theological opponents were Arians and Sabellians. The Ecumenical Council of Constantinople (381) authorised their orthodoxy and in particular their teaching on the Holy Spirit.

Celsus (2 CE): Pagan philosopher, probably Platonic, author of *True Word against Christians*, the oldest literary attack on Christianity, but of which only fragments survive. Celsus criticised in particular Christian doctrine of Incarnation and Crucifixion.

Cyprian (d. 258): Bishop of Carthage, a convert to Christianity and great admirer of Tertullian. He escaped the Decian persecution (250) and continued to govern his church from exile by letters. When he returned (251), he found a number of Christians who had lapsed from their faith and also encountered some who had received easy forgiveness from their confessors. Cyprian was strongly opposed to this practice and soon two councils (251, 252) declared that lapsed Christians should be accepted back into the Church only after appropriate penance. Cyprian was martyred in Carthage in 258. Among his many letters and theological treatises, the most significant are *On the Unity of the Church* and *On the Lapsed*. As a theologian, he promoted the idea of re-baptism of heretics who wanted to join the church, as in his view sacraments administered by heretics were invalid. His theory of the church argued strongly that 'outside of the church there is no salvation' (Lat. *salus extra ecclesia non est*) and highlighted the role of validly ordained ministers.

The Didache (1st half of the 2 CE): A short Christian handbook on the morals and the organisation of the church, dealing with matters such as baptism, fasting, prayer, the Eucharist and issues to do with prophets, bishops and deacons. It is an important source of knowledge on early stages in the development of liturgy and administration in the church, which is not yet fully conceptualised in this phase of theology.

Docetism: An early Christian alternative Christology. According to Docetic theology, Jesus Christ was a purely divine being who had only 'appeared' (Gr. *dokeo*, 'to appear' or 'to seem') in the body.

Ebionitism: A Judeo-Christian opinion expressed by the Ebionites (Hebr. 'the poor men') that the Saviour was only human (i.e. the son of Joseph and Mary), not divine, but possessing some charismatic gifts which distinguished him from other people. This Christological doctrine was another version of adoptionism.

Epistle of the Apostles (*c.* 150–170): An apocryphal document recording the conversation between the Risen Lord and the Apostles. Its theological and polemical aim seems to be to attack Gnostic tendencies in Christianity. It promotes faith in Christ's real incarnation and resurrection.

Epistle of Barnabas (70–135): A Christian document without clear indication of authorship. It promotes perfect wisdom (Gr. *gnosis*) of the economy of salvation. It is made up of two parts: the first (Ch. 1–7) is dogmatic, with criticism of Jewish ceremonial law; the second part (Ch. 18–21) is moral, aiming to promote the freedom of Christians from the Mosaic regulations. The author tries to explain to his readers the real nature of the Old Testament. He explains how the Law should be understood allegorically as metaphors for Christian virtues and institutions. Thus he uses a series of symbolic explanations of how the Old Testament prefigures, for example, Jesus Christ, his Passion and the Church. In the final part, the author repeats the teaching of the first part by borrowing from another document (the *Didache*) the description of the two ways, the way of light and the way of darkness.

Epistle to Diognetus (150–225): A document written by an anonymous apologist who addresses a pagan intellectual and explains the ethos of Christianity and a Christian style of life. In its last part, the document present a mature theology of the divine Logos, the source of all knowledge and life.

Epiphanius (*c.* 315–403): Bishop of Salamis, promoter and defender of the Nicene Creed, and author of the *Panarion* ('Medicine Chest') known as *Refutation of all Heresies*, in which he attacked every heresy known to him from the beginning of the Church.

Gnosticism (Gr. *gnosis*, 'knowledge'): A complex religious movement which had also a Christian form originating in the teaching of a particular theologian. Crucial importance was attached to the revelation of 'secret knowledge' (Gr. *gnosis*) about the origin, structure and purpose of the world. As a theology, Gnosticism was an amalgam of philosophical speculation, Jewish vocabulary, Greek mythologies and Christian elements. Characteristics of Gnosticism were the notion of the 'Unknowable God', and a highly complex spiritual hierarchy of beings separated from visible reality. At the core of the Gnostic myth or mythology is a story about the original catastrophe that created the visible universe. Human beings are held in a prison-like place, however through the discovery of 'gnosis' or the divine element in each person, it is possible to escape from this level of reality to the original, natural unity with the divine. The divine Redeemer was an emissary from the higher world who came to show us how it is possible to redeem ourselves as he did in Jesus of Nazareth.

Hermas (1st half of the 2 CE): One of the Apostolic Fathers, author of the *Shepherd*, which contains a series of visions and promotes Christian ethics. In its inner literary structure the document is divided into three sections: five *Visions*, which represent a Jewish-Christian apocalyptic, twelve *Mandates* or *Commands* in the form of Jewish-Hellenistic homily and ten *Similitudes* (parables). Each part addresses different theological issues: the renewal of the Church and the role of penance; the moral Christian life, emphasising the value of developing virtues and finally the narrative is summed up with a eulogy of life in penance, while exercising the virtues.

Hippolytus of Rome (*c.* 170–236): Regarded as the most important theologian of the third century, defender of orthodoxy and the first 'Antipope'. His principal work is the *Refutation of all Heresies*. When Zephyrinus was Bishop of Rome (198–217), he declined to react against some modalist theologians in the city. Hippolytus came into conflict with Zephyrinus, standing against him and presenting him as theologically and administratively incompetent and unworthy to govern the Church of Rome. When the deacon Callistus was elected as the next leader of the Christian community in Rome (217–222), Hippolytus left the communion of the Roman church and had himself elected Antipope by a group of his sympathisers. He continued in opposition during the reigns of the two immediate successors of Callistus, Urban (222/223–230) and Pontianus (230–235). As Antipope he was banished to Sardinia, but soon afterwards he became reconciled with the legitimate Bishop and the Church of Rome.

Ignatius of Antioch (*c.* 35–110): One of the Apostolic Fathers, Bishop of Antioch, writer and martyr, under the reign of Trajan (98–117) the author of seven epistles to various churches and to Bishop Polycarp of Smyrna. Ignatius' theology of the Church (ecclesiology) highlighted her unity secured by its episcopal function and a monarchical type of episcopacy.

Irenaeus of Lyons (*c.* 130–200): Born probably in Asia Minor (Smyrna?), later elected Bishop of Lyons (*c.* 177/8). He wrote *Against the Heresies*, which defended the faith of the 'Catholic' Church against Gnostic misinterpretations. He was also the author of *Proof of the Apostolic Preaching*, which explains in a positive way the theological content of Christian faith. Irenaeus was of the first theologians of the Great Church who presented a systematic exposition of 'catholic' theology against his Gnostic opponents.

Jerome (*c.* 342–420): An outstanding Christian exegete and theologian, for some time a hermit in the Syrian desert, who also produced the translation of the Bible into Latin known as the *Vulgate*. He was the author of many theological commentaries on the Scriptures, various letters, and an important biographical work on ecclesiastical writers (*Lives of the Illustrious Men*).

Justyn the Martyr (*c.* 100–162/168): The most famous Apologist. He was the author of the *1* and *2 Apology* addressed to pagan readers, and also wrote the *Dialogue with Trypho*, in which he defends the claim of Christian truth against its Jewish opponents.

Marcion (d. *c.* 160) of Sinope in Pontus: Christian theologian who joined the Christian community in Rome around 140. His main views were that Christian theology is based on the Gospel of Love as opposed to the Jewish theology of the Law. Inspired by Paul's distinction between 'the letter' and 'the spirit', Marcion consequently rejected the Old Testament, which in his view expressed the works of the Demiurge that is the God of the Law. Only the God revealed in Jesus, that is the God of Love, was the true object of Christian worship.

Martyrologies: Collections of records of Christian martyrs which began to be composed from the 4 CE to promote the Christian ideal of suffering for faith during earlier persecution.

Melito (d. *c.* 190): Bishop of Sardis, the author of *Paschal Homily*. Melito promoted the concept of Christ's divinity and humanity (God-made-man) and so is seen as a representative of 'proto-orthodox' Christology, which opposed to Gnostic theories of salvation.

Methodius of Olympus (d. *c.* 311): Bishop of Lycia and possibly a martyr. He wrote the *Symposium* or *the Banquet of the Ten Virgins*, which presents the union of Christ with the Church in the metaphor of marriage. He was a critic of the doctrine of transmigration of the souls and purely spiritual resurrection, while highlighting the role and value of the physical body in the eschatological existence.

Millenarianism: Belief in a specific eschatological end of the visible world at the second coming of Christ, when he will destroy evil powers and establish his reign of a thousand years with all his saints and at the end will take them to heaven. Among proto-orthodox Christians some inclination towards this belief is expressed in Justin Martyr, Irenaeus of Lyon, Tertullian and Hippolytus of Rome.

Modalism: An early Christian theory of the Holy Trinity which emphasises the unity of the divine Trinity, rejecting its plurality. There is *one* God, however he revealed himself in three different 'ways' or 'modes', as the Father, as the Son, and ultimately as the Holy Spirit. Among modalist theologians were Noetus, Praxeas and Sabellius. Modalism was a version of 'monarchianism'.

Monarchianism (Gr. *monarchia*, 'sole principle' or 'rule'): A theological theory of the Holy Trinity current during the 2 CE and 3 CE which stressed the unity of God as against Marcion's or Gnostic dualism. In one of its variations monarchanism represented an analogical view to 'modalism'.

Montanus (2 CE): Christian prophet and theologian, founder of Montanism. Montanus was a convert when he first began to prophesy (dervish-like behaviour) in Phrygia (Asia Minor). The same prophetic gift was believed to have descended upon his two companions, the prophetesses Maximilla and Prisca or Priscilla.

Montanism: A second-century apocalyptic movement. Adherents were known first as Phrygians, or 'those among the Phrygians', then as Montanists. They proclaimed the imminent outpouring of the Holy Spirit on the Church, of which the ecstatic prophesy of Montanus and his two female companions was the first sign. Very soon this charismatic group became an autonomous Christian sect developing radical, ascetic characteristics (e.g. disallowing second marriages, tightening rules on fasting, forbidding escape from persecution) and spreading to the Western part of the Roman Empire, including North Africa. In Carthage, the Montanists attracted the attention of Tertullian, who joined this movement, leaving the Catholic Church and becoming a follower of Montanus.

Nag Hammadi Library: A collection of 13 codices with 52 tractates. The tractates are written mainly in Coptic (a later translation of the original Greek documents), with some in Greek. The whole collection dates to fourth century, however it contains writings produced in the second and third centuries by various authors representing different traditions of Gnosticism. The 'library' was found near Nag Hammadi (Chenoboskion) in upper Egypt in 1945/6 and offers unique insights into early Christian theologies as well as some information on non-Christian theologies.

Neo-Platonism: A generic term denoting the revival of Platonic doctrine, with some modifications, from the third to sixth centuries. The originator of Neo-Platonism was Plotinus (*c.* 205–270), whose works were edited by Porphyry of Tyre (*c.* 232–303). The crucial doctrine of Neo-Platonism is based on the existence of the One, the metaphysical Source of beings from which all reality emanated and to which it will return. The One or the Good, the perfect supra-being, begets in his own image the second being, known as the Mind (Gr. *Nous*), and then the Mind contemplating its perfect Origin begets the Soul (Gr. *Psyche*) or world-soul. The Soul is the cause of the rest of the universe; the lesser beings and the heavenly bodies. Since human beings possess reason/mind, they may develop ethical, intellectual and spiritual lives, and this will help them ascend towards the higher reality of ideas or even in ecstasy achieve union with the One. This process of conversion to the One is based purely on human intellectual skills and moral, natural effort, as pagan Neo-Platonism did not refer to any category of 'grace' or 'help' from the One.

Noetus of Smyrna (*c.* 200): Christian theologian who taught the doctrine of the suffering of the divine Father (Lat. *patripassianism*) who was incarnated and then was crucified and died. He rejected the theory of the incarnation of the divine Word.

Novatian (3 CE): Roman presbyter, orator and theologian, author of the treatise *On the Holy Trinity* and various letters. He was a founder of a rigorist Christian group, who strongly opposed any indulgence for lapsed Christians. The Novatianists, although they remain orthodox in their doctrine, were excommunicated from the Great Church.

Odes of Solomon: 42 hymns (1 or 2 CE) with some expressions suggesting links with Gnostic theology. They present various themes, for instance 'esoteric knowledge', 'incarnation', 'eulogy of what is higher', 'spiritual milk and virgin birth', 'ascension of the soul', 'union with the beloved' and 'the triumph of the Redeemer'.

Patristics/Patristic theology (Lat. *pater*, 'father'): The theology of the first part of the first millennium that begins with the post-New Testament documents (e.g. *1 Clement*) and ends with the decrees of the ecumenical Councils of Ephesus (431) and Chalcedon (451). The study of Patristic literature is closely related to the history of the Church, history of late Hellenistic philosophy (mainly Neo-Platonism) and with study of the development of doctrine (ecumenical councils, creeds).

Philo of Alexandria (*c.* 20 BCE–*c.* 50): Jewish philosopher, theologian and exegete. He was the most significant scholar of Hellenised Judaism of his period, who left, particularly to the Patristic theologians, a substantial legacy of concepts (e.g. Logos as the intermediary by whom may be known the transcendent God) and methods of interpretation of the Scriptures (e.g. allegory). His eclectic, academic approach to the Scriptures combined the Hebrew revelation with a mainly Platonic framework of metaphysics. His influence was especially significant on the Alexandrian school of theology (Clement of Alexandria, Origen), as well as on some Latin theologians (St Ambrose).

Praxeas (*c.* 200): Christian theologian who arrived from Asia in Rome, where he suffered persecution because of his teaching. His doctrine is known from Tertullian's polemic *Against Praxeas*, in which Praxeas is accused of the erroneous view on crucifixion of the Father (Lat. *patripassianism*), which as a doctrine was another version of modalism.

Sabellius (3 CE): Christian theologian, representative, if not the founder, of the modalist variation of Monarchianism theology. Little is known of his life.

The Septuagint (abbreviated as 'LXX', i.e. 'seventy'): The title given to the most important Greek translation of the Old Testament. The Septuagint has its origin in Alexandria, Egypt and was composed between 300–200 BC. It was used among Hellenistic Jews spread throughout the Roman Empire. According to the *Letter of Aristeas*, it was believed that 72 Jewish scholars from Jerusalem were commissioned to carry out the task of translation and that the task was completed in 70 days. The LXX differs from the Hebrew Bible in its inner order, since it abandoned the classical distinction between the three sections of the Old Testament: 'Law', 'Prophets' and 'Writings'. Also, the LXX contains some additional books which are not found in the Hebrew Bible, but which were circulated among the Hellenised Jews. These books are known as the 'apocrypha'. The early Christian church inherited the LXX version of the Old Testament, and the New Testament writers quoted the Old Testament literature from the LXX. Later, the Christian theologians of the Patristic period almost all regarded the LXX as the standard version of the Old Testament.

Sibylline Oracles (2 BCE–2 CE): Collection of supposed Jewish and Christian prophecies of the sibyls (divinely inspired clairvoyants), which were widely circulated in Antiquity. Various books of the collection predict the collapse of Rome and the pagan empire. These poetic, visionary treatises were very popular among the Church Fathers.

Tatian (*c.* 160) 'the Syrian': Christian Apologist, a pupil of Justin Martyr. Tatian is known as a radical opponent of Greek culture, particularly philosophy, and as the founder of an extreme ascetic Gnostic community (the 'Encratites') who rejected wine and marriage. He is also the author of *Discourse to the Greeks* and *Diatesseron*, ('Out of four') a history of Christ's life based on the four Gospels.

Tertullian (*c.* 160–225): Inventor of Latin theology, an excellent orator who produced a significant number of controversial, mainly apologetic, treatises. He coined important Latin terms such as 'trinity' and 'person' which would later play an important role in the development of doctrine, as well as making some famous statements (e.g. 'What is there in common between Athens and Jerusalem? between Academy and the Church?'). After his conversion from paganism to Christianity he promoted and defended Christian faith against Gnostics, Jews and pagans. Later in his life, he converted to Montanism (c. 217) and advocated the idea of strict discipline, attacking, for instance, Callistus, the Bishop of Rome, for his view that mortal sin can be forgiven after a canonical penance.

Theophilus of Antioch (2nd half of 2 CE): The sixth Bishop of Antioch in Syria, one of the most significant Apologists. His chief work addressed *to Autolycus* presents anti-Gnostic polemic and develops orthodox theology of God and salvation, including creation of the world 'out of nothing'.

Valentinus (2 CE): Christian theologian, a native of Egypt who moved *c.* 140 to Rome, where he founded his own theological school, later recognised as Gnostic and heretical. His theology is based on sophisticated speculation about the origin of the world and salvation. His Christology presented a variation of Docetism.

Chronology of Quoted Documents and Theologians[1]

300–200 BCE	The *Septuagint* is composed in Alexandria.
c. 20 BCE–c. 50	Philo of Alexandria
c. 30	Execution of Jesus of Nazareth
c. 35	Conversion of Paul
	Ignatius, the Bishop of Antioch was born
c. 50	Paul writes his first *Epistle to Thessalonians*[2]
Before 66	*Gospel according to Mark*
70	Fall of Jerusalem. *Gospel according to Matthiew*
70–135	*Epistle of Barnabas*
c. 85	*Gospel according to Luke.* Marcion is born
c. 80–90	*Gospel according to John*
c. 90	'Synod' of Jamnia (Yavenh) or the meeting of the rabbis established the canon of OT and produces a document expelling Christians from the Jewish community[3]
95–97	*First Epistle of Clement of Rome*
98–100	*Second Epistle of Clement of Rome*
2 BCE–1 CE	*First Book of Enoch*[4]
2 BCE–2 CE	*Sibylline Oracles*[5]
1–2 CE	*Odes of Solomon*[6]
1 CE to early 2 CE	*Sophia of Jesus Christ*[7]
100	*Ascension of Isaiah*; some of its fragments are from second BC, while the final redaction took place from fifth to sixth CE[8]
First half of 2 CE	Hermas, *The Shepherd*
	Epistles of Ignatius, the Bishop Antioch
110	Martyrdom of Ignatius
117–138	Aristides of Athens, *Apology* addressed to Hadrian

c. 132–138	Basilides teaches in Alexandria
130–150	Valentinus teaches in Rome, previously in Alexandria
c. 140	Marcion active in Rome
c. 150	*The Didache*
150–250	*Apocalypse of Peter*[9]
150–170	*Epistle of the Apostles*[10]
150–225	*Epistle to Diognetus*
150–850	*The Greek Apocalypse of Ezra*[11]
c. 155	Tertullian is born
c. 160	Martyrdom of Polycarp, Marcion dies
161–180	Marcus Aurelius. Growth of Montanism. Justin Martyr writes his *Dialogue with Thrypo* and *Apologies*
	Celsus writes *True Word against Christians*[12]
Second half of 2 CE	*Gospel of Peter,*[13] *Second Treatise of the Great Seth.*[14]
c. 160	Tatian the Syrian, writes *Discourse to the Greeks* and *Diatesseron*
c. 160	Tertullian was born
162–168	Martyrdom of Justin Martyr
161–169	Martyrdom of Carpus, however the written record is composed later (4 CE?)
177	Athenagoras of Athens, *On the Resurrection* and *Embassy* addressed to Marcus Aurelius
177–178	Irenaeus becomes the Bishop of Lyons
Late 2 CE	*Treatise on the Resurrection*[15]
180	Theophilus of Antioch, the author of *to Autolycus*
c. 190	Irenaeus of Lyons composes his *Against Heresies.* Melito, the Bishop of Sardis and the author of the *Paschal Homily* dies
2/3 CE	*Testimony of Truth*[16]
3 CE (215 CE?)	*The Apostolic Tradition* contains the Old Roman baptismal Creed
3 CE	*Martyrdom of Saint Perpetua and Felicitas*[17]
c. 200	The original Greek version of the *Gospel of Thomas*[18] *Protoevangelium of James.*[19] Noetus of Smyrna teaches his doctrine. Praxeas active in Rome
c. 217	Tertullian becomes Montanist

c. 217	Callistus I becomes the Bishop of Rome (217–22)[20]
249	Cyprian becomes the Bishop of Carthage
250	Persecution of Christians. Growing controversy between Carthage and Rome over the treatment of returning lapsed Christians
c. 250	Novatian active in Rome writes *On the Holy Trinity*
c. 250–325	Lactantius
254–325	*Teaching of Silvanus*[21]
c. 254	Stephen the Bishop of Rome (254–57)[22]
Second half of 3 CE	*Gospel of Philip*[23]
258	Martyrdom of Cyprian of Carthage
Late 2 CE to early 3 CE	*Apocryphon of James*[24]
Early third CE	The Greek version of *Apocryphon of John.*[25]
311	Methodius of Olympus, the author of the *Symposium* dies
c. 315–403	Epiphanius of Salamis
c. 315–367	Hilary of Poitiers
325	Council of Nicaea
c. 345–410	Rufinus of Aquileia
5 CE	The final redaction of the *Acts of Pilate*[26]

Notes

1 This table is based on B. Altaner and A. Stuiber, *Patrologie : Leben, Schriften und Lehre der Kirchenvaäter,* (Freiburg im Breisgau: Herder), 1978 and Ch. Kannengiesser, ed. *Handbook of Patristic Exegesis. The Bible in Ancient Christianity,* vol. 1–2, (Leiden: Brill,) 2004.

2 Dating of the New Testament documents follows *The New Oxford Annotated Bible. New Revised Standard Version with the Apocrypha,* ed. M. Coogan (Oxford: Oxford University Press, 2001, 3rd ed).

3 See Chapter 1.

4 See Chapters 6 and 8, notes.

5 See Chapters 7, 8 notes and 13.

6 See Chapters 6, 9 and 13.

7 See Chapter 7.

8 See Chapter 7.

9 See Chapters 5 and 7.

10 See Chapters 7 and 11.

11 See Chapter 13.

12 See Chapter 6.

13 See Chapters 6 and 7.

14 See Chapter 5.

15 See Chapter 12.

16 See Chapter 4.
17 See Chapter 13.
18 See Chapter 11.
19 See Chapter 4.
20 See Chapters 10 and 11.
21 See Chapter 6.
22 See Chapter 10.
23 See Chapters 4, 9 and 13.
24 See Chapter 7.
25 See Chapter 6.
26 See Chapter 5.

Resources on the Internet

1 Bibliography of the history of Christian Thought with Special Emphasis on the Patristic Era:
http://www.bethel.edu/~rakrob/files/PATRISTC.htm
2 Bibliography: General Works on the Early Church:
http://camellia.shc.edu/theology/Early%20Church.htm
3 The Christian Classics the Ethereal Library:
http://www.ccel.org/
4 Early Christianity – general resources (North American Patristic Society):
http://moses.creighton.edu/NAPS/napslinks/
main.htm#msb
5 Guide to Early Christian Documents (including the Creeds):
http://ccat.sas.upenn.edu/jod/christian-history.html#creeds
6 The Fathers of the Church ('New Advent'):
http://www.newadvent.org/fathers/
7 The Nag Hammadi Library:
http://www.gnosis.org/naghamm/nhlalpha.html
8 Non Canonical Documents:
http://www.bible-history.com/resource/ch_non.htm
9 Hellenistic Judaism (from Jewish Encyclopedia):
http://www.jewishencyclopedia.com/
view.jsp?letter=H&artid=567
10 Late Hellenistic Philosophy: Neoplatonism:
http://www2.nd.edu/Departments/Maritain/etext/
hwp114.htm
and more:
http://www.rep.routledge.com/article/A130

Notes

Introduction

1   Philip Schaff in J. Pelikan and V. Hotchkiss (eds), *Creeds and Confessions of Faith in the Christian Tradition*, vol. 1 (New Haven/London: Yale University Press, 2003), p. 667.

2   Interestingly, as noted by Pelikan, the Apostles' Creed has no similar authority among the Easter Orthodox Churches, see *Creeds and Confessions*, p. 668.

3   For a more systematic presentation of the Apostles' Creed, see J.N.D. Kelly, *Early Christian Creeds* (London: Longmans Green and Co, 3rd edn, 1972), pp. 368–434; L.H. Westra, *The Apostles' Creed. Origin, History and Some Early Christian Commentaries* (Turnhaut: Brepolis Publishers, 2002).

4   Kelly, *Early Christian Creeds*, pp. 411–420.

5   Cf. Pelikan, *Creeds and Confessions*, p. 667

6   Cf. Kelly, *Early Christian Creeds*, p. 369.

7   See the next Chapter.

8   See R. Williams, 'Does it make sense to speak of pre-Nicene orthodoxy?', in *The Making of Orthodoxy. Essays in Honour of Henry Chadwick*, ed. R. Williams (Cambridge: Cambridge University Press, 1989), pp. 1–23.

9   A. Cameron, *Christianity and the Rhetoric of the Empire. The Development of Christian Discourse* (Berkeley/Los Angeles/Oxford: University of California Press, 1991), p. 21.

Chapter 1: I Believe in God

1   Trans. J.N. Kelly (London: Longmans Green and Co, 1955), p. 32.

2   Such as for example: the Antiochene Creed (325 and 341), the Nicene Creed (380) or the best known Constantinopolitan Creed (381).

3   As noted by J.N.D. Kelly, *Early Christian Creeds* (London/New York /Toronto: Longmans, Green and Co, 1952), p. 101, the primary source for the text of the Old Roman Creed comes from the treatise *Commentarius in Symbolum Apostolorum* written by Rufus at the beginning of 5 CE.

4   *The Apostolic Tradition of St Hippolytus*, ed. G. Dix (London: Society for Promoting Christian Knowledge, 1937), pp. 36–37, modified. The authorship of Hippolytus is now under new scrutiny.

5   The term 'paganism' is a Christian coinage, which represents the whole spectrum of Roman cults. The term is rather problematic, as it covers the whole

non-Christian system of religious worship and expresses a negative assessment of those beliefs. For more information, see G. Clark, *Christianity and Roman Society. Key Themes in Ancient History* (Cambridge: Cambridge University Press, 2004), pp. 35–37.

6　On this subject, see R.L. Fox, *Pagans and Christians in the Mediterranean World from the Second Century AD to the Conversion of Constantine* (London: Penguin Books, 1988, reissued in 2006), pp. 419–492; R.L. Wilken, *The Christians as the Romans saw them* (New Haven/London: Yale University Press, 2003, 2nd edition); G. Clark, *Christianity and Roman Society*, pp. 16–21.

7　For basic information, see P. Fredriksen and J. Lieu, 'Christian Theology and Judaism' in R.G. Evans, ed., *The First Christian Theologians. An Introduction to Theology in the Early Church* (Malden/Oxford/Carlton: Blackwell, 2004), pp. 85–101 with bibliography. More advanced in J.M. Lieu, 'The Parting of the Ways: Theological Construct or Historical Reality?' in *Neither Jew Nor Greek? Constructing Early Christianity* (London/New York: Continuum/T&T Clark, 2002), pp. 11–29 and J.M. Lieu, *Made Not Born: Conclusions*, in *Christian Identity in the Jewish and Graeco-Roman World* (Oxford: Oxford University Press, 2004), pp. 298–316.

8　For more detail on 'the third race' as a synonym of Christianity, see J.M. Lieu, 'The Race of God-Fearers', in *Neither Jew Nor Greek?*, pp. 49–68.

9　Fox makes the following observation: 'Pagans performed rites but professed no creed nor doctrine. They did pay detailed acts of cult [. . .], but they were not committed to revealed beliefs in the strong Christian sense of the term. [. . .] There was also no pagan concept of heresy'. Cf. R.L. Fox, *Pagans and Christians*, p. 31.

10　Cf. E. Ferguson, *Backgrounds of Early Christianity* (Grand Rapids, Michigan: Eerdmans Publishing Company, 3rd edn, 2003), p. 173. Other features of Hellenistic-Roman religion were: 1. monotheistic trend; 2. weakening anthropomorphism and the worship of 'power'; 3. deification of virtues or benefits; 4. demonising aspect of religion; 5. belief in power of fate; 6. astrology; 7. the role of magic; 8. the social character of religion and therefore the crucial role of the public cult; 9. growing significance of 'chosen relationship', which denotes appearance of new grouping of worshippers based on their role/profession; and 10. lack of direct connection between religious cult and morality. Cf. E. Ferguson, *Backgrounds of Early Christianity*, pp. 173–177.

11　Cf. Wilken, *The Christians*, pp. 54–59.

12　For more information, see Glossary.

13　Philip S. Alexander, 'The Parting of the Ways', in *Jews and Christians. The Parting of the Ways A.D. 70 to 135*, ed. J.D.G. Dunn (Grand Rapids, Michigan/Cambridge, UK: W.B. Eerdmans Publishing Company, 1999), p. 6.

14　See further comments in J.M. Lieu, 'The Parting of the Ways', p. 26.

15　This opinion originates in Plato's *Republic*, VI. 509 D-511 C and the classical distinction between four grades of cognition: 1. imagining (Gr. *eikon*) 2. belief/faith (Gr. *pistis*), 3. discursive thinking (Gr. *dianoia*), 4. knowledge and certainty (Gr. *episteme*), based on reason.

16　*De Pulsuum Differentis*, 2.4 and R.L., Wilken, *The Christians*, pp. 72–93.

17　Cf. *Nero*, 16. Tacitus (1 CE). The situation of Christianity changes radically during the reign of Nero (1 CE) when this religion became known to the Roman authorities and was punished. Lucius Apuleius (2 CE) in *Metamorphoses*, 9.14

sarcastically describes a baker's wife, a Christian woman, noting: 'she also despised the gods and instead of a certain religion she claimed to worship a god whom she called "only" God'. Lucian of Samosata (2 CE), characterised the Christians in this way: 'Furthermore their first lawgiver convinced them that they are each other's brothers after they once deny the Greek gods and break the law and worship that crucified sophist and live according to his laws.' Cf. *De Morte Peregrini*, 5, Aelius Aristides (1 CE). Cf. Justin, *1 Apology* (hereafter: *1 Apol.*) 1.6; Athenagoras of Athens, *Embassy for the Christians* (hereafter: *Leg.*), 4–8. Cf. Plutarch, *On Superstition*, which may have influenced the pagan reception of Christianity.

18 H. Musurillo *The Acts of the Christian Martyrs* (Oxford: Clarendon Press, 1972), (hereafter: *The Acts.*).

19 Musurillo notes that Eusebius *Church History* (hereafter: *HE.*), 4.15.18 points to the three martyrs directly after Polycarp and Pionius, who were executed under the rule of Marcus Aurelius (2 CE).

Chapter 2: The Father Almighty, Creator of Heaven and Earth

1 There is ongoing discussion on the definition of 'Gnosticism' (Gr. *gnosis*, 'a special knowledge'). For more information, see the Glossary and Ch. Markschies, *Gnosis. An Introduction*, trans. J. Bowden (London/New York: T&T Clark/Continuum, 2003), pp. 1–27. More advanced readers may consult K. Rudolph, *Gnosis. The Nature and History of an Ancient Religion*, trans. R. McLachlan Wilson (Edinburgh: T & T Clark, 1983).

2 See the Introduction, 3.

3 Cf. the basic review of this position in E. Pagels, *The Gnostic Gospels* (London: Penguin Books, 1990), reprint, pp. 71–88.

4 As an introduction to Irenaeus' life and work, see E. Osborn, 'Irenaeus of Lyons' in R.G. Evans, ed., *The First Christian Theologians. An Introduction to Theology in the Early Church* (Malden/Oxford/Carlton: Blackwell, 2004), pp. 121–126. For more advance readers: E. Osborn, *Irenaeus of Lyons* (Cambridge: Cambridge University Press, 2001).

5 Against Heresies (hereafter: *AgainstHer.*) *1.11.1*.

6 Cf. so-called *Ptolemy's Version of the Gnostic Myth*, preserved by Irenaeus, *Against Her.*, 1.1.1–1.8.5; *Gospel of Truth*, 24.6; 42.16-17.

7 Cf. D.J. Good, 'Gender and Generation Observations on Coptic Terminology, with Particular Attention to Valentinian Texts', in K.L. King, ed., *Images of the Feminine in Gnosticism* (Philadelphia: Fortress Press, 1988), pp. 23–40 (hereafter: *Images.*).

8 For more information on the Nag Hammadi Library, see the Glossary.

9 For example, *The Apocryphon of John*, 2.26–4.24. For more information, see A.H.B. Logan, *Gnostic Truth and Christian Heresy. A Study in the History of Gnosticism* (Edinburgh: T&T Clark, 1996), pp. 76–82.

10 For example, Tertullian, *Prescription of Heretics* (hereafter: *Prescrip.*) 41; *On the Veiling of Virgins* (hereafter: *On Veiling*) 9; Irenaeus, *AgainstHer.* 1.25.6. More: E. Schüssler Fiorenza, 'Word, Spirit and Power: Women in Early Christian Communities,' in R.R. Ruether and E. McLaughlin, eds. *Women of Spirit* (New York: Simon and Schuster, 1979), pp. 29–70.

11 *Gospel according to Thomas* (hereafter: *GosThom.*), saying 101.

12 *Gospel of Philip* (hereafter: *GosPhil.*), 52.21.

13 For example, *Three Steles of Seth*, 123.16. Cf. K.L. King (ed.), 'Sophia and Christ in Apocryphon of John', in *Images of the Feminine in Gnosticism* (Harrisburg: Trinity Press International, 2000), pp. 158–176.

14 For example, Ptolemy's version of the Gnostic Myth, in Irenaeus, *AgainstHer.*, 1.1.1–1.8.5.

15 For example, *Apocalypse of Adam*, 81.2-3. On the use of this metaphor in Gnostic narratives see L. Abramowski, 'Female Figures in the Gnostic Sondergut in Hippolytus' Refutation', in *Images.*, pp. 136–152.

16 For example, *Trimorphic Protennoia*, 35.1-24.

17 It also may be concluded that Gnostic Christians were more open to their sexuality, at least through explicit sexual language related to theology. Cf. R. Smith, 'Sex Education in Gnostic Schools', in *Images.*, pp. 345–360.

18 Cf. the Glossary.

19 Previous to that, among the Apostolic Fathers, Clement of Rome in his *Epistles to Corinthians* uses some formulas that make a distinction between God, the Father and the Son. In this document the title 'God' applies only to the Father who is also described as 'the Creator' and 'the Governor' of the world. Cf. 33.2; 38.3; 52.1.

20 For an introduction to Justin' life and work, see E. Osborn, 'Justin Martyr' in R.G. Evans, ed., *The First Christian Theologians. An Introduction to Theology in the Early Church* (Malden/Oxford/Carlton: Blackwell, 2004), pp. 115–120 with bibliography.

21 *Dialogue with Trypho* (hereafter: *Dial.*) 1.3; Cf. *1 Apol.*, 12.9; 32.10; 36.2; 40.7; 44.2; 46.5; 61.3.10.

22 *2 Apol.*, 2.19.

23 Cf. *Timaeus*, 28C.

24 *To Autolycus* (hereafter: *Autol.*) 1.4.

25 *Autol.*, 1.5.

26 *Autol.*, 1.7.

27 Cf. *Autol.*, 2.38 and in *Recognitiones*, 29; cf. Justin, *1Apol.*, 28.4; Athenagoras, *On the Resurrection of the Dead* (hereafter: *Res.*) 19.

28 *1 Clement*, intro., 2.3; 8.5; 32.4; 56.6; Polycarp, *Ep.Philip.*, intro., *Mart.Polycarpi*, 14.1; *Didache*, 10.3; Hermes, *Shepherd.*, 3.3.5; *Mandate*, 7.4; *Epistle to Diognetus*, 7.2; Theophilus, *Autol.*, 1.4.

29 *Autol.*, 3.9.

30 *Leg.*, 8.

31 *Autol.*, 1.4; 2.34.

32 *Autol.*, 1.11

33 *Autol.*, 1.7.

34 Justin, *2Apol.*, 4.2.

35 *1 Apol.*, 43.1.

36 *1 Apol.*, 6.1.

37 Justin believed that God is 'transcendent, eternal, passionless' (*1 Apol.*, 12; *2 Apol.*, 12), 'unchangeable' (*1 Apol.*, 13) and 'incorruptible' (*Dial.*, 5). God, in Justin's view, is 'compassionate' (*Dial.*, 108), 'the Father and Creator of all' (*1 Apol.*, 8, *Dial.*, 140), 'the Father and Lord of all' (*1 Apol.*, 12; 32), 'the Father and King of heavens' (*2 Apol.*, 12), 'Father of all' (*1 Apol.*, 12; 14; 65; *2 Apol.*, 6, 9; *Dial.*, 7, 33, 56).

38 Irenaeus underlined the role of the Son who reveals the Father while the Father remains invisible in his Son, *AgainstHer.*, IV.4.2; 6.6; God's care V.15.2. The *Proof of the Apostolic Preaching* (hereafter: *Proof.*) explains further characteristic of God as the Father and his providence over the created world, Chapter 8.

39 Cf. *Against Praxeas* (hereafter: *AgainstPrax.*).

40 Cf. Hippolytus, *Against Noetus* (hereafter: *AgainstNoet.*).

41 *Dial.*, 16; 22; 38; 83; 89; 142.

42 *1 Apol.*, 14; 16.

43 In addition to the previous references see *Dial.*, 5; 6; *1 Apol.*, 19.

44 *1 Apol.*, 10; *2 Apol.*, 4.

45 *Dial.*, 1.

46 For an introduction to the crucial connection between early Christian theology and philosophy of this period, see J.M. Rist 'Christian Theology and Secular Philosophy', in R.G. Evans, ed., *The First Christian Theologians. An Introduction to Theology in the Early Church* (Malden/Oxford/Carlton: Blackwell, 2004), pp. 105–114.

47 *AgainstHer.*, 2.10.3; 1.9.2; 2.47.2.

48 *AgainstHer.*, 5.4.2.

49 *AgainstHer.*, 2.34.4.

50 *AgainstHer.*, 4.38.3; 41.1.

51 *AgainstHer.*, 4.36.6.

52 *AgainstHer.*, 2.10.3.

53 *AgainstHer.*, 2.2.4.

54 As an introduction to Tertullian's life and work, see E. Osborn, 'Tertullian', in R.G. Evans, ed., *The First Christian Theologians. An Introduction to Theology in the Early Church* (Malden/Oxford/Carlton: Blackwell, 2004), pp. 143–149. For more advanced readers, E. Osborn, *Tertullian. First Theologian of the West* (Cambridge: Cambridge University Press, 1977).

55 *AgainstPrax.*, 1; 2; 16; 27; 21; *AgainstNoet.*, 8.

56 *AgainstPrax.*, 10. Cf. *On the Flesh of Christ* (hereafter *Flesh*), 3.

57 *Flesh.*, 17.

58 *AgainstNoet.*, 6.

59 For an introductory information, see E., Ferguson, *Backgrounds of Early Christianity* (Grand Rapids, Michigan: Eerdmans Publishing Company, 3rd edn, 2003), pp. 241–243.

60 For an introduction, see B. Layton, *The Gnostic Scriptures. A New Translation with Annotations and Introduction* (London: SCM Press, 1987), pp. 14–15.

61 See, J. Pelikan, *The Emergance of the Catholic Tradition (100–600). A History of the Development of the Doctrine*, vol. 1 (Chicago/London: The University of Chicago Press, 1975) pp. 73–74. For more advanced readers, see the article on Marcion, in H. Räisänen, 'Marcion' in *A Companion to Second-Century Christian 'Heretics'*, eds. A. Marjanen, P. Luomanen, 'Supplements to Vigiliae Christianae', vol. 76 (Leiden: Brill, 2005), pp. 100–124.

62 *Against Marcion* (hereafter: *AgainstMarc.*) 1.

63 *AgainstMarc.*, 2.

64 *AgainstMarc.*, 2.

65 Cf. *Autol.*, 1.5.

66 Cf. *Timaeus*, 28C.

67 *AgainstHer.*, 2.1.1. Trans. *Ante-Nicene Fathers* – modified (hereafter: *ANF.*).
68 *AgainstHer.*, 3.25.3.

Chapter 3: And in Jesus Christ, His only Son our Lord

1 Cf. *The Martyrdom of Carpus, Papylus and Agathonicê*, 2 in H. Musurillo, *The Acts of the Christian Martyrs* (Oxford: Clarendon Press, 1972), p. 31.

2 To illustrate this tendency we can point to the following titles: The *Messiah/ Christ* (e.g. Jn 1.41; Rom. 9.5); *The Prophet* (e.g. Mk 9.7; Lk. 13.33; Jn 1.21; 6.14); *The Priest* (e.g. Jn 17), and *The King* (e.g. Mt. 2.2; 21.5; 27.11). Jesus is introduced as *The Son of David* (e.g. Mt. 9.27; 12.23; 15.22; Lk. 1.32; Rom. 1.3; Rev. 5.5); *The Suffering Servant* (e.g. Mt. 12.18; Mk 10.45; Lk. 24.26) and *The Son of Man* (e.g. Mk 2.10; 2.28; 10.45; 14.21; Lk. 9.58; 12.19; 19.10; Jn 3.13–14; 6.62–63; 8.6).

3 More in M. de Jonge, 'The Earliest Christian Use of Christos: Some Suggestions' in *Jewish Eschatology, Early Christian Christology and the Testaments of the Twelve Patriarchs. Collection of Essays of Marinus de Jonge* (Leiden: Brill, 1991), pp. 102– 124.

4 Among early Jewish-Christian documents, the direct identification of *Jesus of Nazareth* with the figure of *the Messiah*, appears already in *The Epistle of Barnabas* (*c.* 115–117) in 7.8–11, 8.1-2, 12.2.5 when the author argues for signs hidden in the Old Testament signs pointing to Jesus as *the Christ.*

5 For more information, see R.S. MacLemman, *Early Christian Text on Jews and Judaism*, Brown Judaic Studies 194 (Altanta: Scholars Press, 1990), pp. 49–88 and T. Rajak, *Talking against Trypho. Christian Apologetic as Anti-Judaism in Justin's Dialogue with Trypho the Jew*, in M. Edwards, M. Goodman and S. Price, eds., *Apologetics in the Roman Empire: Pagans, Jews, and Christians* (Oxford: Oxford University Press, 1999), pp. 59–80.

6 For example, *Dial.*, 36; 39; 49; 89; 90; 110.

7 For example, Dial., 36; 39; 49; 89; 90; 110.

8 *AgainstHer.*, 3.18.7; *Proof,* 37; 97.

9 *Proof.*, 30; 53; 71; *AgainstHer.*, 3.18.7.

10 *AgainstHer.*, 4.6.6; 4.20.7.

11 *AgainstHer.*, 5.1.1.

12 *AgainstHer.*, 3.19.1: 'For it was for this end that the Word of God was made man, and He who was the Son of God became the Son of Man, that man, having been taken into the Word, and receiving the adoption, might become the Son of God. For by no other means could we have attained to incorruptibility and immortality, unless we had been united to incorruptibility and immortality.' Trans. *ANF.*

13 For general reading see R. Grant, *Gods and the One God. Christian Theology in the Graeco-Roman World* (London: SPCK, 1988), pp. 62–68.

14 The title 'Son of God' is messianic. In the Hebrew Bible, Israel is the 'son': For example, Exod. 4.22; Hos. 11.1; Jer. 3.19; 31.9.20. In the Hebrew Bible, the title was also applied to the angels: Pss. 29.1; 89.7; Job 1.6; to the king Ps. 2.7 and possibly to the priests: Mal. 1.6. In the NT the title expresses self-understanding of Jesus during his messianic mission, for example Mt. 11.27; Mk 13.32. In the light of many statements Jesus is the Son of God (Jn 20.17) united with his Father Jn 5.19; 16.32 through his will Jn 4.34; 6.38; 7.28; 8.42; 13.3, which is also reflected by his actions: Jn 14.10. The title also implies a unity of being and

nature with the Father, a uniqueness of origin and pre-existence: Jn 3.16. More: M de Jonge, 'The earliest Christian use', pp. 135–144.

15 Cf. the important testimony in Ignatius, *Ep.Ephesians*, 20.2.

16 *Leg.*, 10.

17 Cf. Eusebius, *HE.*, 3.27.4. More information on Ebionites can be found in S. Häkkinen, 'Ebionites', in *A Companion to Second-Century Christian 'Heretics'*, eds. A. Marjanen and P. Luomanen, 'Supplements to Vigiliae Christianae', vol. 76 (Leiden: Brill, 2005), pp. 248–278.

18 I refer to only few selected examples of the alternative, later level as 'heretical' Christologies. Furthermore, I do not discuss in detail the early Latin doctrines of Novatian, Lactantius and Hilary. These theologies are presented by L. Ayres, *Nicaea and its Legacy. An Approach to Fourth-Century Trinitarian Theology* (Oxford: Oxford University Press, 2006), pp. 70–76.

19 Cf. the Glossary.

20 Cf. *Against.Noet.*, 1 and 2; Tertullian, *AgainstPrax.*, 1.

21 Hereafter: *OnHer.*, 9.7.

22 *Against.Noet.*, 8.

23 *Against.Noet.*, 15.

24 This view is known as 'patripassianism', that is 'suffering of the Father', see the Glossary ('Noetus') and *AgainstPrax.*, 1.

25 *AgainstPrax.*, 90, 21.

26 *AgainstPrax.*, 5.

27 *AgainstPrax.*, 8. More on Tertuallian's Christology in E. Osborn, *Tertullian, First Theologian of the West* (Cambridge: Cambridge University Press, 1997), pp. 121–143.

28 *AgainstPrax.*, 13.

29 *AgainstPrax.*, 13.

30 From many studies, I would like to recommend: W.A. Meeks, *The First Urban Christians. The Social World of the Apostle Paul* (Yale: Yale University Press, 1983); E. Stegemann, *The Jesus Movement: A Social History of its First Century* (Minneapolis, MN: Fortress Press, 1999).

31 For a basic introduction, see J.M. Dines, *The Septuagint* (London: T&T Clark, 2004), then N.F. Marcos, 'The Septuagint and Christian Origin', in N.F. Marcos, *The Septuagint in Context. Introduction to the Greek Versions of the Bible*, trans. W.G.E. Watson (Leiden: Brill, 2001), pp. 305–363.

32 More on the role of the *LXX* in formation of early Christian Christology in the next Chapter.

33 More on that problematic translation in R. Hanhart, 'Introduction. Problems in the History of the *LXX* Text from Its beginning to Origen' in his *The Septuagint as Christian Scripture. Its Prehistory and Problem of its Canon* (Edinburgh: T&T Clark, 2002), pp. 7–9.

34 For example, Philo of Alexandria in his work *On Noah's Work as a Planter*, 86 explains the Greek title *Kyrios* applied to God as 'the divine Governor of the world'.

35 *Mart.Conon*, 4.2.20, Cf. *Mart.Pionius*, 9.8; See parallel in *2 Clement*, 9.10–11: 'Let us, then, give Him everlasting praise, not only from our mouth, but also from our heart, that He may receive us as sons. For the Lord said: 'those who do the will of my Father are my brethren'.

36 Ignatius, *Ep.Ephesians*, 7.2; Irenaeus, *Proof.*, 88; *AgainstHer.*, III.20.4; Tertullian,
    Against Marcion (hereafter: *AgainstMarc.*), 3.19; 4.22.
37 For example, Ignatius, *Ep.Ephesians*, 1.1; Justin, *1 Apol.*, 33.7; *Dial.*, 8.2; Irenaeus,
    AgainstHer., 1.3.1; 7.2; Tertullian, *Against the Jews* (hereafter: *AgainstJews.*), 10.11.
38 See more in J.T. Carroll, *The Return of Jesus in Early Christianity* (Peabody, Mass:
    Hendrickson Publishers, 2000); Ch. E. Hill, *Regnum Caelorum: Patterns of
    Millenial Thought in Early Christianity* (Michigan Grand Rapids: William B.
    Eerdmans Publishing Company, 2001).

Chapter 4: Who was Conceived by the Holy Spirit, Born of the Virgin Mary

1   Trans. *ANF.*
2   The belief in the Holy Spirit is discussed in Chapter 8.
3   Cf. S. Benko, *The Virgin Goddess. Studies in the Pagan and Christian Roots of Mari-
    ology* (Leiden: Brill, 1993), pp. 196–265.
4   The earliest reference to *Docetic* Christology can be found in 1 Jn 4.2–3 and 2 Jn
    7-11.
5   See the previous Chapter.
6   I use the inverted commas by the name of Isaiah as modern scholarship
    ascribes this passage to the prophet called 'Trito-Isaiah', for more detail see, C.
    Westermann, *Isaiah 40–66. A Commentary*, trans. D.M.G. Stalker (London: SCM
    Press, 1969), pp. 295–296.
7   *Proof.*, 88; 94; *AgainstHer.*, 3.20.4.
8   *AgainstMarc.*, 4.22.11.
9   A note must be made at this point. At this stage the narrative of the Apostles'
    Creed shows some inconsistency in its literary composition. We approach the
    mystery of *the Holy Spirit* and his/her intervention, but we still must wait till
    almost the end of this credal formula to acknowledge his/her existence. This
    lack of consistency can be explained in the historical development of various
    theological statements that are combined in the Creed. The main debate in the
    first and second centuries was related to the nature of God, his relationships
    with the world, and then, to Jesus Christ as God's Son and the Saviour. These
    were the themes of continual discussion at this time and therefore *the Holy Spirit*
    appears here at this point as if 'on the margins' of the main Christological
    narrative.
10 For example, Plutarch, *Numa*, 4.4 suggests that a woman can become pregnant
    by 'a divine spirit' and what follows is 'virgin birth'; Philo of Alexandria knows
    the notion and applies it to the metaphorical birth of the virtues in *Cherubim*,
    40–52. Justin knows about pagan analogies to 'virgin birth', *Dial.*, 67; *1 Apol.*,
    22.2.5; 54.8. According to the Greek mythology Zeus begot Apollo, Athena,
    Dionysius, Heracles.
11 Gen. 6.1-4; Bar 3.26-28; Sir 16.7.
12 Cf. the Glossary.
13 *Ep.Ephesians*, 18.2, in *The Apostolic Fathers. Greek Texts and English Translations*, ed.
    and revised by M.W. Holmes (Grand Rapids, MI: Baker Books, 1999); cf. 7.2;
    Ep.Trallians, 9.1; *Ep.Smyrnaeans*, 1.1.
14 *Ep.Ephesians*, 19.1.

15 *Ep.Ephesians*, 19.1.

16 *Ep.Ephesians*, 19.3.

17 Cf. *Epistle of the Apostles* (*c.* 150 CE), 3; Aristites of Athens (first half of the second century), *Apology*, 15.1; *The Apostolic Tradition*, 21.12–18; Melito of Sardis, *On Faith, On the Soul and the Body;* Pseudo-Melito, *On the Passage of the Blessed Virgin Mary.*

18 Irenaeus' oeuvre contains a number of references and critic of *Docetic* Christology, see for instance, *AgainstHer.*, 1.23.2; 26.1; 2.24.4; 3.11.3; 16.1; 18.3–6; 22.1–2; and his response by confession of the real incarnation in: 1.10.1; 3.4.1–2.

19 *Proof.*, 40; 53; 54; 57; 59; 63.

20 For example, *AgainstHer.*, 1.7.2; 5.1.2 and 3.

21 *AgainstHer.*, 3.19.1; 2; 3; 21.1; 4; 5; 6; 10; 22.1; 4.

22 Isa 7.13 in *AgainstHer.*, 3.19.3.

23 This is the purpose of the whole 21st chapter of the third book of *AgainstHer.*

24 That was the issue of the controversy around the title 'God-bearing' (Gr. *theotokos*) applied to the Virgin Mary and the Nestorian crisis addressed by the Council of Ephesus (431 CE).

25 *1 Apol.*, 33.

26 *1 Apol.*, 33.

27 *1 Apol.*, 66; 77.

28 It is probably from the Greek title *parthenos* that some Jewish sources in the third and later centuries speculate about Jesus' disreputable origin as a son of a Roman solder called 'Pantera'. Cf. an anti-Christian document *Acts of Pilate*, 2.3, Eusebius, *EH.*, 9.5.1. The echo of this accusation can be heard in Origen, *Against Celsus*, 1.28; 32; 69. (hereafter: *AgainstC.*).

29 Cf. G.D. Dunn, *Tertullian* (London – New York: Routledge, 2004), pp. 13–18.

30 *AgainstMarc.*, 3.8; 5.14.

31 *AgainstMarc.*, 4.10 in *Adversus Marcionem*, ed. and trans. by E. Evans (Oxford: Clarendon Press, 1972).

32 *Flesh*, 18.5.

33 *Flesh*, 7.23; *AgainstMarc.*, 4.19. The theological formula of 'the perpetual virginity of Mary' declared by the third Canon of the Lateran Council (469 CE) magnified her status as the virgin 'before' (Lat. *ante partum*), 'during' (Lat. *in partu*) 'and after' (Lat. *post partu*) the birth of Jesus. This pronouncement created also one of our problems with the imagery of Mary, a Jewish woman, who by Patristic theologians was put into the ideological role of the most important guardian of Jesus' humanity.

34 *AgainstPrax.*, 2.1.

35 Cf. the Glossary.

36 For more information on this notion and theology, see K. Rudolph, *Gnosis. The Nature and History of Gnosticism*, trans. R. McLachlan Wilson (Edinburgh: T&T Clark, 1998), pp. 121–131

37 Cf. *GosPhil.*, 59.6–11. For more detail on this Gnostic document, see W.W. Isenberg, *Introduction*, in *The Nag Hammadi Library in English*, ed. J.M. Robinson (New York: Harpers Collins Publishers, 1990), pp. 139–141.

38 *GosPhil.*, 55.27–28.

39 *GosPhil.*, 55.23-31 trans. W.W. Isenberg, in *The Nag Hammadi Library in English.*

40 More on feminine character of the Holy Spirit in Chapter 8.

41 See the basic information in Ch. Markschies, *Gnosis*, trans. J. Bowden (London-New York: T&T Clark, 2003), pp. 89–94. More detail on Valentinus' tradition in I. Dunderberg, 'The School of Valentinus' in *A Companion to Second-Century Christian 'Heretics'*, eds. A. Marjanen, P. Luomanen, 'Supplements to Vigilae Christianae', vol. 76 (Leiden: Brill, 2005), pp. 64–99.

42 *GosPhil.*, 55.31.

43 *GosPhil.*, 55.33–36; 73.10.

44 *GosPhil.*, 71.5.18.

45 *GosPhil.*, 70.34–71.2

46 For the basic information about this document see B.A Pearson, I*ntroduction*, in *The Nag Hammadi Library in English*, ed. J.M. Robinson (New York: Harpers Collins Publishers, 1990), pp. 448–449.

47 *Testimony of Truth* (hereafter: *Testim. Truth.*) 39.29–31.

48 *Testim. Truth.*, 45.9–11.

49 *Testim. Truth.*, 45.14.

50 *Testim. Truth.*, 45.17–18

51 *Testim. Truth.*, 30.20–22.

52 More in: P. Brown, *The Body and Society: Men, Women and Sexual Renunciation in Early Christianity* (London/Boston: Faber and Faber, 1988).

53 Brown, *The Body and Society*, pp. 273–274.

54 Brown quotes E. A.W. Budge, *Miscellaneous Coptic Texts in the Dialect of Upper Egypt* (London: British Museum, 1915), p. 655 and 641 in Brown, *Body and Society*, pp. 273–274.

55 Cf. *Ineffabilis Deus*, the Apostolic Constitution issued by the Pope Pius IX in 1854.

Chapter 5: Suffered Under Pontius Pilate, was Crucified, Dead and Buried

1 Trans. M.W. Holmes, *The Apostolic Fathers. Greek Texts and English Translations* (Grand Rapidis, MI: Baker Books, 2004), p. 185.

2 The famous inscription on a block of limestone, which was found at Caesarea in 1961 states that Pilate's title was *praefectus* and not *procurator* of Judea. The *praefectus*' concerns were limited to essentials, mainly the maintenance of law and order, judicial matters and the collection of taxes. To enable him to carry out his duties he possessed supreme administrative power in the province.

3 Cf. J.K. Elliott, ed., *The Apocryphal New Testament: a Collection of Apocryphal Christian Literature in an English Translation* (Oxford: Clarendon Press/New York: Oxford University Press, 1993); J.K. Elliott, ed., *The Apocryphal Jesus: Legends of the Early Church* (Oxford/New York: Oxford University Press, 1996).

4 Cf. J. Quasten, *Patrology*, vol. 1 (Westminster, Maryland: Newman Press, 1986), p. 118.

5 For example, *Ep. Magnesians*, 13.1.

6 For example, *Ep. Trallians*, 6.1.

7 Cf. *Ep. Trallians*, 9.1 in *The Apostolic Fathers. Greek Texts and English Translations*, ed. and revised by M.W. Holmes (Grand Rapids, MI: Baker Books, 1999).

8 Cf. *Ep. Smyrnaeans*, 1.2.

9 Cf. *Ep.Magnesians*, 11.1.
10 Cf. *Ep.Smyrnaeans*, 2.1. Trans. in *The Apostolic Fathers*.
11 We know from Irenaeus' own testimony in his *Letter to Florinus* that he was born in Asia Minor, cf. Eusebius, *HE.*, 4.1.4. However Irenaeus' opposition to Docetism did not come as a memory of his childhood in Asia, but he did encounter some Docetic Christians among his flock in Gaul.
12 Cf. *Proof.*, 74; 77; 97. Cf. *AgainstHer.*, 2.22.4–6.
13 Cf. *AgainstHer.*, 1.7.2.
14 Cf. *AgainstHer.*, 1.25.6; 1.27.2.
15 Cf. *AgainstHer.*, 3.4.2.
16 Cf. *AgainstHer.*, 3.12.3.
17 Cf. *AgainstHer.*, 3.12.5.
18 Cf. *Proof.*, 71.
19 Cf. *AgainstHer.*, 3.12.9.
20 For more information, see M. Franzmann, *Jesus in the Nag Hammid Writings* (Edinburgh: T&T Clark, 1996), pp. 137–159 with references to the Gnostic documents.
21 Cf. 56.6–19.
22 The important connection between the proto-orthodox fascination with Jesus' painful death and idealisation of martyrdom is discussed by E. Pagels, *The Gnostic Gospels* (London: Penguin Books, 1990), pp. 89–114.
23 For example, *GosThom.*, 17; 77.
24 For more detail, see R. Valantasis, *The Gospel of Thomas* (London/New York: Routledge, 1997), pp. 8–12.
25 For example, the general setting of *The First Apocalypse of James* (hereafter: *1 Apoc.Jas.*). More on this document W.R. Schoedel, *Introduction* in J.M. Robinson, ed., *The Nag Hammadi Library* (New York: HarperSan Francisco, 1990), pp. 260–262.
26 Cf. 81.4-24. Trans. J. Brashler and R. Bullard, in *The Hag Hammadi Library*.
27 See Chapter 1.
28 Cf. 13.
29 Cf. 35; 48.
30 *Dial.*, 30.
31 Cf. 95.
32 Cf. 76.
33 Cf. *Dial.*, 30; 49; 121; 125; 131 and *2 Apol.*, 8.
34 Cf. *Dial.*, 86.
35 Cf. 21.18, see also *AgainstMarc.*, IV.42.1.
36 *Apology*, 21.24. Trans. T.R Glover, in *Apology. De Spectaculis*, 'Loeb Classical Library' (London: Cambridge, Mass: Harvard University Press, 1953).
37 *Apol.*, 32.
38 *Antidote for the scorpion' sting* (hereafter: *Scorp.*), 14.1.
39 In another treatise, *Against the Jews* (8.18), Tertullian emphasised the dissimilarity between the Jews and *Pontius Pilate*. Jews were directly responsible for Christ's crucifixion. On Tertullian's references to the Jews, see G. D. Dunn, *Tertullian* (London/New York: Routledge, 2004), pp. 47–51.
40 Cf. Quasten, *Patrology*, p. 118.
41 Tertullian's went through two conversions in his dramatic life, first from

paganism to Christianity, then, from mainstream Christianity to Montanism. Therefore it is dangerous to label him as a representative of the proto-orthodox theology. Some of his works written in 'catholic phase' represent this trend, but later, his conversion to Montanism disallowed his authority as one of the Latin Fathers of the Church. For more information, see G.D. Dunn, *Tertullian*, pp. 3–11.

Chapter 6: He descended into Hell; on the Third Day He Rose Again from the Dead

1 *Odes of Solomon*, trans. J.H. Charlesworth, in *The Old Testament Pseudepigrapha*, vol. 2, ed. J.M. Charlesworth (New York: Doubleday, 1985), p. 771. More on this document, see J.H. Charlesworth, *Introduction*, in *The Old Testament*, pp. 725–734.
2 Rufinus, *Commentary*; Note 98, p 121; see more in J.N.D. Kelly, *The Early Christian Creeds* (London: Longmans, Green and Co, 1972), pp. 378–382.
3 From enormous literature of the subject, I would like to recommend a collection of papers published as *The Bible in Greek Christian Antiquity*, 'The Bible Through the Ages', ed. and trans. P.M. Blowers (Notre Dame: University of Notre Dame Press, 1997).
4 Cf. J.J. Collins, 'Death and afterlife', in *The Bible World*, ed. J. Barton, vol. 2 (London/New York: Routledge, 2002), pp. 359–361; more detail in P. Johnston, *Shades of Sheol: Death and Afterlife in the Old Testament* (Leicester: Apollos, 2002).
5 Cf. J.H. Charlesworth, *The Old Testament Pseudepigraphia, Apocalyptic Literature and Testaments*, vol. 1 (New York: Doubleday, 1983), Ch. 60.5–25; 64; 79.26.
6 Cf. 10.8–10.
7 Cf. Eph. 4.9–11.
8 Cf. 41–42.
9 Cf. Hermas, *The Shepherd, Similitudes* (hereafter: *Sim.*) 9.16.5–7. For more information, see the Glossary.
10 A similar concept is expressed by another apocryphal document from the second century (possible from Asia Minor), the *Epistle of the Apostles* (26–27), showing that the idea of the apostolic mission in the underworld was part of a widespread theology. But also see Tertullian, *On the Soul*, 55.
11 For other documents representing this point of view, see *Apocryphon of Jeremiah*, quoted by Irenaeus, *AgainstHer.*, 3.20.4; 4.22.1; 33.1; 32.12; 4.31.5 and *Proof.*, 78. More on Jewish-Christian elaboration of the theme in J. Daniélou, *The Theology of Jewish Christianity*, trans. J.A. Baker (London: Darton Longman & Todd Ltd, 1964), pp. 233–248.
12 Cf. Chapter 2 and the Glossary.
13 *Proof.*, 78; *AgainstHer.*, 3.20.4.
14 *AgainstHer.*, 5.16.2–3.
15 *AgainstHer.*, 3.18.6.
16 Cf. 30.35–31.20.
17 Cf. 30.25–30. Trans. F. Wisse, in *The Nag Hammadi Library*, ed. J.M. Robinson (New York: HarperSan Francisco, 1990), for more detail on this document see F. Wisse, *Introduction*, in *The Nag Hammadi Library*, pp. 104–105.
18 Cf. M.L. Peel and J. Zandee, *Introduction*, in *The Nag Hammdi Library*, pp. 379–381.

19 Cf. 104.1–15. Trans. M.L. Peel and J. Zandee, in *The Nag Hammdi Library*.

20 Cf. 32.25–33.5. Trans. S. Giversen and B.A. Pearson, in *The Nag Hammdi Library*.

21 Cf. 29.16–18

22 Cf. 69.12.

23 Cf. 69.20–21.

24 Cf. 42.24–25.

25 Cf. 73.29–30.

26 The theme of resurrection will be discussed more fully in Chapter 12.

27 This title was discussed in Chapter 3.

28 Origen, *AgainstC.*, 2.55. Trans. H. Chadwick, in *Origen. Contra Celsus* (Cambridge: Cambridge University Press, 1965).

29 The variety of early Christian Christologies drafted in the previous chapters exemplify a range of possible understandings of Christ's resurrection. The proto-orthodox, literal interpretation of Christ's bodily resurrection was just one of many.

30 Cf. *AgainstC.*, 1.20. I do not wish to discuss Celsus' philosophical, possible Platonic background, but the belief in reincarnation was a part of Platonic, later Middle Platonic and Neoplatonic eschatology.

31 On the statement *resurrection of the body*, see Chapter 12.

32 This direct connection appears in the earliest Christian documents such as the *Letter of Polycarp to the Philippians*, 2.2.

33 *Proof.*, 38. Trans. J. P. Smith, in *St. Irenaeus. Proof of the Apostolic Preaching*, 'Ancient Christian Writers', no 16 (New York: Paulist Press, 1952).

34 *Proof.*, 41.

Chapter 7: He Ascended into Heaven, and Sits at the Right Hand of God the Father Almighty

1 Trans. M.A. Knibb, in *The Old Testament Pseudepigrapha*, vol.2, ed. J. Charlesworth (New York: Doubleday, 1985), p. 176

2 Cf. Lk. 24.51; Mk 16.19; Acts 1.22.

3 Cf. Acts, 2.32–35 and Phil. 2.6–11; Jn 16.28; 20.17.

4 Cf. *A Dictionary of Christian Theology*, ed. A. Richardson (London: SCM Press, 1969), p. 76, where the editor states: 'It is not generally understood that the Bible itself has no one cosmology but several. Hebrews were not interested in such matters and borrowed their cosmological ideas from their contemporaries such as Babylonians or the Greeks. Nor is it generally recognisable that the so-called cosmology of the three-storey universe is not that of the Bible but that of the late mediaeval world-view. This was a synthesis of Greek and biblical ideas, but it owes more to the Aristotelian-Ptolemaic theory of the universe than it does to the Bible'. More in D. Farrow, *Ascension and Ecclesia. On the Significance of the Doctrine of the Ascension for Ecclesiology and Christian Cosmology* (Edinburgh: T&T Clark, 1999).

5 This passage was often quoted by Paul in Rom. 8.4; Eph. 1.20; 1 Cor. 15.25; and is an important reference to the *Letter to the Hebrews*, 1.13; 8.1; 10.12; 12.2. Christians identified 'a human King' from the Psalm, with the eschatological Messiah: Jesus Christ. As to the idiom 'to sit at right hand' in the Old Testament it

symbolised the highest honour (1 Kings 2.19) or, as in 1 Sam. 2.8, the highest exultation.

6   The theme of being taken up appears in Acts 1.2, 11, 1 Tim. 3.16; 'exultation of Christ' in Acts 2.33; 5.31; 'to ascent' Acts 2.34; J 3.13; 6.62; 20.17. Eph. 4.8–10.

7   Mt. 22.44, 26.64; Mk 16.19; Rom. 8.34; 1 Cor. 15.25; Eph. 1.20; Col. 3.1; Heb. 1.3; 10.12.

8   The construction of the scene in Acts 1.9–11 when Jesus is taken up in the presence of his apostles remains the narrative from 2 Kings 2.11–12.

9   Isa. 14.15.

10 For example, *Ascension of Romulus* (Livius, *History of Rome*, 1.16).

11 Among many passages from the Scripture there is no clear distinction between these two events: Acts 2.32, Rom. 8.34; Col. 3.1; Phil. 2.9; 1 Tim. 3.16; Eph. 1.20; 1 Pet. 3.22. However, there is a distinction between resurrection and ascension in theological terms.

12 For example, *The Sophia of Jesus Christ*; more on this document in D.M. Parrott, *Introduction*, in *The Nag Hammadi Library*, ed. J.M. Robinson (New York: Harper-San Francisco, 1990), pp. 220–221.

13 This suggestion comes from the fourth-century Syriac document *The Testament of our Lord*.

14 Cf. J. Daniélou, *The Theology of Jewish Christianity*, trans. J.A. Baker (London: Darton Longman and Todd Ltd., 1964), p. 249.

15 Cf. 15.9. Trans. *The Apostolic Fathers. Greek Texts and English Translations*, ed. and revised by M.W. Holmes (Grand Rapids, MI: Baker Books, 1999).

16 The symbol of the 'eighth day' or the Ogdoad was also characteristic to the Christian Gnostic eschatology, however in the present context its Jewish-Christian provenience is more significant.

17 *Ascension of Isaiah*, 11.17.

18 Cf. 15.

19 For instance *Ascension of Isaiah*; the documents mention 'seven heavens' on occasion of Isaiah's vision (8.7), his ascension (9.1–42) and in relation to Christ's incarnation (10.17) and ascension of Christ (11.22–32). The highest, the seventh heaven, is the realm of God, as the lowest heavens are inhabited by various groups of angels. In comparison with this tradition St Paul speaks about 'the third heaven' (2 Cor. 12.2-3); *Pseudo-Clementines*, 9.3 about 'two heavens'; and *2 Enoch*, 3–20 presents more details on distinction of 'seven heavens'.

20 For example, Irenaeus, *Proof.*, 9.

21 *Dial.*, 41.

22 *Dial.*, 56 and 127.

23 *1 Apol.*, 45.

24 *1 Apol.*, 36.

25 *Proof.*, 83. Trans. J. P. Smith, in *St. Irenaeus. Proof of the Apostolic Preaching*, 'Ancient Christian Writers', no. 16 (New York: Paulist Press, 1952).

26 *Proof.*, 85.

27 Cf. *AgainstHer.*, 1.10.3; 3.23.3; 4.40.1; 5.26.2.

28 *Proof.*, 85.

29 *AgainstHer.*, 2.20.2.

30 Cf., 4.14.1.

31 On Irenaeus' idea of final destiny of Christ's enemy see the next Chapter.

32 Cf. 51 and 38.

33 *AgainstPrax.*, 12.3.

34 *AgainstMarc.*, 5.19.5.

35 *AgainstMarc.*, 4.20.5.

36 Cf. Chapter 3 and the Glossary.

37 *AgainstPrax.*, 30.

38 Cf. 119.10. Trans. D.M. Parrott in *The Nag Hammadi Library*.

39 Cf. 2.1–25.

40 Interestingly, the *Ascension of Isaiah* mentions 545 days, which may suggests some common source of this number.

41 Cf. 10.15.

42 Cf. 15.10.

43 Cf. 15.15–20.

44 Cf. 14.20–15.5. Trans. F.E. Williams in *The Nag Hammadi Library*, more on the provenience of this document see F.E. Williams, *Introduction*, in *The Nag Hammadi Library*, pp. 29–30.

45 Cf. 15.15–20.

46 However, for instance *The Book of Thomas the Contender*, 143.8 goes further and presents the theory of the last judgment.

Chapter 8: From Thence He shall come to Judge the Living and the Dead

1 Trans. J.H. Crehan, in *Embassy for the Christians. The resurrection of the dead*, 'Ancient Christian Writers', ed. J. Quasten and J.C. Plumpe, vol. 23 (London: Newman Press, 1956).

2 The motif of the last judgment and its dramatic circumstances, including destruction of the world by fire, was very popular in apocalyptic literature (1 BCE–3 CE) and some of its symbols inspired the New Testament images ('eternal fire', 1 Enoch 10.13 and Mt. 25.41) as well as the early Christian theologians. For more detail see J.J. Collins, 'Sibylline Oracles' in J.H. Charlesworth, ed., *The Old Testament Pseudepigrapha. Apocalyptic Literature & Testaments*, vol. 1 (New York: Dounleday, 1983), p. 323.

3 For example, the idea of 'the last judgment' represented by Matthew 25.31–46 shows parallels to 1 Enoch 69.26–28. For more advanced readers, I would like to recommend D.W. Kuck, *Judgment and Community Conflict Paul's Use of Apocalyptic Judgment Language in 1 Corinthians 3:5–4:5* (Leiden: Brill, 1992).

4 Cf. M. Simonetti, *Biblical Interpretation in the Early Church*, trans. J.A. Hughes (Edinburgh: T&T Clark, 1994).

5 More on eschatology in Chapter 13.

6 *Ep.Ephesians*, 11.1.

7 Cf. 4.9; 6.13

8 Cf. 16.2.

9 *Vis.*, 3.8.9.

10 Cf. *Mart.St.Carpus, Papylus and Agathonice*, 4; *Mart.Holy Martyrs Justin*, 5.

11 *Leg.*, 12.

12 Cf. 12.

13 Cf. 18.

14 Cf. 18.
15 Cf. 18.
16 Cf. 19.
17 *1 Apol.*, 19; 52.
18 Cf. 19, 52.
19 Cf. 20.
20 *1 Apol.*, 28; *Dial.*, 141.
21 *1 Apol.*, 45; *Dial.*, 67.
22 *1 Apol.*, 52.
23 Justin underlines this perspective in his *2 Apol.*, 9.
24 *Dial.*, 34; 64; 121.
25 In *Dial.*, 133 a special attention is paid to the Jews who will be judged and punish if they reject repentance for killing Christ the Messiah.
26 *Dial.*, 135.
27 *Dial.*, 45; 117; 120; 121; 122.
28 Cf. *On the Resurrection* (hereafter: *OnRes.*), 17.9.
29 *1 Clement*, 5.4–7; 6.1; 50.3.
30 *AgainstMarc.*, 4.10.12; *OnVeiling*, 1.3; *AgainstPrax.*, 2.14; *Prescrip.*, 13.5. Not all Tertullian's opponents shared the same view. For instance, the Gnostic document, *The Book of Thomas Contender*, openly proclaims the forthcoming of the Day of Judgment (141.14) bringing just reward or punishment for people (141.32–41; 145.12–16).
31 On 'millenarianism' see the glossary.
32 *AgainstHer.*, 5.27.2.
33 *AgainstHer.*, 5.28.1–2.
34 *2 Apol.*, 7; *Dial.*, 88; 102; 141.
35 *1 Apol.*, 12; 43.
36 *1 Apol.*, 17.
37 *2 Apol.*, 6.
38 *Dial.*, 52.
39 *Dial.*, 44.
40 *AgainstHer.*, 5.29.1.
41 Cf. 4.37.1.
42 Cf. 4.37.4.
43 The distinction between 'image' and 'likeness' is based on Gen. 1.26. The two stages of the human journey towards spiritual maturity appear in *AgainstHer.*, 5.6.1; 5.11.2; 5.16.2; *Proof.*, 11.
44 *AgainstHer.*, 5.60.2.
45 Cf. 4.37.6.
46 Cf. 3.19.1.
47 Cf. 4.22.1.
48 Cf. 3.5.2.
49 *On the Soul*, 21
50 *Exhortation*, 2.
51 Cf. 2.6.

Chapter 9: I Believe in the Holy Spirit

1 Cf. Chapter 4.
2 Lewis Ayres provides an interesting example of that pre-Nicene ambiguity on the nature of the Spirit. In fourth century in Egypt, there were Christians who believed in the humanity and divinity of Jesus Christ, but they thought of the Spirit as a created and superior angel in reference to 1 Tim. 5.12, cf. L. Ayres, *Nicaea and its Legacy. An Approach to Fourth-Century Trinitarian Theology* (Oxford: Oxford University Press, 2004), p. 211.
3 Cf. Hermas, *The Shepherd, Vis*, 5.2; *Sim.*, 7.1; 8.1.2; 8.3.3; 8.4.1.
4 Cf. Hippolytus, *OnHer.*, 9.13.2-3. Hippolytus' report refers to the teaching of a certain Alcibiades of Apamea in Syria who represented yet another Jewish Christian school of theology.
5 Cf. G.W.H. Lampe, *The Seal of the Spirit. A Study in the Doctrine of Baptism and Confirmation in the New Testament and the Fathers* (London: Longmans, 1951), pp. 193–222.
6 *1 Clement*, 58.2.
7 *1 Clement*, 8.1; 13.1; 16.2; 63.2.
8 *Ep.Ephesians*, 18.2.
9 *Ep.Philadelphians*, Introduction.
10 *Ep.Philadelphians*, 7.1–2.
11 Hermas, *Sim.*, 5.6.
12 *Sim.*, 5.5.
13 *Leg.*, 7.2; 9.1.
14 Cf. 10.3.
15 Wis. 7.25.
16 *Autol.*, 1.7; 2.15.18.
17 *1 Apol.*, 6; 31; 35; *Dial.*, 49.
18 *1 Apol.*, 44; 56; *Dial.*, 4;7; 25; 32; 34; 36; 37; 38; 52; 54; 55; 56; 61; 73; 74; 77; 84; 88.
19 *Or.*, 13.3.
20 *1 Apol.*, 61.
21 *1 Apol.*, 33.
22 *1 Apol.*, 61, 65; 67.
23 The complexity of Gnostic cosmologies and cosmogonies in which either Wisdom/Sophia or female Holy Spirit took part, presented by K. Rudolph, *Gnosis. The Nature & History of Gnosticism*, trans. R. McLachlan Wilson (Edinburgh: T&T Clark, 1998), pp. 71–87.
24 I must note that in Semitic languages the word for 'spirit' is feminine gender, but in the Greek (the *LXX*) is neutral. The Jewish authors who translated the Hebrew text and notions into Greek were limited in expressing the Holy Spirit in the feminine by the constraints of the language.
25 Cf. The Coptic *GosThom.*, 101.
26 Cf. 71.15–20.
27 Cf. 59.35–60.1.
28 Cf. 64.22–31.
29 Cf. 59.20.
30 Cf. 60.30. Trans. W.W. Isenberg, in *The Nag Hammadi Library*, ed. J.M. Robinson (New York: Harper San Francisco, 1990). For more analytical presentation,

see J.J. Buckley, ' "The Holy Spirit is a Double Name" Holy Spirit, Mary and Sophia in the *Gospel of Philip*', in *Images of the Feminine in Gnosticism*, 'Studies in Antiquity & Christianity', ed. K.L. King (Harrisburg: Trinity Press International, 2000), pp. 211–227 and response by K. Rudolph, pp. 228–238.

31 For example, the *Trimorphic Protennoia*, 35.1–24; the *Thunder, Perfect Mind*, 13.16–16.24.

32 Cf. *AgainstHer.*, 1.30.3.

33 Cf. *The Panarion* (hereafter *Panarion*), 19.4.1; 30.17.6.

34 *Odes.*, 19.1–5.

35 Cf. the Glossary. For more advanced readers, see A. Marjanen, 'Montanism: Egalitarian Ecstatic "New Prophecy", in *A Companion to Second-Century Christian 'Heretics'*, eds. A. Marjanen, P. Luomanen, 'Supplements to Vigiliae Christianae', vol.76 (Leiden: Brill, 2005), pp. 185–212.

36 Eusebius, *HE.*, V, 17:2–3.

37 Cf. Epiphanius, *Panarion.*, 48.11. Trans. F. Williams, in *The Panarion of Ephiphanius of Salamis. Books II and III*, 'Nag Hammadi and Manichean Studies', vol. 36 (Leiden: Brill, 1994).

38 *Expressis verbis* this formula will appear in the Creed of the Council Constantinople I (381).

39 *AgainstHer.*, opens with this confession in 1.10.1 and closes in 5.20.1.

40 Cf. 4.20.1; 5.1.3; 5.1; 6.1; *Proof*, 11.

41 Cf. 5.

42 Cf. 6 but also 2; 5; 42; 49.

43 Cf. 6; 89; 90; 93.

44 Cf. 42.

45 Cf. 6; 90; 93.

46 *AgainstHer.*, 5.8.1.

47 *Proof.*, 97.

48 Cf. 99.

49 Cf. 42.

50 *AgainstHer.*, 5.12.2.

51 Cf. 5.36.8.

52 Cf. 3.17.3.

53 Cf. 3.6.4.

54 Cf. 5.18.1.

55 Cf. 3.17.3.

56 Cf. 4.6.3; 6.6.

57 Cf. 1.10.3; 4.6.3; 19.2; 20.4 and 5; 4.19.3; 20.4; 20.6 and 7.

58 The first article is based on faith in One God, the second – in Jesus, the Son of God, the third – in the Holy Spirit who 'prophesised through the prophets'. Cf. *Proof.*, 6.

59 *Proof.*, 7. Trans. J. P. Smith, in *St. Irenaeus. Proof of the Apostolic Preaching*, 'Ancient Christian Writers', no. 16 (New York: Paulist Press, 1952).

60 *AgainstHer.*, 5.9.2.

61 *AgainstHer.*, 5.8.1.

62 Cf. Chapter 3 and the Glossary.

63 *AgainstNoet.*, 10.

64 Cf., 8.

65 Cf. 14.
66 Osborn notes: 'What then did Tertullian achieve? He handed on a form of discourse, which opened the way to further development and above all a formula, 'one substance in three persons'. [. . .] Trinity is less the existence of three heavenly beings, than a new way of believing in one God'. In E. Osborn, *Tertullian* (Cambridge: Cambridge University Press, 1977), p. 138.
67 Further comments in Osborn, *Tertullian*, pp. 116–143.
68 *AgainstPrax.*, 12.
69 That is sharing omnipotence as a specific feature of the divine 'propriety' in *AgainstPrax.*, 7.
70 Cf. J. Pelikan, *Christianity and Classical Culture* (Yale: Yale University Press, 1993), pp. 231–247 and Ch. A. Hall, *Learning theology with Church Fathers* (Illinois: Inter-Varsity Press, 2002), pp. 101–120. The summary of the Cappadocians' theology can be found in F.M. Young, *The Making the Creeds* (London: SCM Press, 1993), pp. 53–57.
71 *AgainstPrax.*, 6–7.
72 Cf. 11.

Chapter 10: The Holy Catholic Church [The Communion of Saints]

1 The addition 'the communion of saints' appears in the Apostles' Creed and is absent in the Old Roman Creed. Following Kelly's exposition I accept its first appearance in the local synod held in Nimes in 394. Cf. J.N.D. Kelly, *Early Christian Creeds* (London: Longmans, Green and Co, 1972), pp. 388–397. It is quite difficult to establish the exact source of this statement. Kelly refers to Dom Morin's plausible hypothesis tracing the notion back to the invective found in Cyprian of Carthage's correspondence in *Ep.* 69.9, namely, *communio malorum* 'Communion of Evil People', which gave some inspiration to the rhetorical use of the opposite term. However, as the idiom has a later origin than the current chorological frames, I will omit from my reflection.
2 Trans. P.A-S.
3 Trans. in M. Bévenot, *Cyprian. De Lapsis and De Ecclesiae Catholicae Unitate* (Oxford: Clarendon Press, 1971).
4 Hermas, *Sim.*, 9.1.1.
5 *Dial.*, 123. More on the subject, J.M. Lieu, 'The Forging of Christian Identity and the Letter to *Diognetus*', in *Neither Jew nor Greek? Constructing Early Christianity* (London: T&T Clark, 2002), pp. 171–189.
6 For example, Irenaeus, *AgainstHer.*, 3.17.1.
7 Hippolytus, *Exposition of Daniel*, 4.59.4.
8 Methodius of Olympus, *Symposium*, 3.8.72.
9 *AgainstMarc.*, 1.28.2.
10 *2 Clement.*, 14.
11 Ignatius, *Ep.Ephesians*, Introduction. Trans. M.W. Holmes, in *The Apostolic Fathers. Greek Texts and English Translations* (Grand Rapids: Baker Books, 1999).
12 *Vis.*, 2.4.1.
13 *Vis.*, 1.3.4.
14 *Vis.*, 1.1.6; 4.1.3.

15 *AgainstHer.*, 3.24.1.
16 *AgainstHer.*, 4.33.8.
17 *AgainstHer.*, 1.10.1.
18 Hippolytus, *OnHer.*, 9.12; Tertullian, *On Modesty* (hereafter: *OnMod.*), 21. More
    on this controversy in introduction to next Chapter.
19 *On the Baptism* (hereafter: *Bapt.*), 8.4.
20 *On Idolatry* (hereafter: *Idol.*), 24.4.
21 *On the Crown* (hereafter: *Corona.*), 11.4.
22 *On the Mantle*, 6.2.
23 *Apol.*, 45.1.
24 *OnMod.*, 14.17.
25 For example, *On Monogamy* (hereafter: *Monog.*), 11.2; *OnMod.*, 1.8.
26 *Apol.*, 2.18; 39.4; 46.7; *Prescript*, 3.6, *OnMod.*, 19.26.
27 Cf. Jerome, *On the Illustrious Men*, 53.
28 More details cf. W.H.C. Frend, *Martyrdom and Persecution in the Early Church. A
    Study of a Conflict from the Maccabees to Donatus* (London: Basil Blackwell, 1965).
29 Cf. the introduction to Cyprian's theology of baptism in S.G. Hall, *Doctrine and
    Practice in the Early Church* (London: SPCK, 1992), pp. 85–94.
30 Cf. *Epistle* (hereafter: *Ep.*), *Ep.*, 17.1.
31 Cf. *OnMonog.*, 7.9.
32 Cf. *On the Unity of the Catholic Church*, 6. Trans. M. Bévenot, *Cyprian. De Ecclesiae
    Catholicae Unitate* (Oxford: Clarendon Press, 1971).
33 Cf. *Ep.*, 73.21.
34 Cf. *Ep.*, 69.7; 71.1.
35 The controversy between Cyprian and Stephen, the Bishop of Rome, led to the
    question of the personal holiness of the minister who administers the sacra-
    ment. Much later, the Roman Catholic Church reaffirmed that 'the state of
    grace', that is personal holiness, is not a prerequisite for valid administration of
    the sacrament. Cf. the *Council of Trent*, session VII, Can.12, *De bapt.*, Can. 4.

Chapter 11: The Forgiveness of Sins

1 Cf. J.N.D. Kelly, *Early Christian Creeds* (London: Longmans, Green and Co,
   1972), p. 82.
2 Cf. Hermas, *The Shepherd, Vis.* 1.1.6.
3 Hippolytus, *OnHer.*, 9.7.
4 *OnHer.*, 9.7.
5 *OnHer.*, 9.7.
6 For more, see T. Wiley, *Original Sin: Origins, Development, and Contemporary
   Meaning* (New York: Paulist, 2002).
7 Cf. the term 'sin' in *The Dictionary of the Old Testament, Pentateuch*, ed. T.D.
   Alexander, D. Baker (Leicester: Inter Varsity Press, 2003) and *Dictionary of Biblical Theology*, ed. X. Léon-Dufour (Maryland: The Word Among Us, 1988).
8 For more information, see T. Buckley, *Seventy Times Seven: Sin, Judgment and
   Forgiveness in Matthew* (Collegeville: Liturgical Press, 1991); C.F.D. Moule, *Forgiveness and Reconciliation and other New Testament themes* (London: SPCK) 1998.
9 Cf. 'list of sins' in 1 Cor. 5.10–12; 6.9–10; 2 Cor. 12.20; Gal. 5.19–21; Eph. 5.3;
   Col. 3.5; 1 Tim. 1.9–10; 2 Tim. 3.2-5; Tit. 3.3.

10 The possible question why Christian rhetoric stressed so much the issue of the sin in its effort to spread the 'Good News' finds its answer in R.L. Fox, *Pagans and Christians in the Mediterranean World from the Second Century AD to the Conversion of Constantine* (London: Penguin Books, 2006), pp. 64–101.

11 By 'anti-Jewish' I mean the rhetoric against Judaism as a competitive religion to Christianity.

12 Cf. 11.1. Trans. M.W. Holmes, in *The Apostolic Fathers. Greek Texts and English Translations* (Grand Rapids: Baker Books, 1999).

13 Cf. 11.11.

14 Cf. 5.1.

15 Cf. 6.11.

16 E.g. *Dial.*, 54.

17 *1 Apol.*, 61.

18 The metaphor of baptism as an 'illumination' (Heb. 6.4) was a common theme of various early Christian groups, such as Jewish, proto-orthodox and Gnostic Christians, and shared the semantic cf. *Odes of Solomon*, 10.7; 15.3; 21.5; 32.1; 40.6 36.3.

19 *1 Apol.*, 61.

20 E.g. *Didache*, 7.1.

21 *1 Apol.*, 61; 65.

22 For the Scriptural references, see Mt. 18.15–17; 1 Cor. 5.1–13.

23 *Ep.Philipians*, 8.

24 *Ep.Philipians*, 6.1, 11.

25 Cf. *Mand.*, 4 3.1. Trans. Holmes, in *The Apostolic Fathers*.

26 Cf. 4.3.6.

27 *Sim.*, 8.11.1.

28 *Vis.* 2.2.2–4; 3.4; *Mand.*, 4.1.8.

29 For more, see R. Valantasis, *The Gospel of Thomas* (London: Routlege, 1997), pp. 7–19.

30 For this motif, see *The Hymn of The Pearl*, 109.35, in B. Layton, *The Gnostic Gospels. A New Translation with Annotations and Introduction* (London: SCM Press, Ltd, 1987), pp. 366–376; *GosThom*, logion 13; *The Book of Thomas the Contender* (hereafter: *ThomCont.*), 140.10–14.

31 According to Clement of Alexandria, that was the belief of Basilides, cf. *Stromateis*, 4.82.1; on forgiveness of sins in Basilides' theology, see *Stromateis*, 4.153.4.

32 Origen, *Commentary in Romans*, 4.4; 3.6.

33 Cf. Irenaeus, *AgainstHer.*, 3.4.3; Tertullian, *AgainstValentinians*, 4.1–2. This story could be a part of a legend, but still it shows strength of his reputation not only among his disciples.

34 Cf. *AgainstHer.*, 1.21.2–3.

35 Cf. *The Valentinian Exposition. On the baptism A*, 40.30–41.38.

36 Tertullian, *OnBaptism.*, 16.1; Cyprian, *Ep.*, 73.22; *MartyrdomPerp.Fel.*, 21.2.

37 As we know a little about Tertullian's life it is hard to draw a chronological line between his 'catholic' and Montanist periods. It is rather through his works that we can detect two different stages of his theology. In a recent publication, Dunn notes: 'The notion that Tertullian's Montanism meant that he ever left the Church is one that does not seem sustainable today' in *Tertullian* (London: Routledge, 2004), p. 6 and the author refers to D. I. Rankin,

Tertullian and the Church (Cambridge: Cambridge University Press, 1995), pp. 27–38.

38 *OnMod.*, 7.
39 Cf. 1.
40 *On Penitence* (hereafter: *OnPen.*), 9.1–6.
41 *OnMod.*, 2.12–15.
42 Cf. 1.19.
43 Cf. 18.18.
44 Cf. 9.20; 21.14.
45 Cf. 3.3; 19.28.
46 Cf. 18.18.
47 Cf. 17.8.
48 Cf. H. von Campenhausen, *Ecclesiastical Authority and Spiritual Power in the Church of the First Three Centuries* (Peabody: Hendrickson Publishers, 1977), pp. 124–148.
49 Cf. 21.10.
50 Cf. 21.17.
51 Cf. 21.16.

Chapter 12: The Resurrection of the Flesh

1 For more information, see B.C. Walker, *The Resurrection of the Flesh in the Western Christianity, 200–1336* (New York: Columbia University, 1995), C. Setzer, *Resurrection of the Flesh in Early Judaism and Early Christianity: Doctrine, Community and Self-definition* (Boston: Brill, 2004).
2 Cf. Chapter 6.
3 Cf. Chapter 8.
4 Cf. Chapter 13.
5 'Eschatology' denotes a branch of theology, which deals with the doctrines of 'the last things' (Gr. *ta eschata*), that is the second coming of Christ, universal judgment and destiny of humanity after it (heaven or hell).
6 For more, see J.J. Collins, *Death and Afterlife, in The Biblical World*, ed. J. Barton, vol. 2 (London/New York: Routledge, 2002), pp. 363–366. Collins notes: 'It has been often claimed that Jewish eschatology is distinguished from Greek by its emphasis on the resurrection of the flesh in contrast to the immortality of the soul, an emphasis that has obvious implications, however, is far too simple and fails to do justice to the kind of belief that emerges in the book of Daniel and *Enoch*. While this is not the Greek idea of immortality of the soul, neither is its resurrection of the flesh. (. . .)' Collins sums up the development of the Jewish theology: 'The ultimate goal of life has been changed from prosperity in the land and the succession of the generations to a spiritual for existence beyond the grave.' Cf. p. 366.
7 Cf. Chapter 6.
8 'Everlasting life' becomes explicit with Dan. 12.2 which has the only mention of 'everlasting life' in the Hebrew Bible. Isa. 26.19, probably related to national 'resurrection', as did Ezek. 37, though it needs to be noted that Ezek. 37 refers to unburied dead bodies not to those in Sheol. Ezek. 18 is usually seen as making the point that those in exile need to take responsibility for their own condition and not blame it on the sins of the previous generation. The emphasis

on individual responsibility caused difficulty however if as previously believed Sheol was the common destiny of good and bad alike. It became a particular issue during the Maccabaean revolt in the 2 BCE when Jews who kept faithfully to the requirements of the Torah were martyred for their faith. In the meantime Hellenistic Judaism was influenced by idea of the immortality of the soul (Wis. 3). I own this helpful comment to Dr Allan Jenkins.

9 For more information see Ph. S. Johnston "Shades of Sheol Death and Afterlife in the Old Testament" (Downers Grove, Ill: Inter Varsity Press, 2002).

10 Cf. D.M., Stanley, *Christ's Resurrection in Pauline Soteriology* (Rome: Pontifical Biblical Institute, 1961) and M.E. Dahl, *The Resurrection of the flesh. A Study of 1 Corinthians 15* (London: SCM Press, 1962).

11 As it is suggested by A.J.M. Wedderburn, *Baptism and Resurrection: Studies in Pauline Theology and Its Graeco-Roman Background* (Tübingen: Mohr Siebeck, 1987), pp. 6–37.

12 Cf. *Embassy*, 'To the Emperors Marcus Aurelius Anoninus and Lucius Aurelius Commodus, conquerors of Armenia and Sarmatia, and more than all, philosophers'.

13 Cf. 4, see also 8. Trans. Robert Donaldson. This argument comes back with the next wave of pagan criticism, see Origen' *AgainstC.*, 5.14 and Methodius of Olympus, *Res.*, 1.20.

14 Cf. 8; 11.

15 Cf. 10.

16 Cf. 10; 12.

17 Cf. 15.

18 Cf. 18.

19 Cf. 13.

20 *Dial.*, 139.

21 Cf. 113.

22 *1 Apol.*, 18.16.

23 Cf. 69.

24 Justin the Martyr shared belief with other early Christians in 'millenarianism', that is thousand years of Christ's reign on earth in a Jerusalem, for example *Dial.*, 80.5; 81.4. Some problems with this belief are highlighted by L.W. Barnard, *Justin the Martyr: His Life and Thought* (Cambridge: Cambridge University Press, 1967), p.165.

25 Cf. *Dial.*, 31; *1 Apol.*, 51.8–9; 52.3.

26 *Dial.*, 81.

27 Cf. 80.

28 It seems that in Justin's eschatology two parallel options are possible. One, that at the end of time there will be common resurrection of all people to judgment and then the thousand years reign of the saints with the Lord in Jerusalem, after which they all will enter into the eternal kingdom, while the wicked will be sentenced to punishment as long as God recognises it as necessary. Secondly, that the kingdom of God and the eternal punishment will be immediate without any intermediary period as presented by *Apologies*.

29 *AgainstHer.*, 1.24.5; 1.27.3.

30 For example, *GosPhil.*, 73.1–3.

31 *Panarion*, 40.2.5.

32 *OnHer.*, 5.8.22–24.
33 Cf. 45.15–46. Trans. M.L. Peel, *The Nag Hammadi Library in English*, ed. J.M. Robinson (New York: Harpers Collins Publishers, 1990).
34 Cf. 48.3–11.
35 Cf. 1.
36 Cf. 2.
37 Cf. 35.
38 Cf. 15.3.
39 Cf. 11.3.
40 Cf. 6.
41 *Res.*, 8. Trans. E. Evans, *Treatise on the resurrection* (London: SPCK, 1960).
42 Cf. 15, 59.3; see his *Apol.*, 48.4; *Testimony of the soul*, 4.1; *AgainstMarc.*, 4.34.
43 Cf. 50.2.
44 For example, *AgainstMarc.*, 4.10; *AgainstPrax.*, 2.14.
45 *Res.*, 9.2.
46 Cf. 11.1.
47 Cf. 18.
48 Cf. 49.
49 Cf. 52; 62.

Chapter 13: And Eternal Life. Amen

1 Trans. H. Musurillo, *The Acts of the Christian Martyrs* (Oxford: Clarendon Press, 1972), p. 111.
2 See the previous Chapter.
3 Cf. J.J. Colins, 'Death and Afterlife', in *The Biblical World*, ed. J. Barton, vol. 2 (London/New York: Routledge, 2002), pp. 357–375.
4 *Sibylline Oracles* (hereafter: *Or.Sib.*) 8.335–355.
5 *Or.Sib.*, 8.240–245, see also the *Greek Apocalypse of Ezra*, 4.36.
6 Cf. 5.24–25.
7 For example, *Or.Sib.*, 2.196–210, 252–254, 313–316.
8 For example, the *Greek Apocalypse of Ezra*, 2.29, 34.
9 *Or.Sib.*, 3.768–795, Trans. J.J. Collins, in *The Old Testament Pseudepigrapha. Apocalyptic Literature & Testaments*, ed. J.H. Charlesworth, vol. 1 (New York: Doubleday, 1983), cf. *1 Enoch*, 60.24.
10 *Or.Sib.*, 2.325–329.
11 Cf. 4.12; 5.9; 7.2; 21.1.3. The immanent coming of the Lord's judgment is rather commonplace among early Christian documents. Its best expression can be found in *Didache*, 16. For more advanced study of the theme, see V. Balabanski, *Eschatology in the Making, Mark, Matthew and the Didache* (Cambridge: Cambridge University Press, 1997).
12 Cf. 16.3–5.
13 Cf. 2.1; 4.9.
14 Cf. 28.1–4.
15 Cf. 21.1.
16 Cf. 15.8. More on the appearance of the metaphor of the 'eighth day' (Gr. *Ogdoad*) in early Christian documents see J. Daniélou, *The Theology of Jewish Christianity* (London: Darton Longman & Todd Ltd, 1964).

17 Cf. 36.1–2; 21.6–8.
18 Cf. 25.8.
19 Cf. 15.8.
20 Cf. 21.3 also 'the Lord's garment' in 11.11; 21.3; 25.8.
21 Cf. 1.1; 5.12; 9.8–11; 17.1; 20.7.
22 Cf. 7.4 and 6. Trans. J.H. Charlesworth, in *The Old Testament Pseudepigrapha. Apocalyptic Literature & Testaments*, ed. J.H. Charlesworth, vol. 2 (New York: Doubleday, 1985).
23 Cf. 40.6.
24 Cf. 25.12.
25 *Dial.*, 80.
26 Cf. 113; 139.
27 *Dial.*, 45; *1 Apol.*, 21.
28 *1 Apol.*, 10.
29 *1 Apol.*, 12; 28.1; 52.3; *2 Apol.*, 7; *Dial.*, 45.
30 Cf. 6.1–9.
31 Cf. 2.24 and 26.
32 *Treat.Res.*, 44.31; *On the Origin of the World*, 127.14–17; *GosPhil*, 67.15–18; *The Tripartite Tractate*, 122.19-23.
33 Cf. 44.27–29; 45.14–15; 45.25–26.
34 Cf. 49.9–30.
35 Cf. 67.14–30; 84.20–86.8. Within the Valentinian tradition, some theories of eternal peace paid special attention to the metaphor of the 'bridal chamber'. Cf. *GosPhil.*, 65.11; 67.5; 67.16; 67.30; 69.25; 69.27; 72.22; 76.5; 82.16–17; 82.18; 82.24; 86.5.
36 Cf. 81.34–82.14.
37 *ThomCon.*, 141.4–18; 141.32–142.2.
38 Cf. 142.11–143.7.
39 *AgainstHer.*, 2.30.9.
40 Cf. 4.40.1; 5.28.1–2.
41 Cf. 5.27.2.
42 *AgainstHer.*, 4.38.3. More information in E. Osborn, *Irenaeus of Lyons* (Cambridge: Cambridge University Press, 2001), pp. 211–216.
43 *AgainstHer.*, 4.20.5–7.
44 Cf. 5.12.4.
45 *Proof.*, 40.
46 *AgainstHer.*, 5.5.2.
47 Cf. 5.33-35.
48 Cf. 5.35.2; 5.36.1.
49 Cf. 5.36.1–2.
50 Cf. 5.27.2; 4.37.7; 4.38.3.
51 Cf. 5.27.2.
52 Cf. 5.7.2.
53 Cf. 5.36.3.
54 *OnPan.*, 2.
55 *AgainstMarc.*, 2.11.
56 *AgainstHermogenes.*, 3.3.
57 *AgainstMarc.*, 3.24.

58 *Bapt.*, 8.
59 *AgainstMarc.*, 3.24; *Res.*, 58; 62.
60 *Res.*, 32.6.
61 *Apol.*, 50.2.
62 *To the Martyrs*, 3.3.
63 *Res.*, 40.9.
64 *Scorp.*, 6.7.
65 *Prescrip.*, 13.1.

Conclusion

1 *On the Divine Images*, 20 in *On the Divine Images, Three Apologies against those who attack the Divine Images*, trans. D. Anderson (Crestwood, NY: St. Vladimir's Seminary Press, 1980), p. 20.
2 Cf. 23.

Bibliography

All quotations from the Old and New Testament follow:

The New Oxford Annotated Bible. New Revised Standard Version with the Apocrypha, ed. M.D. Coogan (Oxford: Oxford University Press, 2001).

I. Helpful, basic resources quoted in the study:

The Ante-Nicene Fathers, ed. A. Roberts and J. Donaldson (Edinburgh: Clark, 1885).

The Apocryphal New Testament: a Collection of Apocryphal Christian Literature in an English Translation, J.K. Elliott, ed. (Oxford: Clarendon Press – New York: Oxford University Press, 1993).

The Apostolic Fathers. Greek Texts and English Translations, ed. M.W. Holmes (Grand Rapidis, MI: Baker Books, 2004).

The Apostolic Tradition of St Hippolytus, ed. G. Dix (London: Society for Promoting Christian Knowledge, 1937).

Athenagoras of Athens, *Embassy for the Christians. The resurrection of the dead,* trans. J.H. Crehan, in 'Ancient Christian Writers', ed. J. Quasten and J.C. Plumpe, vol. 23 (London: Newman Press, 1956).

The Biblical World, ed., J. Barton, vols I–II (London – New York: Routledge, 2002).

Cyprian of Carthage, *Cyprian. De Lapsis and De Ecclesiae Catholicae Unitate,* trans. M. Bévenot (Oxford: Clarendon Press, 1971).

189

Dictionary of Biblical Theology, ed. X. Léon-Dufour (Maryland: The Word Among Us, 1988).

A Dictionary of Christian Theology, ed. A. Richardson (London: SCM Press, 1969).

The Dictionary of the Old Testament, Pentateuch, ed. T.D. Alexander, D. Baker (Leicester – Inter Varsity Press, 2003).

Irenaeus of Lyons, *Proof of the Apostolic Teaching*, trans. J.P. Smith, 'Ancient Christian Writers', no 16 (New York: Paulist Press, 1952).

The Nag Hammadi Library, ed. J.M. Robinson (San Francisco: HarperCollins Publishers, 1990).

The Old Testament Pseudepigraphia, Apocalyptic Literature and Testaments, vol. 1 (1983), vol. 2 (1985), ed. J. Charlesworth (New York: Doubleday).

Origen, *Against Celsus*, trans. H. Chadwick (Cambridge: Cambridge University Press, 1965).

The Panarion of Ephiphanius of Salamis. Books I–III, 'Nag Hammadi and Manichean Studies', trans. F. Williams, vol. 36 (Leiden: Brill, 1994).

Rufinus, *A Commentary on the Apostles' Creed*, trans. J.N.D. Kelly (London: Longmans, 1955).

Tertullian, *Treatise on the resurrection*, trans. E. Evans (London: SPCK, 1960)

II. References quoted in the book

Abramowski, L., 'Female Figures in the Gnostic *Sondergut* in Hippolytus's Refutation', in K.L. King, ed., *Images*, pp. 136–52.

Alexander, Ph.S., 'The Parting of the Ways', in *Jews and Christians. The Parting of the Ways A.D. 70 to 135*, ed. J.D.G. Dunn (Grand Rapids, Michigan/Cambridge, UK: W.B. Eerdmans Publishing Company, 1999), pp. 1–25.

Ayres, L., *Nicaea and its Legacy. An Approach to Fourth-Century Trinitarian Theology* (Oxford: Oxford University Press, 2006).

Balabanski, V., *Eschatology in the making, Mark, Matthew and the Didache* (Cambridge: Cambridge University Press, 1997).

Barnard, L.W., *Justin Martyr: His Life and Thought* (Cambridge: Cambridge University Press,1967).

Benko, S., *The Virgin Goddess. Studies in the Pagan and Christian Roots of Mariology* (Leiden/New York/Köln: E.J. Brill, 1993).

Blowers, P.M., ed. and trans. *The Bible in Greek Christian Antiquity*, 'The Bible Through the Ages' (Notre Dame: University of Notre Dame Press, 1997).

Brown, P., *The Body and Society: Men, Women and Sexual Renunciation in Early Christianity* (London/Boston: Faber and Faber, 1988).

Buckley J.J. '"The Holy Spirit is a Double Name": Holy Spirit, Mary and Sophia in the *Gospel of Philip*', in K.L. King, ed., *Images*, pp. 211–27.

Buckley, T., *Seventy Times Seven: Sin, Judgment and Forgiveness in Matthew* (Collegeville: Liturgical Press, 1991).

Cameron, A., *Christianity and Rhetoric of Empire: The Development of Christian Discourse* (Berkeley/Los Angeles: University of California Press, 1991).

Campenhausen, H. von, *Ecclesiastical Authority and Spiritual Power in the Church if the First Three Centuries* (Peabody: Hendrickson, 1997).

Carroll, J.T., *The return of Jesus in Early Christianity* (Peabody, Mass: Hendrickson Publishers, 2000).

Clark, G., *Christianity and Roman Society* (Cambridge: Cambridge University Press, 2004).

Collins, J.J., 'Death and Afterlife', in J. Barton, ed., *The Biblical World*, vol. 2 (London/New York: Routledge, 2002).

Daniélou, J., *The Theology of Jewish Christianity*, trans. J.A. Baker (London: Darton Longman & Todd Ltd, 1964).

Dines, J.M., *The Septuagint* (London: T&T Clark, 2004).

Dunderberg, I., 'The School of Valentinus' in A. Marjanen and P. Luomanen, eds., *A Companion to Second-Century Christian 'Heretics'*, pp. 64–99.

Dunn, G.D., *Tertullian* (London/New York: Routledge, 2004).

Elliott, J.K., ed., *The Apocryphal Jesus: Legends of the Early Church* (Oxford/New York: Oxford University Press, 1996).

Evans, R.G., ed., *The First Christian Theologians. An Introduction to Theology in the Early Church* (Malden/Oxford/Carlton: Blackwell, 2004).

Farrow, D., *Ascension and Ecclesia. On the Significance of the Doctrine of the Ascension for Ecclesiology and Christian Cosmology* (Edinburgh: T&T Clark, 1999).

Ferguson, E., *Backgrounds of Early Christianity* (Grand Rapids, Michigan: Eerdmans Publishing Company, 3rd edn, 2003).

Fox, L.R., *Pagans and Christian in the Mediterranean World from the Second Century AD to the Conversion of Constantine* (London: Penguin Books, 1988).

Franzmann, M., *Jesus in the Nag Hammadi Writings* (Edinburgh: T&T Clark, 1996).

Fredriksen P. and Lieu, J., 'Christian Theology and Judaism' in R.G. Evans, ed., *The First Christian Theologians*, pp. 85–101.

Frend, W.H.C., *Martyrdom and Persecution in the Early Church. A Study of a Conflict from the Maccabees to Donatus* (London: Basil Blackwell, 1965)

Good, D. J., 'Gender and Generation: Observations on Coptic Terminology, with Particular Attention to Valentinian Texts', in K.L. King, ed., *Images of the Feminine in Gnosticism* (Philadelphia: Fortress Press, 1988), pp. 23–40

Grant, R., *Gods and the One God. Christian Theology in the Graeco-Roman World* (London: SPCK, 1988)

Häkkinen, S., 'Ebionites', in A. Marjanen, P. Luomanen, *A Companion to Second-Century Christian 'Heretics'*, pp. 248–78.

Hall, Ch.A., *Learning theology with Church Fathers* (Illinois: InterVarsity Press, 2002).

Hall, S.G., *Doctrine and Practice in the early Church* (London: SPCK, 1992).

Hanhart, R., 'Introduction. Problems in the History of the *LXX* Text from Its beginning to Origen', in *The Septuagint as Christian Scripture. Its Prehistory and problem of its Canon* (Edinburgh: T&T Clark, 2002), pp. 7–9.

Hill, Ch. E., *Regnum Caelorum: Patterns of Millennial Thought in Early Christianity* (Michigan Grand Rapids: William B. Eerdmans Publishing Company, 2nd edn, 2001).

Johnston, P., *Shades of Sheol: death and afterlife in the Old Testament* (Leicester: Apollos, 2002).

Jonge, M., de 'The earliest Christian use of *Christos* some suggestions' in *Jewish Eschatology, Early Christian Christology and the Testaments of the Twelve Patriarchs. Collection of Essays of Marinus de Jonge* (Leiden: Brill, 1991).

Kelly, J.N.D., *Early Christian Creeds* (London: Longmans Green and Co, 3rd edn, 1972).

King, K.L., *Images of the Feminine in Gnosticism* (Philadelphia: Fortress Press, 1988)

—— , 'Sophia and Christ in Apocryphon of John', in *Images*, pp. 158–76.

Kuck, D.W., *Judgment and Community Conflict Paul's Use of Apocalyptic Judgment Language in 1 Corinthians 3:5–4:5* (Leiden: Brill, 1992).

Lampe, G.W.H., *The Seal of the Spirit. A Study in the Doctrine of Baptism and Confirmation in the New Testament and the Fathers* (London: Longmans, 1951).

Layton, B., *The Gnostic Scriptures. A new Translation with annotations and Introduction* (London: SCM Press, 1987).

Lieu, J.M. 'The Parting of the Ways: Theological Construct or Historical Reality?' in *Neither Jew Nor Greek? Constructing Early*

Christianity (London/New York: Continuum/T&T Clark, 2002).

——, 'The Forging of Christian Identity and the Letter to *Diognetus*', in Neither Jew nor Greek? *Constructing Early Christianity*, pp. 171–89.

——, 'Made Not Born: Conclusions, in: *Christian Identity in the Jewish and Graeco-Roman World* (Oxford: Oxford University Press, 2004).

Logan, A.H.B., *Gnostic Truth and Christian Heresy. A Study in the History of Gnosticism* (Edinburgh: T&T Clark, 1996).

MacLemman, R.S., *Early Christian Text on Jews and Judaism*, Brown Judaic Studies 194 (Altanta, Georgia: Scholars Press, 1990).

Marcos, N.F., 'The Septuagint and Christian Origin', in N.F. Marcos, *The Septuagint in Context.Introduction to the Greek Versions of the Bible*, trans. W.G.E. Watson (Leiden: Brill, 2001), pp. 305–63.

Marjanen, A., 'Montanism: Egalitarian Ecstatic "New Prophecy", in A. Marjanen and P. Luomanen, eds., *A Companion to Second-Century Christian 'Heretics'*, pp. 185–212.

Marjanen, A., Luomanen, P., eds., *A Companion to Second-Century Christian 'Heretics'*, 'Supplements to Vigiliae Christianae', vol. 76 (Leiden: Brill, 2005), pp. 100–124.

Markschies, Chr., *Gnosis. An introduction*, trans. J. Bowden (London/New York: Continuum/T&T Clark, 2003).

Meeks, W.A., *The First Urban Christians. The Social World of the Apostle Paul* (Yale: Yale University Press, 1983).

Moule, C.F.D., *Forgiveness and Reconciliation and other New Testament themes* (London: SPCK, 1988).

Musurillo, H., *The Acts of the Christian Martyrs* (Oxford: Clarendon Press, 1972).

Osborn, E. F., *Tertullian. First Theologian of the West* (Cambridge: Cambridge University Press, 1977).

——, *Irenaeus of Lyons* (Cambridge: Cambridge University Press, 2001).

——, 'Justin Martyr' in R.G. Evans, ed., *The First Christian Theologians*, pp. 115–20.

——, 'Irenaeus of Lyons' in R.G. Evans, ed., *The First Christian Theologians*, pp. 121–6.

——, 'Tertullian' in R.G. Evans, ed., *The First Christian Theologians*, pp. 143–9.

Pagels, E., *The Gnostic Gospels* (London: Penguin Books, 1990).

Pelikan, J., *Christianity and Classical Culture* (Yale: Yale University Press, 1993).

——, *Credo. Historical and Theological Guide to Creeds and Confessions of faith in Christian Tradition* (New Haven/London: Yale University Press, 2003).

Pius IX, *Ineffabilis Deus*. The Apostolic Constitution, 1854.

Quasten J., *Patrology*, vol. 1 (Westminster, Maryland: Newman Press, 1986).

Räisänen, H., 'Marcion' in A. Marjanen and P. Luomanen, eds., *A Companion to Second-Century Christian 'Heretics'* (Supplements to Vigiliae Christianae), vol. 76 (Leiden: Brill, 2005), pp. 100–124.

Rajak, T., 'Talking against Trypho. Christian Apologetic as Anti-Judaism in Justin's Dialogue with Trypho the Jew', in M. Edwards, M. Goodman and S. Price, eds., *Apologetics in the Roman Empire: Pagans, Jews, and Christians* (Oxford: Oxford University Press, 1999), pp. 59–80.

Rist J.M., 'Christian Theology and Secular Philosophy', in R.G. Evans, ed., *The First Christian Theologians*, pp. 105–14.

Rudolph, K., *Gnosis. The Nature and History of an Ancient Religion*, trans. R. McLachlan Wilson (Edinburgh: T & T Clark, 1983).

Schüssler Fiorenza, E., 'Word, Spirit and Power: Women in Early Christian Communities,' in R.R. Ruether and E. McLaughlin, eds., *Women of Spirit* (New York: Simon and Schuster, 1979), pp. 29–70.

Setzer, C., *Resurrection of the body in early Judaism and early Christianity: doctrine, community and self-definition* (Boston: Brill, 2004).

Simonetti, M., *Biblical Interpretation in the Early Church*, trans. J.A. Hughes (Edinburgh: T&T Clark, 1994).

Smith, R., 'Sex Education in Gnostic Schools', in: K.L. King, ed., *Images*, pp. 345–60.

Stanley, M.D., *Christ's Resurrection in Pauline Soteriology* (Rome: Pontifical Biblical Institute, 1961).

Stegemann, E., *The Jesus movement: a social history of its first century* (Minneapolis, MN: Fortress Press, 1999).

Valantasis, R., *The Gospel of Thomas* (London/New York: Routledge, 1997).

Walker, B.C., *The resurrection of the body in the Western Christianity, 200–1336* (New York: Columbia University, 1995).

Wedderburn, A.J.M., *Baptism and Resurrection: Studies in Pauline Theology and Its Graeco-Roman Background* (Tübingen: Mohr Siebeck, 1987)

Westermann, C., *Isaiah 40–66. A Commentary*, trans. D.M.G. Stalker (London: SCM Press, 1969).

Westra, L.H., *The Apostles' Creed. Origin, History and some Early Christian Commentaries* (Turnhaut: Brepolis Publishers, 2002).

Wiley, T., *Original Sin: Origins, Development, and Contemporary Meaning* (New York: Paulist, 2002).

Wilken R.L., *The Christians as the Romans saw Them* (New Haven: Yale University Press, 2nd edn, 2003).

Williams, R., 'Does it make sense to speak of pre-Nicene orthodoxy?', in R. Williams, ed., *The making of Orthodoxy Essays in Honour of Henry Chadwick* (Cambridge: Cambridge University Press, 1989), pp. 1–23.

Young, F.M., *The Making the Creeds* (London: SCM Press, 1993).

Indices of Ancient Theologians and Documents

Acts of Pilate 48, 160, 172
Apocalypse of Peter 51, 69, 159
Apocryphon of James 74, 160
Apocryphon of John 61, 62, 160, 165, 166
Apostolic Tradition 5, 8, 48, 147, 159, 163, 171
Aristides of Athens 35, 147, 148, 158
Ascension of Isaiah 59, 67, 69, 158, 176, 177
Athenagoras of Athens 19, 76, 79, 88, 122, 147, 148, 159, 165

Basilides 148, 159, 183

Callistus I, the Bishop of Rome 102, 109, 151, 156, 160
Cappadocian Fathers 96, 148, 181
Celsus 63, 64, 65, 149, 159, 171, 175
1 Clement (the Letter of the Romans to the Corinthians) 134, 155, 166, 178, 179
Clement of Alexandria 155, 183
Cyprian of Carthage 105, 106, 149, 160, 181, 182, 183

Didache 10, 69, 79, 97, 147, 149, 150, 159, 166, 183, 186

Epiphanius of Salamis 90, 125, 150, 160, 180
Epistle of Barnabas 10, 69, 111, 133, 147, 150, 158, 168
Epistle of the Apostles 69, 108, 150, 159, 171, 174
Epistle to Diognetus 147, 150, 159, 166, 181

First Book of Enoch 59, 158

Gospel of Nicodemus 48
Gospel of Peter 59, 69, 159
Gospel of Philip 42, 43, 90, 136, 160, 166, 180
Gospel of Thomas 114, 159, 173, 183

Hermas 59, 79, 100, 113, 115, 147, 151, 158, 174, 179, 181, 182
Hilary of Poitiers 160, 169
Hippolytus of Rome 109, 126, 147, 151, 153, 160, 163, 166, 167, 179, 181, 182

Ignatius of Antioch 38, 39, 40, 47, 48, 49, 50, 79, 88, 99, 100,

196